Feeding the Other

Food, Health, and the Environment

Series Editor: Robert Gottlieb, Henry R. Luce Professor of Urban and Environmental Policy, Occidental College

For a complete list of books published in this series, please see the back of the book.

Feeding the Other

Whiteness, Privilege, and Neoliberal Stigma in Food Pantries

Rebecca de Souza

The MIT Press
Cambridge, Massachusetts
London, England

This book was set in ITC Stone Serif Std and ITC Stone Sans Std by Toppan Best-set Premedia Limited.

Credit: Natalie Diaz, "Why I Hate Raisins" from *When My Brother Was an Aztec*. Copyright © 2012 by Natalie Diaz. Reprinted with the permission of The Permissions Company, Inc., on behalf of Copper Canyon Press, www.coppercanyonpress.org.

Library of Congress Cataloging-in-Publication Data

Names: De Souza, Rebecca, author.
Title: Feeding the other : whiteness, privilege, and neoliberal stigma in
  food pantries / Rebecca de Souza.
Description: Cambridge, MA : MIT Press, [2019] | Series: Food, health, and
  the environment | Includes bibliographical references and index.
Identifiers: LCCN 2018036775| ISBN 9780262039819 (hardcover : alk. paper) |
  ISBN 9780262536769 (pbk. : alk. paper)
Subjects: LCSH: Food banks--Minnesota--Case studies. | Poor--Minnesota--Case
  studies. | Stigma (Social psychology) | Social stratification. |
  Paternalism. | Racism.
Classification: LCC HV696.F6 D399 2019 | DDC 363.8/8309776--dc23 LC record
available at https://lccn.loc.gov/2018036775

To people all around the world who wake up every morning anxious about what their children will eat.

Contents

Series Foreword

Feeding the Other: Whiteness, Privilege, and Neoliberal Stigma in Food Pantries is the fifteenth book in the Food, Health, and the Environment series. The series explores the global and local dimensions of food systems and the issues of access; social, environmental, and food justice; and community well-being. Books in the series focus on how and where food is grown, manufactured, distributed, sold, and consumed. They address questions of power and control; social movements and organizing strategies; and the health, environmental, social, and economic factors embedded in food system choices and outcomes. As this book demonstrates, the focus is not only on food security and well-being but also on economic, political, and cultural factors and regional, state, national, and international policy decisions. Food, Health, and the Environment books therefore provide a window into the public debates, alternative and existing discourses, and multidisciplinary perspectives that have made food systems and their connections to health and the environment critically important subjects of study and for social and policy change.

Robert Gottlieb, Occidental College
Series Editor (gottlieb@oxy.edu)

Acknowledgments

I am thankful for the support and insights of the countless individuals I have encountered in my professional and personal life: colleagues, professors, students, interviewees, leaders, legislators, activists, family, friends, and ministers. I am also thankful for the people who have stood in my way—ignoring, silencing, and greatly underestimating me—because that has just made me think harder and do more.

A special thank you to my participants who shared their stories with me—your voices have been with me for half a decade now and I know them so well. I have worried a lot about how to represent you and your stories. I hope that there is truth somewhere between our voices and that I have done justice to your stories. Thank you to Chum and Ruby's Pantry–Duluth for letting me into your midst and allowing me to do this research. I am forever grateful for your generosity to me and to the community.

I would like to thank the Institute for Advanced Study at the University of Minnesota, the EVCAA Research and Scholarship Grant program, and the Small Seed Grant program at the University of Minnesota, Duluth (UMD), for partially funding this project. Thank you to UMD's College of Liberal Arts for providing me with a single-semester leave to work on this research. A warm thank you to my colleagues in the Department of Communication for your kindness every day. To Drs. Michael Sunnafrank, Elizabeth Nelson, and David Gore: Despite institutional constraints, you have created a space where intellectual creativity can flourish. Thank you for your many subversions.

Thank you to my beloved, Adam Pine. I found you in Duluth, and for that I love this city. Thanks for the countless conversations about research, unofficial peer reviews, and introducing me to critical geography! Thank you for decentering whiteness in our home and for your steadfast commitment to sharing the load. Because you worked on the "concrete particulars" of our lives—cooking, cleaning, and looking after our kids—I could write this book. Your abundant spirit and side-splitting comedy know no bounds. Dominic and Franka, thank you for constantly interrupting my work with demands for tight huggies, butt-cheek jokes, loud wailing, sickness, and building "Wegos." You are *all* life and *all* joy. This book was written between when you both were born, and I am so grateful that I got to do both in my life: have babies and write this book.

Thank you to my parents, Winston and Celeste, who are unique in every way—kind, generous against their own interests, and quirky—you are the constant backdrop to my life. To my siblings, Aaron and Sarah, you are both so strong and so blessed, even amid the hard tests that life has given you. You are with me every day. To my family in America—Donald, Sharon, Nicola, Susan, Caitlin, Alayna, and Robbie. To all my nieces and nephews—Andrew and Lexi, Daniel and Derek, Felix, Benji, and Hazel. You are all too sweet. This book would not have been possible but for my particular history and biography inscribed within me. For this, I am grateful to my ancestors who I never knew and to my grandparents, Mark and Rose Lobo and Frank and Charlotte de Souza, who were born and lived in places like Goa, Zanzibar and Pakistan and who did things like work in the railways and for the telegraphs and made spectacular wedding gowns and wedding cakes: workers, artists, intellectuals, always resilient, and always people of faith.

I would like to thank all the teachers, professors, and mentors I have had along the way. A special thanks to my professors at Purdue University—Steve Wilson and John Sherry—who taught me how to do good research and how to write well. I owe a massive debt of gratitude to my mentor, Dr. Mohan Dutta, who cleared the way and smoothed the paths for us brown folks in a very white discipline of communication. You taught me the importance of having a voice, listening to people's voices, and using those voices for justice. A warm thank you to my students who, through impassioned conversation and debate have given me deep insight into the workings of discourse, ideology, and whiteness.

To the strong white women of faith in Duluth: Charlotte Franz, Kathy Nelson, Jackie Falk, and Lee Stuart. Your sermons, our conversations, and your steadfast commitment to poor citizens and antiracism were in my mind as I wrote this book—I think you will hear your voices in these pages.

A special thank you to Dr. Robert Gottlieb, who I did not know and who did not know me, but who received this manuscript with few words and a professional openness that quite frankly shocked me. It reminded me of why my mother pushed me to come to the United States: as she frequently stated with annoying confidence, *"There*, people will recognize you for your merit, Becky." A warm thank you to Beth Clevenger, Anthony Zannino, Kathleen Caruso, and Melinda Rankin for all your editorial guidance—your work is on point! Your professionalism has made this process relatively painless—and the book is stronger because of you.

Above all, thank you to my Christ. You take rubbish and turn it into something. You open the eyes of the blind and let us see you. I am grateful for the ways in which you allow privilege and powerlessness to maneuver in my life all the time. As I say sometimes standing, but mostly always in tears: "For I know whom I have believed, and am convinced that He is able to keep what I have entrusted to Him against that day" (2 Timothy 1:12).

1 Introduction: Neoliberal Stigma, Food Pantries, and an Unjust Food System

Like so many things, it [WIC] really played a vital role in being able to get food and keeping my kids and myself fed. At the same time, there was always stigma attached to it. From the case manager to what they would call the "income maintenance" people. So you go into the government services building and you fill out this form and the person on the other desk is not nice. Not always but often and actually outright cruel a lot of times. I've had that experience. And then you go to the grocery store and with your food stamps, you buy soda and chips, people look at you and glare at you. But if you buy fruits and vegetables, they're pissed off at you because you're buying things that they can't afford. And so, no matter what you do, there's always this "hmmph." ...

I mean, if you look back historically what we were founded on, the Puritan beliefs, you work hard and you're going to get somewhere. That's a myth. I mean, the truth is that it is a wonderful myth and it's a wonderful thing to believe in because a small percentage of people will work really hard and everything is going to fall into place. The majority of people are going to work really hard, but they're not going to have opportunities to meet their needs. So they need assistance. There's this idea that you've got some kind of character flaw or there's something wrong with who you are and the decisions you've made. That's unfortunate. I don't know if that has changed at all. It's been a long time since I've had food stamps. It's been a long time since I've had WIC.

—Trinity, African American female, Ruby's Pantry client

Trinity has certainly hit the nail on the head. Trinity is an occasional client of Ruby's Pantry (RP), a food pantry run by a faith-based organization (FBO), where she pays twenty dollars in exchange for a large quantity of industrial food. Trinity was just one of the many women interviewed for this study who articulated so precisely the many ways in which she experiences stigma today. A shortage of resources means that Trinity must utilize charitable and government food assistance programs to feed her family. Quite ironically, the burden of stigma is most deeply experienced in her attempts to alleviate food insecurity. It is not the lack of food but the interactions she engages in to procure food that are stigmatizing. Suspicion surrounds her. As described in the excerpt, as a young working mum struggling to make ends meet, Trinity signed up for the Women, Infants, and Children (WIC) government food assistance program that provides food support to pregnant women. The WIC office was just one of many places where she felt devalued. But this was not all. Negative assumptions follow Trinity around multiple sites and spaces—from the benefits office to the grocery store. We are not privy to exactly what happened at the grocery store but may wonder what about Trinity makes her a "mark"? Is it because she uses an Electronic Benefits Transfer (EBT) card that disburses her food benefits? Is it because she has three children? Is it because she is Black[1]? Or is it because she has potato chips in her cart and fresh fruit? Most likely, it is a combination of all of the above.

Trinity identifies puritanical beliefs, the myth of the American dream, and more recent public health discourses as reasons for the stigma—and she is exactly right. Erving Goffman (1963, 3), who pioneered the scholarly work on stigma, defined *stigma* as a "deeply discrediting" attribute, by which stigmatized individuals are believed to possess a characteristic or a trait conveying a "devalued social identity." However, Goffman also argued that the issue at hand was not the attribute itself, but how such attributes came to be devalued or discredited in society. More recently, sociologists Richard Parker and Peter Aggleton, in their work on the stigma of HIV and AIDS, argued that stigma was not so much about marks, but about social processes linked to power and domination that conferred negative meanings to marks, a phenomenon they referred to as the "political economy of stigma" (Parker and Aggleton 2003; see also Parker 2012). This is certainly the case here. Trinity is caught in a web of powerful political narratives, in which deep-seated ideologies interwoven through politics, religion, and race come together to justify negative perceptions about people like her—poor people, women, welfare recipients, and Black women on welfare. To be clear, stigmatizing narratives follow poor whites around as well, but they are intensified in the presence of darker skin tones.

What Is This Book About?

This book is about *food justice* and, more precisely, the stigmatizing narratives that surround people who are hungry and food insecure. Gottlieb and Joshi (2010, 6) define *food justice* as "ensuring that the benefits and risks of where, what, and how food is grown and produced, transported and distributed, and accessed and eaten are shared fairly." This is clearly not the case in the United States, which has one of the highest rates of hunger and food insecurity among developed nations. That rate increased from 10.5 percent in 2000 to about 12.5 percent in 2015 and has stayed roughly unchanged since then. Poor households, single parents, and communities of color are disproportionately affected. Food insecurity is almost three times higher among African American households (26.1 percent) and Hispanic households (23.7 percent) compared to white households (10.6 percent). Food insecurity is at 23.1 percent for households with children headed by a single man and a whopping 34.4 percent for households with children headed by a single woman (Coleman-Jensen, Gregory, and Singh 2014). Regional and local-level data put food insecurity among Native populations anywhere between 30 and 50 percent (Blue Bird Jernigan et al. 2013). Food insecurity also results in health disparities—dramatically different physical health outcomes for different populations—thus violating the basic human rights of individuals (Chilton and Rose 2009).

In this book, I argue that stigmatizing narratives about those who are hungry and food insecure—that is, poor people, women, and racial minorities—serve to uphold and legitimize the unjust food system. I use the term *neoliberal stigma* to refer to a particular kind of Western and American narrative that focuses on individualism, hard work, and personal responsibility as defining attributes of human dignity and citizenship. When people do not live up to these parameters, for reasons out of their control, they are *marked* as irresponsible, unworthy, and "bad citizens," creating the "Us and Them" phenomenon. This book speaks to the burden of stigma that people who are raced, classed, and gendered face at the intersections of these identities in their attempts to manage hunger and food insecurity. This research project adds to the growing body of work on food justice by analyzing the stigma of food assistance—as well as the neoliberal turn that stigma takes within these contexts. Stigma is a sharp, poisonous undercurrent that runs rampant in the lives of the hungry and food insecure in the United States and yet one that is concealed and underestimated. By unpacking and interrogating discursive practices within food pantry spaces, this work continues the long journey toward food justice.

Despite several decades of calling for a new food system, issues of food access continue to be met with technical, informational, and therapeutic solutions focused on distributing surplus industrial food, increasing health awareness, and building food skills among poor citizens. These are small-scale and short-sighted solutions that place the burden of solving the problem of hunger on local communities and individuals, while state and corporate actors renege on their responsibilities. In this book, I argue that stigmatizing narratives that circulate around the hungry serve to uphold the unjust food system and forestall systemic change. Therefore, to bring about broader systemic change, we first need to shift the narratives around *what causes hunger* and *who the hungry are*. Just as racial ideologies and representations hold the racial structure in place (e.g., Hall 1997), so too do stigmatizing ideologies about the hungry hold the food system in place. This book is about unpacking how these discourses emerge and the expression they take so as to reconfigure the food system in the interests of justice.

Building off the political economy of stigma framework, this book shows that the process of stigmatization is entirely dependent on access to social, economic, and political power, which allow groups to identify difference, construct stereotypes, and separate people into categories. Scholars point out that stigma is as much about power and privilege as it is about marginalization and disenfranchisement (Link and Phelan 2014). The process of categorization after all is an exercise of power, although one that may be subverted by those who are marked (Crenshaw 1991). Stigma is about white privilege and systems of whiteness—the ordinary power ordinary white people have to control values, institutions, and environments. Stigma is about systemic patriarchy and the unearned privilege and priority given to male voices, issues, and worldviews.

Communication is central to the production of stigma, and thus stigma is about *discursive privilege*—the power to tell a story about who the Other is and who "We" are. Stigma is about the power to create narratives of similarity and difference, narratives of Us and Them, and use these stories to legitimize oppression. Stigma is witnessed in the way the media show up after the big food festival in North Minneapolis is over, a festival which was attended by several hundred "bright, shining, beautiful Black and brown faces," as food advocate Aliyah said, to write about the one gunshot that rang out six hours later. Aliyah exclaimed: "We sent them press releases, why did they not write a story about the festival, but came running with their cameras when they heard about the gun shot." Stigma is about the power to present and represent—the power to mark, assign, stereotype, and frame issues, people, and situations in particular ways. Stigma is about the power to levy accusations, to cast suspicion, and to be heard. Stigma is the power to shut up and silence others.

Trinity's words in the opening excerpt get at the many ways in which people who use food assistance programs are stereotyped and caged within discursive boxes today, such that they are symbolically and materially violated even before they can speak. In her voice, we hear the multiplicative burden of oppression that food insecure women of color face. We hear logic and reason. We hear vision. However, this is a voice we rarely hear in the public sphere—a voice that is silenced, eclipsed, and invisible amid the frenzy of political discourses out to trap her. From a food justice lens, it is my argument that her voice must no longer be silenced, but instead be central to all discussions and actions surrounding food policy.

In this study, food pantries provide the starting point for the analysis of neoliberal stigma because they are the cornerstone of the government's strategy to "end hunger." Today, rather than legal entitlements, charitable food assistance programs have come to *stand in* for the state and function as arms of the government (Poppendieck 1999; Riches and Silvasti 2014). Although food pantries are at the very bottom of the totem pole in the food system, they are vital components in the system. Food pantries, though small individually, provide the largest-scale means to manage hunger. Of those needing emergency food assistance during the year, 92 percent obtain food from food pantries (Comstock and Pesheck 2013). Feeding America (FA) is a nationwide network of two hundred food banks operating sixty thousand food programs, of which approximately thirty-five thousand are food pantries. These programs alone serve roughly forty-five million people each year. In addition to these programs, there are pop-up and ad hoc food pantries that do not belong to the FA network. Despite the number of food pantries around, this colossal structure of the food system is frequently sidestepped in the literature. Food pantries are often exempt from critical interrogation because they are run by charitable organizations and enshrined in religious and moral discourses; 51 percent of FA programs rely entirely on volunteers, and 62 percent are run by faith-based organizations. Discourses of charity and good works make it really hard to critique these spaces, and, as a result, the many injustices of the food system remain hidden from view. Furthermore, because the functions of food pantries have been narrowly described in terms of "collecting and distributing food," they are rarely viewed as sites for organizing and activism.

This book is an invitation to think about food pantries not as charitable spaces, but as political and politicized spaces with the potential for activism and advocacy. I use the term *political* to refer not to voting behaviors or identification with political parties per se, but to deeply ingrained worldviews and ideological assumptions we hold about the world—in this case, views about the problem of hunger and food insecurity, its causes and solutions, and perceptions about who the hungry are. People who enter these spaces as donors, volunteers, or recipients bring with them deep-seated ideologies, social identities, and subjectivities, all of which inform practice. The organizations themselves have particular worldviews and visions that reflect underlying political ideologies. In these charitable enclaves, kindness and care coincide with racism, paternalism, and systems of poverty governance, as well as resistance to these systems. Although politics is typically concealed in spaces of charity, it does not disappear. Alongside moral and religious values, political ideologies remain an important subtext influencing thoughts and practices. It is my argument that all of these sacred cows need to be made visible and unpacked if we are to move toward a vision of food justice and reimagine food pantries as centers of activism.

This book is about prioritizing and foregrounding the voices, experiences, and realities of people who enter the food system through the backdoor—the food pantries. In a secondary definition, Gottlieb and Joshi (2010, 6) identify *food justice* as "a language and a set of meanings, told through stories as well as analysis, that illuminate how food injustices are experienced and how they can be challenged and overcome." This book, by documenting the voices, experiences, and realities of those who enter the food system through the backdoor, contributes to a more equitable way of knowing the food system—and hopefully a more equitable way of shaping policy. Hunger drives and fundraisers commodify the suffering of the hungry by presenting pathologizing images of the poor, while political discourses portray food insecure people as lacking in discipline, enacting poor food choices, and unconcerned about their health. Food pantries, food banks, hunger coalitions, and even those involved in advocacy such as Feeding America and Hunger Solutions rarely have people who have actually experienced hunger sit on their executive boards; here, too, voices of privilege dominate. Racism and elitism are embedded in the very structure of the food system. Communication scholar Mohan Dutta (2008) argues that the erasure of the voices of people living with hunger is critical to their marginalization. Social change is thus achieved by exposing systems of domination that privilege some forms of meanings over others and replacing them with new sets of meanings.

In this book, the voices of the hungry are foregrounded as they emerge within systems, organizations, and other voices of privilege. This research project interrogates the complex moral judgments made about those who experience hunger at food pantries operated by two faith-based organizations (FBOs) in Duluth, Minnesota (United States), and the ways in which these judgments are expressed organizationally and interpersonally, and internalized within individuals. Through a comparative case analysis, this book presents a rich and layered account of the ways in which neoliberal stigma is produced, reified, and resisted at each food pantry. Two primary research questions guide this study: In what way does the experience of neoliberal stigma intersect with embodied experiences of class, race, and gender? And how do organizational discourses and practices produce, create, and disrupt neoliberal stigma? Scholars argue that there is a tendency to generalize the effects of the neoliberal metanarrative, thereby missing all kinds of ethical and political activism in organizations (Barnes and Prior 2009; Cloke, May, and Williams 2017). Sensitive to this critique, this study unpacks the ways in which ethical engagement is practiced in these settings. So, if food justice is "a language and a set of meanings, told through stories as well as analysis, that illuminate how food injustices are experienced and how they can be challenged and overcome," then my hope is that this book will provide a new set of meanings, stories, and analyses in the interests of justice.

Neoliberal Stigma

The concept of *neoliberal stigma* offers a way to think about stigmatizing narratives in the contemporary political and economic context. David

Harvey (2005, 2) defines *neoliberalism* as "a theory of political economic practices that proposes that human wellbeing can best be advanced by liberating individual entrepreneurial freedoms and skills within an institutional framework characterized by strong private property rights, free markets, and free trade." Neoliberalism has been described as "capitalism with the gloves off" because it promotes the aggressive expansion of business forces without the mitigating balance of nonmarket and democratic forces (McChesney 2003, 8). In a neoliberal era, business forces are more aggressive and face less organized opposition than ever before. Politically, key values of neoliberalism include freedom of choice, market security, laissez-faire, and minimal government intervention; in terms of subjectivities, the main markers include hard work, self-help, and self-reliance (Larner 2000). In the Western context, the neoliberal metanarrative is also linked to notions of citizenship, providing prescriptions about what it means to be a good citizen, where citizenship is tied to economic productivity and making good/ healthy choices, while those who are economically underproductive are marked as lazy, deviant, and irresponsible citizens (Holborow 2015; Rose 1999).

Neoliberal stigma occurs when markers of hard work, personal responsibility, and economic citizenship are applied in a variety of contexts, creating social distance between groups. Within a neoliberal mindset, systemic problems are recast through the process of subjectification, such that a problem like hunger is reframed as a problem *of the hungry*. So when Trinity says, "There's this idea that you've got some kind of character flaw," it falls right within the conceptual framework of neoliberal stigma. Neoliberal stigma can be identified in the discursive practices of framing, blaming, and shaming that cast suspicion on the motives, intentions, and moral character of Others and in so doing silences them. Centering the analysis on neoliberal stigma means attending to the ways in which these communicative processes circulate around the food insecure and operate in the service of power: structures of capitalism, racism, and nationalism.

The concept of neoliberal stigma draws heavily upon the age-old Calvinist distinction between "deserving and undeserving poor." Calvinism, a Christian denomination found in seventeenth-century England, viewed work as an absolute duty, a spiritual end in itself, and the best way to please God. In this European theological framework, later transported to America, those who did not work were damned regardless of whether they were rich or poor, although economic success was seen as a sign of God's election (Waxman 1983). In the 1990s, these distinctions between the deserving and undeserving poor were deployed in the United States to justify welfare reform and usher in a new era of aggressive neoliberal policies. Indeed Parker (2012, 166) notes that "stigma is not a free-floating social phenomenon." Instead, "the period in which a stigma appears and the form it takes are always influenced by historical circumstances" (166).

In using the term *neoliberal stigma*, I cast a wider and more contemporary net. Neoliberal stigma prioritizes work, where work is tied to values of self-sufficiency, personal responsibility, and freedom of choice. In this framework, wealth *is* valued for its own sake—not necessarily because it is an indicator of hard work. Wealth equals accountability. Wealth symbolizes personal responsibility regardless of how the wealth was produced. Wealth humanizes individuals. In the framework of neoliberal stigma, the underlying basis for evaluation is not spirituality alone, but moves between spiritual, economic, and nationalistic worldviews. Thus, the binary of "deserving and undeserving" gives way to the language of hard work, responsibility, entrepreneurialism, nationalism, citizenship, and self-sufficiency. Morality and ethics are not debates about inherent values, character, or behavior, but about the ability to produce value in the marketplace or, conversely, not to detract value from it. Furthermore, neoliberalism, though it purports to be neutral—judging all equally based on economic logic—is in fact not. All are *not* treated equally even in the marketplace. Drawing on the work of critical race scholars, I argue that in the case of neoliberal stigma explicit interpersonal racism, "color-blind" racism, and the racism inscribed in rules and governance procedures are used to discriminate against people of color (Bonilla-Silva 2010; Goldberg 2009). Business, legal, and administrative rationalities become fronts for racism, sexism, and classism. Because of its alleged neutrality, neoliberal stigma finds expression among conservatives, liberals, and across the political spectrum.

The effects of neoliberal stigma on those who are hungry and food insecure are multiple and occur at emotional, social, and political levels. At the emotional level, embarrassment and shame are central to the experience of hunger in the United States today (De Marco, Thorburn, and Kue 2009; Dutta, Anaele, and Jones 2013; Garthwaite 2016). The stigma of hunger leads to a double burden: the economic burden of trying to put food on the table and the psychological burden of knowing that society stigmatizes you as deviant, abnormal, and a bad citizen. Psychological aspects include worry, anxiety, and sadness about the family food supply, feelings of having no choice in the foods eaten, and shame and fear of being labeled as poor (Connell et al. 2005). In general, people who internalize negative stereotypes may experience psychological effects such as poor self-esteem and self-concept, which can result in anxiety and depression (Corrigan, Larson, and Rusch 2009; Miller and Major 2000).

Socially, for individuals whose "spoiled identity" is not known or visible to others, managing information about themselves is a constant struggle to avoid rejection; this might mean concealing information about oneself or preempting stigma by disclosing information about oneself (Goffman 1963; Meisenbach 2010). Stigma fractures communities and keeps individuals disconnected and isolated from each other and mainstream society. Stigma has the ultimate effect of enhancing perceptions of social distance and keeping people away from other people and spaces. Neoliberal stigma and the narratives that come with it are divisive because they script how we think about, communicate, and relate to the paradigmatic Other. Neoliberal stigma creates suspicion and doubt, and it has a silencing effect on individuals and communities.

At the political level, stigmatizing ideologies are sedimented within laws and institutions. Thus, even in the absence of person-to-person stigma, macrolevel structures control and discriminate against communities—a phenomenon referred to as "stigma power" (Link and Phelan 2014). When individuals attempt to remedy their food insecurity, it unleashes the force of these moralizations, be it at the benefits office, the grocery store, or food pantries. Stigma can thus prevent people from accessing and demanding their legal entitlements. This is why Trinity says, "It's been a long time since I've had food stamps. It's been a long time since I've had WIC."

Food, Discourse, and the Political Economy of Stigma

Food *communicates* (Greene and Cramer 2011). The discursive practices surrounding food create and convey meaning and are therefore easily linked to stigma processes. From the absence and presence of food in our daily lives, from the type of food we eat to the quantity and quality of food to where we get our food, food marks us out as rich/poor, weak/strong, intelligent/ignorant, cultured/uncultured, careful/careless, moral/immoral, and healthy/unhealthy. Food communicates through physical inscriptions it makes on and "in" bodies through conditions of emaciation, starvation, anorexia, overweight, and obesity. Particularly with regards to obesity, in the present historical moment, this hypervisible condition is presented as evidence of poor eating habits for which individuals are held personally responsible. Individuals marked by weight are blamed for their intrinsic laziness, lack of desire for self-improvement, weak character, and recalcitrant bodies, meanings which are intensified at the intersections of class and race. In short, our bodies communicate. They tell stories about us—stories that serve as a sharp reminder of how the human body is not a given reality; rather, bodies are inscribed with social and biomedical meanings (Lupton 2003).

Food is political. According to Spurlock (2009, 7), discursive practices surrounding food are neither neutral nor apolitical, but rather "capable of constituting communities and imaginaries, simultaneously drawing and obliterating boundaries." In contemporary society, the relationships among social identity structures of class, race, and gender are increasingly tied to particular food practices. Critical rhetorical scholar Helene Shugart (2014, 8) argues that it is through the realm of food that class is constructed and performed today: "contemporary discourse around good food functions to reinstate and recalibrate the culturally resonant national mythology of class, with a particular eye to the restoration of a middle class." Research by Dougherty et al. (2016) suggests that the way people communicate about food has become a marker of social class. People from different class backgrounds talk about food differently—and especially for middle-class families hit by hard times and unemployment, food represents a particular discursive struggle to manage class location and class slippage.

Food is a marker of citizenship. Through food and food practices, we come to understand who is prioritized and who is an "ideal citizen." Using a rights and responsibility framework, good citizens are those who work hard and do not use food assistance or welfare—a belief that can be traced back to the Calvinist tradition in seventeenth-century England (Waxman 1983). In the UK, geographer and policy analyst Kayleigh Garthwaite (2017) observes that the rise of food banks has been accompanied by myths, moral judgements, and misconceptions about people seeking food. Political narratives—in particular, conservative government rhetoric—invoke Calvinist distinctions between the deserving and undeserving poor and responsibilize individuals for their food bank use. Food pantry users are characterized as selfish and lazy, as those who do not pay for their rent or provide food for their children, but instead spend their money on alcohol, drugs, and large televisions. Similar themes are found in the United States as well. A study by Dutta, Anaele, and Jones (2013) found that stigma was a key reason participants did not use food pantries, *despite* hunger. Perceptions of being lazy acted as barriers to seeking out food pantry support and other resources. As one participant noted: "You are on food stamps, lot of people look down on you. They think that you are lazy." Another participant noted that because of this stigma, "people think that they can just throw food at us" (11).

Food is a marker of *health* citizenship. Good health citizens are expected to care for their bodies so as to limit the harm they might cause to other citizens and the nation state (Petersen and Lupton 1996). Historically, the notion of citizenship has meant participation in political and collective life, but today citizenship means the exercise of healthy and morally sound lifestyle choices even amid the oppressive forces of racism, class inequities, and unhealthy environments. Good citizens are those who make good food choices and do not burden the public health system. While seemingly positive and benign, the "new public health" has shifted the meaning of citizenship to focus on individual and internal responsibilities for health and wellbeing, while sidestepping the role of governments and institutions (Petersen and Lupton 1996). The "good food movement" today, with its directives on what to eat, has broadened the gulf between "good health citizens"—those who follow public health directives and "bad health citizens"—those who do not, the so-called cultural dupes who are enslaved to the system of industrial agriculture (Shugart 2014). This is why Trinity is chastised for "choosing" bad food; the implication is that she is not motivated to take care of her health. Trinity is also chastised for choosing good food, because as a Black woman she falls right into the discursive trope of the "welfare queen," a trope that goes all the way back to the welfare debates of the 1990s. It refers to a woman, usually Black, who in the public imaginary shirks work and abuses the system by buying so-called luxury foods using public tax dollars (McCormack 2004). So, damned if you do, damned if you don't. A variety of discourses come together to stereotype or "fix" Trinity in place—her complexity, her desire, her intellect, and her creativity erased.

The Entrepreneurialism of Hunger Solutions

One of the earliest indictments of the emergency food assistance system was made by Janet Poppendieck (1999) in her book *Sweet Charity? Emergency Food and the End of Entitlement*. Her work examined processes through which emergency food assistance had become a stable and institutionalized feature of the economy to solve the problem of hunger in the United States. She wrote provocatively that "fighting hunger has become a national pastime" (24). The emergency food industry, with its explosion of food banks and church-basement food pantries, holiday giveaways, mail-carrier drives, and soup kitchens, exploded on the scene during the 1980s in conjunction with the government's "roll-back" neoliberal policies that deflected responsibility away from the government. She argued: "The resurgence of charity is at once a *symptom* and a *cause* of our society's failure to face up to and deal with the erosion of equality. ... It creates a culture of charity that normalizes destitution and legitimates personal generosity as a response to major social and economic dislocation" (5; emphasis in original). In her critique, Poppendieck laid out the "seven deadly ins" of charitable food assistance: insufficiency, inappropriateness, nutritional inadequacy, instability, inaccessibility, inefficiency, and finally indignity or the stigma and Us and Them dynamic present in food banks.

Poppendieck's book is one of the most comprehensive critiques of food pantries; however, it has been nearly two decades since she wrote her treatise. Since then, hunger has been on the rise, as have food pantries and food banks. SNAP benefits have been inadequate at meeting people's food needs, so charitable assistance has expanded. In the last decade, the need for charitable food support increased 166 percent, with 92 percent of those needing food during the year obtaining it through the charitable food system (Comstock and Pesheck 2013). In Minnesota, the state where I have lived for the last ten years, food shelves are visited by approximately nine thousand people each day; in 2017, Minnesotans visited food shelves 3,402,077 times, which was the highest number of visits in recorded history—about fifty thousand more visits than the previous high set in 2014 (Hunger Solutions 2018). Hunger Solutions, an advocacy organization notes: "This [2017] marks the seventh consecutive year with more than 3 million visits to our food shelves. In other words, since the recession, over three million food shelf visits has become the "new normal" in Minnesota" (Hunger Solutions 2018).

Indeed, charitable food assistance is a big business today, which takes place through a complex set of public and private/profit and nonprofit partnerships. In his book *Big Hunger*, Andrew Fisher (2017) refers to this as the "hunger industrial complex." This network is made up of private, public, corporate, and community actors who come together to deliver, distribute, or cook food for the hungry and food insecure. Fisher argues that the problematic relationships between government and nongovernment entities have resulted in a self-perpetuating hunger industrial complex, in which antihunger advocates have failed to hold corporations and the government accountable for these larger problems.

A Deer Caught in the Headlights

Although Poppendieck and a host of scholars and activists have called for dismantling the hunger industrial complex and food pantries, this has not happened. In fact, much work is being done to make them bigger, healthier, and more "entrepreneurial" through the use of business practices. There are food pantries that have started to charge a small fee for food, pantries that encourage "work for food," and pantries that use marketing and sales techniques to promote healthy choices. I attended the Food Access Summit 2014: Organize for Equity, held in Duluth, at which only three panels addressed food pantry issues. Despite the *organize for equity* subtitle, each panel focused on the question of how to *improve* food pantries, rather than how to question the inequities that undergird them. The first panel centered on how to operate community gardens for food shelves, another focused on how to promote healthy choices, and a third discussed how to procure culturally appropriate food for African immigrant communities. The Minnesota Food Charter also was presented at this conference, a document which noted the rising problem of hunger; however, here too solutions were restricted to providing healthier and more culturally appropriate foods at food pantries. The charter applauded Minnesota for being a food and farm economic powerhouse—the fifth-largest agricultural economy in the United States—and, no surprise, most of the solutions presented served the interests of agroindustries.

At the same Food Access Summit, a telling moment occurred that high-lighted the superficial interpretation of the phrase *organize for equity*, as well as the problematics of white liberalism. One of the four white female pan-elists was discussing how she procured meat for her food pantry clients—*even venison*, she noted excitedly. After she finished, a hand went up in the audience, from a woman who identified herself as Native. She went on to explain the irony of how she, an indigenous woman, could get a pound of venison from the local food shelf, but not through her own traditional hunting practices. She pointed out that her family was forced to go through numerous hunting and fishing regulatory procedures, including paying for a butcher to carve up the animal. She scoffed, "You know, my commu-nity, we were doing that long before anyone else, as if we need to go to a butcher!"

The panelists were caught off-guard by this woman who, like Trinity, in one brief moment had hit the nail on the head: she'd identified a com-modified food system that makes those who hunt, grow, and produce food starve, while those who have never produced food thrive; a food system that destroys traditional food systems, replaces them with industrial food, and then frames exploited communities as dupes; a food system that is not racially neutral, but that both steals the labor of people of color and then starves them; a food system that is a prime example of the twin forces of capitalism and racism at work. A food system that is made of various actors, who dutifully play their roles and in so doing keep it in place. Yes, there it was. In one fell swoop, this woman challenged centuries of being discur-sively "fixed in place" to make one of the most astute comments at the conference. But her question was met with blank stares, awkward silence, a proverbial deer caught in the headlights moment, and an inevitable topic shift. This was whiteness at its worst: silent, innocent, fragile, powerful, and oppressive. This interaction captured for me the vast social distance that exists within food pantries between givers and receivers and Us and Them; it is a distance that stems from the tyranny of whiteness, color-blind racism, and neoliberal mindsets.

The Study

Relatively new to Duluth at the time, my spouse and I were driving back to our home when we saw a long line of people carrying laundry baskets outside of the First United Methodist Church, locally known as the Coppertop Church. The line went through the parking lot into the street, causing a traffic jam at an already busy intersection. The car registered -5°F, cold even for a December evening in Duluth. We later learned that this line was for the Ruby's Pantry (RP) food distribution, a place where people could pay fifteen dollars and receive thirty to forty pounds of food; the price went up to twenty dollars two years later. The long line, the laundry baskets, and what seemed to be a lot of people lugging pounds of food created a spectacle that was both disturbing and intriguing. I grew up in Bangalore, India, a city of eight million, where hunger and food insecurity are still commonplace experiences. However, the breadlines—and the indignity of breadlines—in a country of wealth, abundance, and the "American dream" were disturbing.

This project is based on four years of ethnographic field work, including in-depth interviews, field work, informal conversations, and surveys with staff and clients.[2] The two food pantries featured in this project—Chum and Ruby's Pantry—vary in religious and political orientation, organizational structure, quantity and quality of food distributed, clientele, and relationship to the state. Chum might be categorized as a traditional food pantry, whereas RP is an example of a type of entrepreneurial food pantry, which uses a quasi-market model to provide food support. Chum is a more politically liberal organization, which applies a social justice orientation to its work and receives funding from a variety of sources, including government funds. RP, on the other hand, is rooted in evangelical conservative leanings, makes no claims about social justice, and positions itself in opposition to government programs.

Reflexivity in the Research Process

My interest in issues of marginality stem from my own markings that occur at the intersection of nation, culture, religion, and race. Growing up middle-class in India meant that structural deprivation was never part of my story, and even today I remain an outsider to poverty—but I understand what it means to be "different." I moved from India to the United States almost fifteen years ago, already inscribed with a complex postcolonial history and biography. In India, my first name was always an immediate marker of my Christian roots and my last name a marker of the nearly five hundred years of Portuguese rule in Goa, the place where my ancestors were born. As part

of a Christian minority in a predominantly Hindu country, I grew up knowing that Christianity was the language of the white colonizer, but also that
Indian Christians were hardly that. The Christ I knew was a "God of the
oppressed," to borrow a phrase from Black theologian James Cone (1997),
the God of struggle, the God of the poor, the God that I rejected many times
to fit in. I grew up experiencing the discursive erasures and microaggressions
common to any minoritized community, but also the radical multicultural-
ism of an ancient and experienced civilization with porous national borders
and easy nationalism—although this is quickly changing with the rise of
Hindu nationalism. Later, as an immigrant in the United States, a woman,
a woman of color, the vector of my marginality was no longer religion but
rather the color of my skin. In graduate school, even as I was serving myself
cheap food from a buffet, a friend of mine—yes, a Black friend—observed
quietly: "You walk around as though you don't know you're different." In
many ways, coming to America was a story of learning how to be raced,
learning how to be hypervisible and invisible, and learning how to be vigilant about my body, my voice, my accent, and the meanings they convey to
the white people sitting in my head and in the playgrounds my children run
around in. Across both continents, patriarchy has been like sinking sand in
my life slowly pulling me down and structuring my thought and behavior
through its hegemonic norms and deft disciplinary tactics.

As is true of most people who share my categories, I am sensitive to the
fact that my body betrays a story, which shows up in the research process.
Indeed, Harding (2004, 138) argues that "understanding ourselves and the
world around us requires understanding what others think of us and our
beliefs and actions, not just what we think of ourselves and them." As I
went about doing this research, I found that people of color were more
likely to disclose their experiences of being raced and racism, whereas
whites were more cautious. Given my visible markers, people were more
likely to assume that I was politically liberal, although for whites this meant
a particular brand of white liberalism, whereas for people of color, liberalism was less about politics and more about an embodied worldview that
emerged from shared experiences of oppression. A few people engaged with
my identity as an immigrant and outsider. For instance, when an African
American man Xavier disclosed to me that he was Muslim, he asked expec-
tantly, "You know about that?" To which I shrugged saying, "Yes I'm from
India." He nodded, pleased to have found someone for whom being Muslim was normal and an everyday occurrence.

In my writing and thinking about issues of food justice, I employ a rather heterodox approach, drawing on social scientific research as well as critical and feminist theorizing about food, race, and the political economy. This interdisciplinary approach provides richness and interpretive power to my analysis, allowing me to bear witness to the meanings, moments, and possibilities that characterize the lives of my participants. That said, I should note that this book is written and produced within institutions of privilege—mostly white and mostly middle class, so the explanations presented are excruciatingly detailed, well accounted for, and painfully justified for the benefit of this audience. Every claim, in particular about whiteness, privilege, and charity, though grounded in data and in the voices of my participants, has been overturned, questioned, and critiqued formally and informally by institutional authorities as well as by budding institutional authorities—my students. I have channeled my frustration into lengthier well-cited explanatory sections. But for this, I apologize to Xavier and many of the other interviewees, for whom these claims would resonate immediately and be commonsense assumptions not requiring detailed explanations. The process has brought to light for me the vast difference in commonsense itself between the privileged and the oppressed.

Feminist theorizing draws attention to how knowledge production is deeply embedded in sensory experience, in which bodies combine with other actants in an environment to become producers of knowledge (Ellingson 2017). In the food pantry spaces that I visited, the material, physiological, and technocratic reality of hunger was palpable. Here rich and poor bodies combined with food, discourses, papers, files, ID cards, badges, numbers, and clips. Hunger showed up in emotive expressions on the faces of mothers and children, in the size of bodies—whether too thin or overweight—in the use of canes, respirators, and wheelchairs, and in the smell of old buildings, stale food, and well-used toilets. On several occasions, this sensory data seeped through my skin, reminding me that discourse and materiality are hopelessly intertwined with bodies in spaces even when we do not mention it. On several occasions, my spouse and I threw away the food that we brought home from RP because we just couldn't bear to pick out the good potatoes from the rotten ones; it was a sign of our class privilege, as well as how marked that food was in our eyes.

Of Sacred Cows and Trigger Warnings

The purpose of this book is not to denigrate the few food pantries, volunteers, or whites depicted in this book, but rather to shed light on a systemic issue: the more than thirty-five thousand food pantries that make up the bottom rungs of the food system. I use the case study methodology to point to specific organizations, pantries, individuals, incidents, and events; however, these data points are meant to illuminate structural patterns of injustice within the food system and to show how individuals and entities participate in these structures. As one food justice advocate I spoke to said: "It's easy for people, especially for white people, to think that institutional racism is a system, that's in this big cloud and that nobody's up there operating it. But what they don't realize is that it's a system built up of tons of people. And that they are part of that system. And, that it's not just about, oh, this person's a Trump supporter, so that's clearly someone that's racist. If you're not actively contributing towards liberating people that have been oppressed, you're part of that system. And, that doesn't make you any better than the person out there saying 'make America great again.'"

This book will make some readers uncomfortable because it might interfere with their sense of selves, their attachment to markers of their own identity, how they were socialized, and their faith beliefs—in particular, if they have worked at, donated to, or volunteered at food pantries. For some, shifting the gaze toward white people will feel uncomfortable—an indicator of their attachment to privilege and the wages of whiteness. For some, the critique of conservative values and the questioning of "good white liberalism" will also hit a nerve—in particular, when pointing out the links between politics, race, and faith. It is my hope that people will push through this discomfort because addressing the issue of hunger and food insecurity necessitates this kind of reflexivity. Talking about injustice necessarily means addressing many of the sacred cows in American life and life in general. The voices of the hungry presented in this book will certainly help with this process.

A Note about Interpretation

Qualitative and ethnographic research, even when it follows specific protocols for data collection, analysis, and presentation, is plagued by questions about interpretation. Readers might ask: How do you know this is what your participants meant? Aren't you reading too much into this? These are good questions because meanings are *polysemous* in that different people take away different meanings from messages. Having said that, reading the data too much (and too deeply) is precisely the power of ethnographic work. As lay people, we do not always have the opportunity to steep ourselves in the voices, the histories, the geographies of other people to figure out what it all means. However, as researchers we do: we get to sit with these voices for years trying to make sense of them. Thus, in this context, the term *interpretation* is not used to refer to personal opinion in an "everything is relative" sort of way; instead, it is a systematic technique to organize, make sense of, and reduce the data.

In this study, I used Charmaz's (2001) constructivist approach to grounded theory to analyze the data.[3] In general, the process involves identifying patterns in the data and substantiating those patterns with internal and external checks (e.g., does this meaning show up in multiple places in the data, and how does this meaning relate to things outside of the data set). This means that any claim made in the study has been substantiated by multiple data points—and I present examples of these in the book. The interview excerpts and quotes are presented mostly verbatim, with a few modifications to allow for readability and clarity. These data points will allow readers to judge for themselves the credibility and trustworthiness of the analysis. That said, whether in constructivist or more positivistic forms of research, the researcher is never a spectator but always implicated in the creative process of doing research, which both presents and constructs events, experiences, and even what comes to be called *data*. Importantly, in my interpretative work, I strive to maintain a social justice sensibility. Frey, Pearce, Pollock, Artz, and Murphy (1996, 115) observe: "The social justice sensibility does not even pretend to be objective, neutral, or dispassionate. ... Rather, social justice research makes an explicit "preferential option" for those who are disadvantaged by prevalent social structures or extraordinary social acts; it emerges from and channels the emotions of the researcher."

The Place

Duluth can be characterized as a socially liberal, midsized city, with a history of deindustrialization, but also with a viable medical, educational, and cultural economy. Duluth is similar to other deindustrialized cities in the Rust Belt, which have experienced economic decline, population loss, and urban decay, but also different because—as Chum's executive director, Lee Stuart, points out—Duluth continues to have a substantial postindustrial economy and a cultural vibrancy. According to Pine (2016), Duluth has done quite well in reimagining and repositioning itself as a postindustrial city. Although unique in many ways, Duluth is not that different from other cities in the nation. Poverty, income and racial disparities, residential segregation, and hunger and food insecurity are significant challenges facing the region.

Duluth lies within St. Louis County and is the third-largest city in Minnesota after Minneapolis and St. Paul. The original inhabitants of the region were members of the Sioux and Ojibwe tribes. Today, Duluth has a population of approximately one hundred thousand. European Americans make up 90 percent of Duluth's population, "two or more races" comprise 3 percent of the population, Native Americans 2.5 percent, African Americans 2.3 percent, and Asians and Hispanics 1.5 percent of the population each. Duluth has a median income of $45,950, about 30 percent lower than the statewide median income, with a median income of $19,844 for people of color (St. Louis County Public Health and Human Services 2013). The prevalence of food insecurity in the state of Minnesota is 10.8 percent, but a Duluth survey found that 20.4 percent of participants were "worried they would run out of food before they could buy more"—an indicator of food insecurity (Kjos et al. 2015). A study in the Lincoln Park neighborhood, classified as a food desert, found that a significant portion of the population (10–15 percent) experienced barriers accessing food. Residents overpaid for food at local convenience stores, and many used food pantries and SNAP benefits to provide for their families (Pine and Bennett 2014).

Duluth is a socially and politically liberal city; even as Trump was elected into office in 2016, the city elected its first female mayor, Emily Larson, who often bikes to work. Duluth tends to have high civic participation and is home to several social service organizations. Rev. David Bard, the former minister of the First United Methodist Church, which hosts RP in Duluth, talked about "a kind of quality of care about folks in Duluth," but said that the city had a long way to go to become that beacon of light Jesus talked about. Indeed, hidden beneath the cloak of white liberalism, most well-to-do residents remain largely illiterate about the ways in which structural racism, classism, and institutionalized patterns of exploitation occur.

The gulf between volunteers and clients at food pantries such as Chum is clear evidence of this kind of socioeconomic and racial separation that exists in Duluth. On the one hand, there is a set of well-to-do, mostly white folks with an interest in the arts, the outdoors, and craft beer. These folks tend to be well-connected to each other and institutions, giving Duluth a small-town feel. They also tend to be socially engaged and put their ethical sensibilities to work in the form of volunteerism and activism. On the other hand, you have a set of people (white and people of color) too poor to participate in the lifestyle the city has to offer, folks who are excluded from full citizenship in the city because of poverty, mental illness, drugs, and homelessness. The people who show up to RP each month are an indicator that poverty and food insecurity are very much part of the white experience as well.

Duluth is often referred to as the "city on the hill" by local residents, an apt phrase because the city is located quite literally on a hill that ends at the shores of Lake Superior. The magnificent lake full of beauty, promise, and irony is visible from almost all corners of the city. During the late nineteenth century, Duluth was the only port in the United States with access to the Atlantic and Pacific Oceans and as such became the site of the prosperous steel, lumber, and shipping industries. The economic downturn of the 1970s and 1980s brought with it the closure of the steel plant and a dwindling population and economy. Bulk carrier ships come in and out of the Duluth harbor for at least nine months of the year, carrying iron ore, coal, and stone from the lower lakes through the Saint Lawrence Seaway and the Soo Locks at Sault Ste. Marie. Today, fog horns can be heard almost all year round; silos loom in the harbor and over the horizon, as do giant piles of taconite, iron ore pellets, and limestone. All this is a ready reminder of the city's industrial heyday, but also of a tenuous present.

Defining Hunger and Food Insecurity

Hunger is the extreme effect of the prolonged and involuntary lack of food, resulting in "discomfort, illness, weakness, or pain that goes beyond the usual uneasy sensation" (USDA 2017a). Typically, by the time someone has experienced hunger, they have already suffered considerable harm, so the term *food insecurity* is used to capture the nutritional, emotional, and mental trauma associated with this broader phenomenon (Coleman-Jensen, Gregory, and Singh 2014). The term *food security* originated in the hallways of international organizations such as the Food and Agricultural Organization (FAO) in response to global threats of hunger, famine, and starvation in the early 1970s. Initial understandings of food security showed concerns for the production and supply of food at a global level; however, in later years, the term *food security* shifted to include a whole nexus of concerns around purchasing power, nutrition, and social control (Patel 2009). Today, the most-cited definition of *food security* in the United States comes from a World Bank (1986, 1) report, which defined it as "access by all people at all times to enough food for an active and healthy life."

An Unjust Food System

The problem of hunger and food insecurity in the United States is surprising because there is no shortage of food in the country. According to the FAO, world agriculture produces enough food to provide everyone in the world with at least 2,720 kilocalories per person per day (Carolan 2011). The United States not only has an abundance of food, but also has the cheapest food in the world: people spend less of their annual income on food here than in any other country. Hunger is not caused by the lack of food in the world but by the inability of people to gain access to the plentiful food that exists—and this is a systemic issue. One of my participants Lara, a woman of color and a local food systems advocate, used a very apt analogy to talk about how far-reaching the food system is, saying, "It's like a weed, where you think you're just getting the little flower, and then you pull it out and it's like a big bulb. And, you pull it out and the weed goes all the way down there [signaling to the other end of the room]." In the food system today, the levers of power are operated not by those who grow and produce food or even by the public who consumes food, but rather by multinational corporations, transnational agencies, lobbyists, and federal and state governments, which together create hunger—with devastating consequences.

Hunger persists because of a variety of interlocking reasons, ranging from the industrialization of agriculture to neoliberal trade agreements to a lack of adequate legal entitlements. Over the last fifty years, there has been a radical shift from viewing food as a public good to viewing it as a commodity to be bought, sold, and traded on the global market. According to environmentalist Vandana Shiva (2008), the food crisis today is the result of the convergence of climate change, peak oil, and globalization, all of which have devastated people's access to food and livelihoods. Agricultural trade liberalization has resulted in a concentration of landholding across nations: while large, export-oriented agricultural industries emerge as winners in the system, small farmers and communities lose their lands, their intellectual property rights, and their rights to grow food (de Souza et al. 2008). In addition, government cuts in agricultural input subsidies have forced farmers to pay more for agricultural inputs while receiving less for their output. As a result, the food system today is highly concentrated, with a small number of companies owning a large market share of grain, meat, and agrichemicals. For example, chickens used to be raised in small flocks by many farmers, but today most are factory farmed in large numbers and are under contract with a few companies, like Tyson.

These processes have had devastating effects on the everyday lives of people—in the United States and globally. As noted earlier, approximately 12 percent of the US population faces hunger and food insecurity, and around forty million people access food assistance programs. Advocates even talk about the fact that farmers in the United States are now using food assistance programs because they are food insecure; farmers grow commodity crops, not food, and as a result cannot disperse food locally to feed people and are food insecure themselves. In India, the country of my birth, the food system has led to an epidemic of farmer suicides; farmers who are unable to pay off debts are killing themselves leaving behind emotionally devastated and financially indentured families and communities (Rastogi and Dutta 2015).

Overall, the fact that not even the richest country in the world can guarantee food security for its citizens signals a failure of public policy. Worldwide, activists have called for restructuring the food system, increasing minimum wage, and increasing legal food entitlements as necessary solutions to hunger. They assert that policy should be centered on a "food-first" principle, rather than a profit-first principle, and should be informed by the right to food, health, and a clean environment (Riches and Silvasti 2014). In the United States, advocates note that changing the food system will require campaign finance reform because our current political representatives speak on behalf of corporations, not people. Food justice requires not only increases in entitlements and wages, but specific policies to advance equity and fix the problem of food deserts, food swamps, residential segregation, and grocery gaps. The good food movement has offered urban gardening, community-supported agriculture, farm-to-school programs, and farmers' markets as solutions to food access, although it notes that such strategies are only possible when resources of money, time, and land are available to communities (Alkon and Agyeman 2011; Allen 1999).

Legal Entitlements and Entitlement Failure

Hunger is neither natural nor inevitable, but rather the product of social and political design. This idea of "entitlement failure" was proffered more than thirty years ago by Nobel Prize–winning economist Amartya Sen (1983), who observed that famines across the world occurred amid ample food supply, even in countries exporting food—a clear example of people's legal rights not being fulfilled. He asserted rather controversially for the time that "the law stands between food availability and food entitlement" (166). This is why butter and wheat were exported during the Irish famine of 1840, even when poor Irish people could not afford these foods. This is also why three million Indians died during the Bengal famine in 1943, even as British Prime Minister Churchill ordered the diversion of food from starving Indians to well-fed British soldiers (Mukerjee 2010).

So what is a legal entitlement? In general, government programs are considered entitlements if legislation requires the payment of benefits to any person or entity. Entitlements are binding obligations on the government, and eligible recipients have legal recourse if the obligation is not fulfilled. Just as employers have legal claims to tax credits, so too do entitlements confer people with *legal* rights to particular credits (Jost 2003).

The United States Department of Agriculture (USDA) is the government agency that manages the issue of hunger and provides nutritional guidelines for the country, among its many other roles. The USDA administers one of the largest food-entitlement programs—the Supplemental Nutrition Assistance Program (SNAP) program, formerly known as the Food Stamp Program. SNAP provides cash benefits to millions of eligible, low-income individuals and families, which can be used to purchase food. SNAP is a needs-based legal entitlement (similar to Medicaid and Supplemental Security Income), which means that SNAP allocations are made through "mandatory spending" and SNAP exists outside of the annual appropriations process. So to say that SNAP is a federal "entitlement" program means that anyone who is eligible can receive benefits; moreover, receiving benefits does not mean someone else is going to lose them.

In 2016, about forty-five million people living in 21.8 million US households participated in the SNAP program, but the rates show decline (Oliveira 2018). There has been a steady decline in SNAP spending due to lower participation rates and a reduction in average benefits. In fiscal year 2017, 42.2 million individuals on average participated in the SNAP program each month—almost 5 percent fewer than in the previous year. The per-person benefits averaged $125.99 per month, which represented a 7 percent drop from 2014 after the end of the Recovery Act benefit increase (Oliveira 2018). According to the SNAP outreach coordinators I spoke to, reasons for low SNAP participation rates include strict poverty governance procedures combined with rock-bottom benefits not worth signing up for, personal shame or embarrassment for using benefits, and moral quandaries people experience due to feeling like they may be taking benefits away from others.

The USDA has other mechanisms by which it provides food support; these programs do not provide cash benefits like SNAP, but provide food—typically industrial food—based on eligibility criteria and need. These programs include The Emergency Food Assistance Program (TEFAP), which provides "emergency food" to people through charitable food support programs such as food pantries and soup kitchens; the Women, Infants, and Children program, which provides food support for pregnant women and children; the National School Lunch Program (NSLP), which provides free and reduced lunch to kids in school; the Commodity Supplemental Food Program (CSFP), which provides food support to elderly people; and the Food Distribution Program on Indian Reservations (FDPIR), which was set up as an alternative to SNAP for American Indian and non-Indian households living on Indian reservations without easy access to SNAP offices or authorized grocery stores.

Industrial Surplus Food

There is little debate today that federal food support programs were developed during the Depression to solve the problems of hunger *and* surplus food. Food is created in such overabundance in the United States that simply redistributing surplus food to the hungry is enough to stave the physiological sensation of hunger—and this is exactly what the government does. Historian Elizabeth Sanders (1999) argued that in the early years, the role of the USDA was to serve the interests of the people that worked the land, but over the next century, it became more involved in overhauling federal farm policy. Policy overhauls were oriented toward supporting industrial agriculture, which employed the use of inputs such as pesticides, fertilizer, and hybrid seeds. Industrial agriculture resulted in the mass production of food and created surpluses of certain kinds of food. By the 1970s, there was a push toward expanding commodity crops (e.g., corn, wheat, rice, and soybeans), with the government subsidizing these crops. The result was more surplus food. In this protectionist system, the government buys back surplus foods from agroindustrial players like Cargill to distribute to vulnerable Americans through a mash-up of food assistance programs designed to manage hunger, such as TEFAP. Gottlieb and Joshi (2010, 77) point out that the USDA combined big agriculture and social welfare programs in a way that said, "Feed the poor and feed school children, but do it with the surplus commodity crops, surplus meat and dairy products."

Aggressive neoliberal policies rolled out in the 1990s, such as the Welfare Reform Act of 1996 and Charitable Choice Legislation in 2002, have meant that in recent years social services including food assistance are almost exclusively delivered by nongovernmental organizations (Bielefeld and Cleveland 2013). In the hunger industrial complex, agricultural and retail industrial players like Dole, Del Monte, Target, Walmart, and Tyson sell or donate surplus foods to food banks, which channel these foods to food pantries, soup kitchens, and other service providers to distribute to the poor. These surplus foods may be commodity crops, foods deemed unfit for retail because of manufacturing errors or damage during shipping and handling, or even failed new food products. Food banks employ high-tech and sophisticated logistical apparatuses to transfer surplus food from the point of origin to the hungry. In the United States, roughly 80 percent of all food banks are affiliated with Feeding America (FA), a national network that procures and redistributes surplus and unsalable food from agrobusinesses and the USDA. Founded in 1979, FA comprises two hundred food banks, which distribute food to around sixty thousand food pantries and meal programs. The majority of FA's partner agencies and food pantries are run by faith-based organizations (FBOs). Across these charitable arenas, thousands of dedicated organizations, staff, and volunteers donate their time and labor to coordinate the delivery of surplus foods to the hungry and food insecure.

The distribution of surplus foods has become increasingly contentious with regards to health. The hunger-obesity paradox—the fact that hungry individuals can also be overweight and obese—is associated with disordered eating, a poor diet, dietary nutrient deficiencies, and low fruit and vegetable intake, all of which increase the risk of obesity and health problems (Dinour, Bergen, and Yeh 2007; Drewnowski and Darmon 2005). To maintain adequate energy, people with limited means select lower-quality diets, consisting of high-energy, inexpensive foods. The frequency of fruit and vegetable consumption declines significantly as food-insecurity status worsens—so the hunger-obesity paradox can at least partially be explained by the fact that low-costs foods are higher in fats, added sugars, and refined grains. These industrially processed foods tend to be cheaper per calorie than nutrient-dense foods such as certain fruits and vegetables. Using food pantries may also contribute to health problems for the same reason; food pantries typically distribute highly processed food with high levels of sodium, fat, and sugar, which can be transported, shelved, and distributed easily, but these foods also result in health issues. There has been research linking programs like SNAP to increased risk of being overweight, although these findings have not been consistent and vary by program and other aspects of the food environment (Dinour, Bergen, and Yeh 2007).

Public health researchers Chilton and Rose (2009) sound a clarion call for hunger and food insecurity to be viewed through a rights or entitlements-based approach. They observe that though the USDA collects data on food insecurity each year and has been publishing its findings for decades, there has been very little change in the prevalence of food insecurity; in fact, the numbers have gone up. The question of who is responsible for creating or enabling a state of food security remains unclear. Chilton and Rose write: "Accountability also implies that, in cases where government does not follow through on appropriate reference goals, there is legal recourse for those affected" (1205).

Poverty Governance and SNAP Fraud

Not only do government entitlement programs provide inadequate food support, but they also subject claimants to harsh systems of *poverty governance*, a term that refers to the way in which the poor are surveilled, disciplined, and brought into submission through stringent and less than adequate social programs. Political theorists Soss, Fording, and Schram (2011, 1) in *Disciplining the Poor* note that poverty programs are not designed to eliminate poverty, but rather "to temper the hardships of poverty and ensure that they do not become disruptive for the broader society." Indeed, the poor are both marginal and central to the social order; marginalized because they are isolated and ignored and exist at the periphery of society, but central, because the burden they bear is necessary for the rest of society to enjoy the life that it does. Given this social structure, social programs are designed to make the poor "more manageable" and to secure their cooperation. To do this, a wide variety of policy and administrative tools are used, including surveillance and penalty systems to keep recipients in check. Soss, Fording, and Schram argue that the convergent forces of poverty governance and neoliberalism have resulted in a "muscular" form of governance that is more normative, dispersed, and diverse in its organization.

Pine (2016) similarly argues that poverty and economic inequality in the United States have been growing in recent decades; however, food assistance programs are strategically designed to keep people food insecure. These programs serve low- and no-income individuals, providing a carefully calibrated ration of food that preempts the physical pangs of hunger but is insufficient for achieving food security. They provide just enough food to keep poor people from starving or protesting in the streets, but not enough for people to live healthy, stress-free, and happy lives. For instance, Pine (2016) observes that maintaining eligibility for SNAP benefits is a time-consuming but necessary part of the lives of food insecure people. The eligibility criteria across multiple programs intersect to create a "porous continuum of care" within which people experiencing food insecurity must constantly maneuver without seeing any real change in the quality of their lives. These programs diffuse disruptive political demands but do not protect people from the nutritional, mental, and emotional trauma of hunger.

Feminist scholar Nancy Fraser (1987) uses the phrase "juridical-administrative-therapeutic state apparatus" (JAT) to theorize the current welfare system that depoliticizes social problems and renders them into individual problems to be administered by highly regulated state machinery. Consistent with the theme of poverty governance, the *juridical* element positions recipients according to a legal system by allowing or denying them rights based on market-driven definitions of citizenship; for instance, in an increasingly neoliberal landscape, the poor only have the right to assistance if they are engaged in economic production. The *administrative* element requires that subjects petition and prove their need to a bureaucratic institution, which decides their claims based on administratively defined criteria. The final *therapeutic* element transposes public and political problems into problems of "mental health" or "character problems," such that solutions to hunger also include attending nutrition classes and mothering instructions. Fraser argues that the JAT "positions its subjects as passive clients or consumer recipients and not as active co-participants involved in shaping their life-conditions. ... It is a form of passive citizenship in which the state preempts the power to define and satisfy people's needs" (115).

Because SNAP is a needs-based entitlement program that *must* be allocated, the only way the government can change the amount spent on the program is by manipulating eligibility criteria and restrictions. So, though the government must provide SNAP benefits, it can control *how much* of these benefits to provide and *to whom*. The criteria can be set to exclude or include more people and/or to be more or less generous in benefits to eligible recipients. As a result, potential SNAP beneficiaries are subjected to rigorous screening procedures to verify eligibility based on income and assets. Households must report their income and other relevant information; the process involves a state eligibility worker, who interviews a household member and verifies the information using third-party data matches, paper documentation, or by contacting a knowledgeable party, such as an employer or landlord. Households must reapply for benefits periodically, usually every six or twelve months, and report any income changes.

SNAP requires that all recipients meet work requirements unless exempted because of age or disability. In addition, Able-bodied Adults Without Dependents (or "ABAWDS" as they are referred to in policy) between the ages of 18 and 49 must meet special work requirements to maintain their eligibility.

Despite the fact that SNAP has one of the lowest fraud rates for federal programs, which fell from four cents on the dollar in 1993 to about one cent in 2006–2008, there is a robust setup to prevent against fraud and abuse (Dean 2016). Per the USDA (2017c), *SNAP fraud* occurs when benefits are exchanged for cash or when people lie on their applications to get benefits—or more than they are supposed to get—or when a retailer has been disqualified from the program for past abuse or falsifying information. In 2014, approximately forty-six million individuals received SNAP benefits, of whom only forty-five thousand individuals were disqualified for fraud—a drop in the ocean. Still, the USDA has over one hundred analysts and investigators across the country who analyze retailer data, conduct undercover investigations, and process cases, including issuing fines and administrative disqualifications. In 2012, SNAP investigations resulted in 342 convictions, including a number of multiyear prison terms and approximately $57 million in monetary results. The USDA website encourages the reporting of fraud stating: "If you see or hear about SNAP fraud, tell us. Help us protect your tax dollars ... We appreciate the help of concerned citizens ... Your report is confidential. Help us Fight SNAP Fraud." Neoliberal ideological formations can also be seen in this clincher on the USDA website: "While SNAP is intended to ensure that no one in our land of plenty should fear going hungry, it also reflects the importance of work and responsibility" (USDA 2017b).

Dominant Hunger Narratives

Dominant hunger narratives in the United States mirror the contradictions and tensions embedded in the food system, a system controlled by the vested interests of multinational corporations, nongovernmental agencies, and federal and state governments. In this political economic context, portrayals of the hungry tend to be informed by the *kinds of solutions being talked about.* Food insecure people vacillate between being portrayed as sympathetic, relatable, and empathetic, or as dishonest, untrustworthy, and shameful welfare abusers, depending on the context. When the context is charity, hunger drives present sympathetic images of the hungry for fundraising purposes and easily sidestep the systemic and political dimensions of food access—often not even known to those participating in the drives. Pathologizing language and imagery are used to pull at the heart strings of citizens and to motivate charitable food donations. These stories portray hunger as a significant problem that *can* be solved by individuals "doing good," when in reality, the hunger problem is far too vast to be solved by charity. When the context is policy and political change, such as an increase in SNAP benefits, then hungry people are demonized and framed as "fraudulent abusers." Charitable solutions are applauded, but broad-based structural solutions—such as increasing the minimum wage, employment, and benefits and restructuring the food system—are met with disdain. The switch between sympathy and disdain in not based on any real difference between "people who are hungry" and "people who are on welfare," but rather this difference is a *socially constructed difference* deployed to justify political projects.

Adding insult to injury, not only are recipients of food drives framed in negative ways, but those who contribute to food drives and food shelves are framed in positive ways. A study by DeLind (1994) interrogated the discursive practices of "commodified giving" used by Michigan Harvest Gathering (MHG), an antihunger campaign, which was a partnership between public, private, and nonprofit institutions. She found that donors and corporations were applauded for their compassion, care, and social responsibility. The givers were framed as "winners" and given public recognition and rewards. Missing from the discourse however was any mention of the profitable partnerships between state, government, and the corporate sector. For instance, the fact that the food bank council employs government grants to clean, sort, haul and transport second grade produce to then deliver to the food banks. DeLind also found that those who experienced hunger were completely absent from the discourse. Press releases did not give the public a sense of the nature, extent or human dilemmas that constituted hunger. While compelling statistics were used to show the extent of the problem, she writes: "Such information does not contribute to the public's ability to understand hunger better. It merely documents hunger's worthiness as an opponent" (61). MHG produced a recipe book for sale, but there were no recipes by the hungry or for hungry people; in fact, ingredients were expensive and elite. No one with any experience of hunger sat on the MHG planning board, instead there were only "distinguished leaders"; the hungry were not present at the celebration receptions, and while mingling with others was encouraged, this did not include mingling with the hungry. DeLind concluded that MHG "selectively dehumanized (or technified) the issue of hunger, while at the same time it personified corporate structures, and justified commercial interests in humanistic terms" (59).

Relevant to this discussion are how portrayals of the poor in a neoliberal era shift between stereotypes of the poor, who are unable to reverse their circumstances to images of the poor as entrepreneurial (Clair and Anderson 2013). For instance, in their study of Heifer International, a religious nonprofit based in the United States, Clair and Anderson (2013) found that the organization portrayed poor communities in Africa as happy, healthy workers, and as "enterprising" people on the cusp of capitalism, who just needed the donation of a cow (or other such animal) to succeed, while complex histories of colonialism and American imperialism were sidestepped. Harter et al. (2004) studied the discursive practices of Streetwise, a Chicago- based nonprofit, who through the publication of a journal by the same name, provides employment opportunities to homeless men and women. They found that the paper was filled with personal stories of men and women recovering from addiction and adverse life experiences. The stories highlighted that it was important to the men and women not simply to be given a handout for selling papers on street corners, but to be treated as business vendors. Homeless individuals were framed as "independent entrepreneurs working their way toward success" (412–413).

Today, charitable organizations face pressure to incorporate business practices and construct the poor as "entrepreneurs," but in so doing engage in practices that forestall systemic transformation. Individuals are portrayed as entrepreneurial, but the enormous challenges that poverty presents to entrepreneurship are ignored. For instance, according to Forbes (2013), the eight key skills successful entrepreneurs require are resiliency, focus, investing for the long term, finding and managing people, sales, staying up to date, self-reflection, and self-reliance. Other skills include personal branding, financial management, stress management, the ability to experiment, and design thinking. Indeed, to expect that a person living in poverty, given a cow or a stack of newspapers, will magically acquire the resources, capital, and networks necessary to move from indigence to becoming a successful entrepreneur of the Forbes-caliber kind is simply insincere.

Across dominant discourses, what is clear is that portrayals of the hungry and the poor are always partial, incomplete, and lacking in depth. Individuals experiencing hunger are either completely erased from the narratives or are stigmatized as victims, perpetrators, and morally flawed individuals. Even when individuals are portrayed positively as entrepreneurs, these portrayals are incomplete as they erase the context within which poverty occurs. These portrayals are unrealistic—and a good example of how the American dream is continuously being repackaged.

Overall, dominant narratives fail to connect with the desires, concerns, complexities, and contexts of hungry individuals. The voices of the hungry are erased and displaced by voices of privilege—and their corresponding values, assumptions, and ideologies. Today, ideological assumptions about how charity coupled with capitalism can solve social and structural problems dominate the discourse. Dominant narratives fail to educate the public on the injustice that permeates the food system. Because of these erasures, stories fail to unite tellers and listeners in ways that illuminate issues of power and control and food injustice; instead, the stories reinforce the division between Us and Them. The result is that well-intentioned people participate in hunger drives and tell their children not to waste food; but since hunger and food insecurity are depoliticized in these discourses, the opportunity for systemic transformation is lost. Delind (1994, 61) describes what an alternative discourse about hunger would look like: "It would mean, among other things, allowing the reasons and relationships that surround hunger to emerge from peoples' lives and not have them institutionally prescribed. To do this would require admitting the perspective, or standpoint, of those who are hungry. It would mean making them visible, validating their insights into the nature of hunger, and honoring their behavioral responses to it."

Hunger in an International Context

In *First World Hunger Revisited,* Riches and Silvasti (2014) show internationally how the rise of neoliberalism in rich, food secure, industrialized nations has been accompanied by the rise of the institutionalization, corporatization, and globalization of charitable food banking. Since the 1990s, food-banking procedures have been institutionalized in countries such as

Canada, Australia, the United Kingdom, and New Zealand, a process pioneered by the United States. Food banking is also on the rise in the welfare states of Finland and Denmark—surprisingly, because food banking runs contrary to the Nordic ideal of universalism, which highlights the public responsibilities of society toward its citizens based on democracy and a commitment to reducing inequities (Silvasti and Karjalainen 2014). In Finland, similar to the United States, food pantries were triggered by a depression in the 1990s but soon became a way to silently fix the holes in the social security system. Even when the economy stabilized, the state argued that it could not afford to increase social security funding. Riches and Silvasti observe that when food aid becomes part of the mission of the third sector, it becomes very difficult to reverse.

In Europe, the growing reliance on the redistribution of surplus food acts as a safety valve for global food markets. For example, the European Union's food distribution program Fund for European Aid to the most Deprived (FEAD) buys up agricultural surplus to balance market fluctuations; this overproduction is later delivered as food aid to Finland and other countries. Riches and Silvasti (2014) argue that the public legitimacy of charitable food assistance points to an interesting contradiction: on the one hand, these governments deny and belittle hunger as a social problem, but at the same time they are involved with strengthening the corporatization and global outreach of food banks through public funding. Of course, where there are welfare cuts and roll-out neoliberalism, there you will also find stigmatizing rhetoric; rhetoric in which welfare and legal entitlements are presented in terms of the moral decline of recipients, who are typically depicted as shirkers—and this is happening across industrialized nations, which have abundant food supplies (Garthwaite 2017; Silvasti and Karjalainen 2014).

The Problem with Charity

From a political perspective, charitable food assistance programs are popular because unlike legal entitlements, they do not rock the boat. As many officials I spoke to said: "Democrats like them because they feed the poor, and Republicans like them because they help big business." In this system, corporate and government interests are promoted, but not the needs and interests of clients. Corporate donors win big: they get to donate outdated, expired, and unsaleable foods to food banks, receive tax write-offs, and be protected from liability via Good Samaritan laws. Food banks and food pantries further contribute to corporate welfare by sparing corporations disposal costs and landfill fees and helping companies forge an image of corporate citizenship (Tarasuk and Eakin 2003, 2005). However, taken together, the hunger industrial complex represents a form of *systemic charity*, a term I use to refer to the large scale and methodical manner in which money, labor, and the good intentions of people are harnessed and channeled in service of the Other through the complex arrangement of people, materials, and organizations. In this hunger industrial complex, charity does not exist outside of a capitalist/neoliberal market logic, but rather charity is very much "capitalism at work." Clair and Anderson (2013, 558) note that charitable organizations "necessarily prop up the weak rafters in a capitalist structure without most donors realizing this implication."

There are several reasons that charity is not an appropriate solution to end hunger. Charity depoliticizes the issue of hunger, making it a personal and a private issue, not a public one (Chilton and Rose 2009; Poppendieck 1999). Unlike entitlements, charity does not confer upon people guaranteed rights, but rather traffics in the language of gratitude. Charity legitimizes the distribution of substandard products and services and makes it impossible to question the giver or the gift. Farmer (2005) observes that charity typically means "doling out the leftovers" in a piecemeal fashion and asking recipients to be grateful for it. He makes a rather chilling observation: "Those who believe that charity is the answer to the world's problems often have a tendency—sometimes striking, sometimes subtle, and surely lurking in all of us—to regard those needing charity as intrinsically inferior. This is different from regarding the poor as powerless or impoverished because of historical processes and events (slavery, say, or unjust economic policies propped up by power parties)" (153). Charity reinforces social distance and hierarchy between givers and receivers and Us and Them (Bourdieu 1990). Consequentially, charity silences civic participation and resistance from those on the receiving end by creating subject positions that furthers their political and communicative disenfranchisement.

Charity is not justice. Communication scholars Frey, Pearce, Pollock, Artz, and Murphy (1996, 111) observe that "social justice is not done when 'we' in our largess donate some of our disposable resources to 'them'; it is done when we act on our recognition that something is amiss in a society of abundance if some of us are well off while others are destitute." Having a social justice sensibility means identifying with others from a position of solidarity; a solidarity that is grounded in the realization that we share a world with others and are thus ethically obligated to listen to and respond meaningfully to their stories. A social justice sensibility requires engagement and action to redress structural inequities, not simply doling out the leftovers. Contrary to dominant discourses about the altruistic nature of charity as "doing good" and "serving the community," charity in its systemic form is an agent of stigma because it produces and reproduces the subordination of particular groups of people through macro-level policies and microlevel practices, and in so doing, charity represents both the outcome of and a precursor to stigmatization.

Rights-Based Perspectives

Rights- and justice-based perspectives focus on equity and therefore provide a counterfoil to charitable approaches to hunger. Poppendieck (1999, 69) notes: "The justice model is associated with dignity, entitlement, accountability, and equity. Its essence is the creation of rights, not only moral rights that may be asserted but also justiciable rights that can be enforced through legal action." Specifically, the right to adequate food, food sovereignty, and community food security perspectives provide a useful entry point for how to think about justice-based solutions. These perspectives outline the root causes of hunger and identify *who* is responsible for facilitating and creating conditions of food security.

The right to adequate food (RAF) was adopted by the United Nations in 1948, when food was seen as a necessary condition to achieve a minimum standard of living: "The right to have regular, permanent and unrestricted access, either directly or by means of financial purchases, to quantitatively and qualitatively adequate and sufficient food corresponding to the cultural traditions of the people to which the consumer belongs, and which ensure a physical and mental, individual and collective, fulfilling and dignified life free of fear" (United Nations Human Rights 2010, 2). The RAF framework maintains that food must be "available, accessible and adequate" (2); thus, violating the right to food can interfere with the fulfillment of human rights, such as the right to health, education, or life, and vice versa. The RAF delineates the role of government in ensuring people's right to food.

Importantly, the right to food is not a right to *be fed*, but the right to *feed oneself* in dignity. The RAF further stipulates that because the private sector plays a significant role in the food system in food production, processing, distribution, and trade, it must also be held accountable for food insecurity, as well as environmental contamination (Patel 2009).

A global movement, *food sovereignty* is defined as "the RIGHT of peoples, communities, and countries to define their own agricultural, labor, fishing, food and land policies which are ecologically, socially, economically and culturally appropriate to their unique circumstances. It includes the true right to food and to produce food, which means that all people have the right to safe, nutritious and culturally appropriate food and to food-producing resources and the ability to sustain themselves and their societies" (NGO/CSO Forum for Food Sovereignty 2002). The notion of food sovereignty arose in the 1970s with a group of Guatemalan Mayan peasant farmers or *campesinos* trying to establish agroecological alternatives to industrial farming practices. Food sovereignty advocates for communities' rights to grow and produce rather than depend on global markets. This movement is not necessarily antitrade but is against dominant global agribusiness systems that devastate the livelihoods of farmers (Patel 2009). The movement rallies against policies from the World Bank and International Monetary Fund that push for neoliberal deregulation and privatization of the agricultural sector. It argues that land grabs by big agribusinesses in the context of an expanding neoliberal agenda have resulted in the consolidation of land ownership and created a peasantry dependent on agribusiness for its survival.

The community food security (CFS) framework emerged in the United States in the early 1970s, inspired by the food sovereignty movements in the Global South (Hamm and Bellows 2003). Food studies scholar Patricia Allen (1999) traces the movement's domestic origins to the 1960s and 1970s civil rights movement and Black power organizations concerned with problems of nutrition for inner-city children. In the CFS framework, food security is defined as follows: "all persons obtaining at all times a culturally acceptable, nutritionally adequate diet through local non-emergency sources" (39). CFS is concerned with ownership of food production and provides a rallying cry against the charitable response to hunger. A CFS approach includes an emphasis on economic and social rights, self-reliance, and a systemic understanding of sustainable natural resource use. Although CFS accounts for the role of government, its primary focus is on culture-centered community solutions and transforming local and regional food systems: the argument being that solutions must go beyond government entitlements to create long-term independence for communities.

Chapter Overview

Through a comparative case analysis, this book presents a multifaceted look at how neoliberal stigma plays out in food pantries. Each chapter showcases the opacity of deep-seated ideological formations; the versatility of neoliberal stigma (how it is used in a variety of contexts); and how race, class, and gender inform the experience and expression of stigma. When the data allow it, the chapters highlight moments of possibility for resisting neoliberal stigma. Each chapter highlights a different facet of injustice that occurs in food pantry spaces and it is my hope that each chapter will provide a slightly different framework for reflection, discussion, and action. The chapters conclude with implications for practice and policy, with the caveat that these are incomplete lists to be used as starting points for further analysis by organizations and advocates.

Chapter 2 charts the key conceptual and interlocking themes in the book: ideology and discourse, neoliberalism, and the stigma of poverty, welfare, race, religion, and gender, all of which work together to produce neoliberal stigma. Chapter 3, the first data chapter, begins by foregrounding the voices of the hungry and food insecure. In the voices of the hungry we hear stories of desire, ambition, and complexity. We hear about the struggles that poor people, people of color, and mothers and fathers face. We also recognize how the problem of hunger is intertwined with physiological health problems, disability, anxiety, stress, depression, lack of social support, institutional failures, and even violence and sexual abuse. Chapter 4 explores the ways in which whiteness, and the problematics of white liberalism play out in the Chum food pantry. Volunteers are caught between multiple discourses of individualism, hard work, and market vocabularies on the one hand and social justice discourses on the other. The chapter highlights the racial distance between volunteers and clients, as well as the discursive practices within Chum that reinforce racial distance. Chapter 5 explores the complexity of neoliberal stigma as it moves between the conservative evangelical Ruby's Pantry home office and the more politically liberal RP food distribution site in Duluth. The chapter highlights discursive practices at RP that make distinctions between the "good kind" of hungry people and the "bad kind" of hungry people—the subtext for which are often age-old racial and gender stereotypes.

Chapter 6 shows how neoliberal stigma surrounding the hungry creates a "culture of suspicion" in food pantry spaces. Clients are vigilant about how they speak and behave, always feeling the threat of stigma against them. The chapter highlights discursive practices that create solidarity and unity on the one hand but fracture communities on the other. Chapter 7 demonstrates how food insecure individuals perform health citizenship despite the crushing burden of material constraint. In the voices of the hungry, we hear how important good food is to them, how they feel more energetic after eating good food, how they enjoy gardening, and the lengths they go to in order to get nutrients into their diets.

The concluding chapter, chapter 8, draws out key findings from the study and ends with ways in which food pantries can be reconfigured in neoliberal times so as to move in the direction of food justice. Drawing on existing theories of social change, I argue that we must use the voices of the hungry and food insecure to reformulate identities and shift dominant narratives that surround the issue of hunger. I present examples of organizations and coalitions, including the Joint Religious Legislative Coalition (JRLC) and Appetite for Change, the work of which is useful for thinking about how to reenvision food pantry spaces.

The Hope: Food Pantries as Allies in Shifting the Narrative

As discussed in the review of the food system, food pantries are small actors in a much larger and unwieldly food system in which the biggest players are federal and state governments, multinational corporations, and transnational agencies and organizations. Food pantries are at the very bottom of the pecking order and in many ways beholden to the system and its rules—at least as far as food collection and distribution is concerned. However, food pantries are also necessary allies in dismantling the food system. Given their ubiquitous presence, food pantries have a tremendous opportunity to define what social justice looks like from a faith-based and humanist perspective and to engage in activism. There are over forty thousand food pantries in the United States. They all have a wide circle of influence because they employ staff and volunteers, serve clients, conduct outreach in their communities, and interact with government stakeholders. Added to that, most food pantries are run by FBOs and have small and large congregations in tow, with well-intentioned folks genuinely interested in reaching out to others. Business has shown itself irresponsible and government has shown itself as business, so FBOs are some of the last spaces to offer countercultural and noncomputational models of living and social exchange. It is my argument that food pantries must organize and assert their moral and ethical power in the food system for change to occur; they must shift the dominant narratives surrounding hunger and take steps toward systemic transformation.

Although it is true that food pantries have few resources to spare and are beholden to the larger food system in place, they can be a formidable force in influencing food justice. Food pantries are at the very frontlines of the hunger epidemic, closest to the people who experience the violence of hunger, so it is my argument that they can be centers for the production of new narratives. They can play an important role in disrupting the stigma that circulates around the poor and hungry—stigmatizing narratives that emerge from politics, religion, and race and that uphold the unjust food system. Fortified by the stories of their clients—clients like Trinity—food pantries can take small steps to act as points of resistance and to eventually bring about the vision of food justice. Food pantries could raise consciousness among their communities with regard to class, race, and gender dynamics. They could be more vigilant about the stories they tell and they could create counterdiscourses to resist political and religious ideologies that stigmatize the poor—themes that are taken up in chapter 8. In the midst of injustice, food pantries could bear witness to the power, agency, and desires of the people who walk through their doors. Although we cannot always claim to understand what hunger and structural violence feel like and we cannot exaggerate our roles as witnesses, we *can* act upon what we have finally recognized with both eyes wide open—as described by Eduardo Galeano in "Celebration of the Human Voice/2": "When it is genuine, when it is born of the need to speak, no one can stop the human voice. When denied a mouth, it speaks with the hands or the eyes, or the pores, or anything at all. Because every single one of us has something to say to the others, something that deserves to be celebrated or forgiven by others" (25). In an unjust food system, food pantries can play a role in recovering the silenced voices and creating new and richly humanizing narratives filled with complex truths and contradictions. In an unjust food system, food pantries can come together and bring disconnected people together to ask questions, to judge, to critique, and to join together in demanding justice, and, in so doing, create great joy, great, great joy in food.

2 Key Conceptual Themes

FROM THE DESK OF LYN SAHR

At Ruby's Pantry we are filling the food gap for thousands of families every month. Although we can provide a moment of happiness for parents by being able to feed their families, as the food goes away ... so goes the happiness. There is an old saying, "If you give a man a fish, he eats for a day. If you teach him how to fish, he eats for a lifetime!" We want to help people along the way to the satisfaction of self-sufficiency. That's one of the reasons we ask for a $20 donation. However, it is an uphill challenge.

There are three types of family situations that we recognize have needs. First, those that are not able to work. These dear folks are special and near to God's heart. Along with churches we are there to help them which is our Biblical responsibility.

The second type is the family situation where the heads of the household are not able to find jobs but they want to work. Shame on us for sending millions of jobs to other countries and taking away the dignity from the parents of children stuck in poverty this way. ...

And then there is the third type of situation, people who do not want to work and will not work. What do we do with this problem? The Apostle Paul writes this: "*On the contrary, we worked night and day, laboring and toiling so that we would not be a burden to any of you. We did this, not because we do not have the right to such help, but in order to make ourselves a model for you to follow. **For even when we were with you, we gave you this rule: 'If a man will not work, he shall not eat'**" (II Thessalonians 3:8–10; emphasis mine).

I know that sounds harsh but the underlying reality is that people cannot find satisfaction without providing for themselves to the best of their ability. ... At Ruby's Pantry we give people the opportunity for dignity and accountability which will help lead to contentment.

—Lyn Sahr, white male, founder of Ruby's Pantry, "From the Desk of Lyn Sahr," August 5, 2015

This letter penned by Lyn Sahr gets right to the heart of neoliberal stigma. Sahr is the founder of Ruby's Pantry (RP) and pastor of a small, conservative evangelical Christian church in Minnesota. Almost every month, Sahr writes letters clarifying RP's mission, vision, and values through a variety of stories, ponderings, and appeals. These letters go out to organizers, volunteers, and staff at RP and are also available online for public consumption. The letters clarify RP's position on the causes of hunger, who is responsible for hunger, and solutions to hunger and, in so doing, shed light on RP's worldview and political orientation. This letter is just one of the millions of texts and artifacts circulating in American society today that reinforces stigma against the poor by focusing on the individual causes of poverty—a mainstay of conservative evangelical discourses. These texts are so ubiquitous that most Americans would either nod in agreement or shrug them off without skipping a beat.

In this chapter, I use Sahr's letter as an entry point to chart out key conceptual themes in this book—ideology and discourse, neoliberalism, the stigma of poverty, welfare, race and gender, and religious theology, all of which work together to produce neoliberal stigma. The goal of this chapter is to answer a rather lofty question: Where does stigma come from? Similar to how structural racism is held in place by racial ideologies, it is my contention that the unjust food system is also fixed in place through ideological assumptions that cohere in each of these themes. These assumptions are not grounded in real facts about people but are socially constructed; in time and with repetition, they become real in people's minds. Furthermore, ideologies become sedimented in policy and therefore impact people in material ways. I should point out that even as I write about each theme separately, they are inextricably linked together and in practice much more difficult to parse out.

"People Who Do Not Want to Work and Will Not Work"

The tension at the heart of this book has to do with the third situation that Sahr describes—"people who do not want to work and will not work." This of course is not a fact, but a social and political myth. In this great American myth, these are the lazy and irresponsible people, "bad citizens," who do not take responsibility for their lifestyles. These are the folks who will do anything to get out of work. They take advantage of the system and live off the labor of good citizens. They do so because they have deep-seated character, moral, and spiritual flaws. This idea or ideological formation that there are people who "do not want to work and will not work" is a formidable one. It is the centerpiece of social and political debates in American society—even when not explicitly stated—and is constantly in circulation in American culture. This fundamental belief informs the way in which Americans give to charity, how they reach out to others, how they behave in work and nonwork environments, how they think about the problem of and solutions to hunger, and how they vote on policy (e.g., Gilens 1999). It can be found most blatantly in conservative discourses, but also in seemingly neutral liberal discourses. This belief is one of the cornerstones of neoliberal stigma.

I define *neoliberal stigma* as the otherizing and social-distancing phenomenon created through neoliberal political economic rationalities that operate across a range of cultural, political, and institutional practices. In the framework of neoliberal stigma, hard work, self-help, and self-reliance take center stage, consistent with Calvinist assumptions. However, in addition to these values, other meanings are attached, such as the glorification of wealth; economic responsibilities of citizenship (i.e., contribution to the bottom line or GDP); entrepreneurialism as a means to solve ethical and systemic issues; and the centrality of "choice" in the marketplace. When individuals fail to live up to the ideals of the marketplace, the consequence is an identification of difference, a separation of people into Us and Them, disapproval, and rejection. People who typically "fail" on neoliberal parameters are poor citizens, people of color, and other exploited groups, because they lack economic wealth—a necessary condition for citizenship in a neoliberal era. In a neoliberal framework, wealth is the unspoken criterion for humanization and the receipt of justice, a calculus, which then allows poor people to be denigrated, dehumanized, and delivered injustice. Neoliberal stigma expresses itself in communicative processes of framing, blaming, shaming, and silencing. However, unlike traditional Calvinist discourses, which tend to be explicit and harsh, neoliberal stigma is flexible and can also be found alongside more compassionate discourses. A key difference between how neoliberal stigma expresses itself via conservatives and liberals is with regards to religion; conservatives tend to believe that prayer and a personal relationship with God can solve problems of structural violence, whereas liberals tend to believe in the sufficiency of science and information in solving structural problems.

In his letter, Sahr weaves political, nationalistic, and theological threads together to explain the causes of hunger. Social distance between Us and Them—the latter being Sahr's third group—is produced through prescriptions about what it means to be a good citizen, where citizenship is tied to economic productivity and work is framed as dignity. In this framework, those who are economically underproductive are marked as lazy, deviant, and irresponsible, and not following God's way. In the opening of the letter, Sahr reinforces a key catchphrase in conservative thought—"teach a man to fish"—which he uses to prioritize individual hard work and entrepreneurialism as opposed to more systemic solutions. Sahr then gives a nod to nationalism by connecting hunger to the outsourcing of jobs: shame on us for causing "American" families to starve. This diatribe erases the fact that hunger in the United States is linked to global hunger—the commodification of food, land grabs by American agroindustries, and neoliberal policies.

The third category of people Sahr describes is a racially coded category; the fact that this racialization is *not* explicit is significant because neoliberal stigma typically occurs in a "color-blind" manner. In the wake of the civil rights era, whites have had a harder time expressing racism for fear of looking bad, but racism has not gone away; rather, it has taken on new forms of expression. Sociologist Bonilla-Silva (2010, 3) observes that the new racial ideology in place today is "color-blind racism" or "racism-lite" in which racial inequality is reproduced by practices that are subtle, institutional, and apparently nonracial: "Instead of relying on name calling (niggers, Spics, Chinks), color-blind racism otherizes softly ("these people are human, too"); instead of proclaiming God placed minorities in the world in a servile position, it suggests they are behind because they do not work hard enough; instead of viewing interracial marriage as wrong on a straight racial basis, it regards it as "problematic" because of concerns over the children, location, or the extra burden it places on couples. Yet this new ideology has become a formidable political tool for the maintenance of the racial order."

Indeed, when it comes to welfare, Gilens (1999) notes that an important reason Americans hate welfare is because of the racialized beliefs the public holds about welfare recipients. He avers that race is the subject just beneath the surface of terms such as *welfare, urban, crime,* and *poverty*—terms used strategically to evoke people of color. The homeless beggar, the welfare queen, the gang member are strongly associated with minorities in the mass media and the public imagination. He writes: "Although political elites typically use a race-neutral language in discussing poverty and welfare, it is now widely believed that welfare is a 'race-coded' topic that evokes racial imagery and attitudes even when racial minorities are not explicitly mentioned" (67).

Several studies in the social sciences confirm these findings; for instance, one survey of racial stereotyping found that the "mere mention" of affirmative action made white respondents significantly more likely to agree with negative racial generalizations like "most blacks are lazy" (Sniderman and Carmines 1997). In short, even though Sahr does not depict the third category of people in explicit racial terms, the implication is clear.

Now we might argue that "Sahr did not mean it this way," or perhaps he is just ignorant, unaware, or politically incorrect. Or perhaps I, the researcher, am reading too much into it. Perhaps. But what is made crystal clear in his letter is his standpoint or positionality in the world. In the arrogance of the writing, in his gaze of Others, Sahr betrays his whiteness. *Whiteness* is a "location of structural advantage," a worldview, standpoint, or "place from which white people look at ourselves, at others, and at society" (Frankenberg 1993, 1). In the social structure, the place or the point where Sahr is standing is right at the top, and he uses this position to gaze down at Others on the rungs beneath. In so doing, Sahr participates in maintaining the social order. Parker and Aggleton (2003, 17) argue that we should see stigma not as isolated phenomena or expressions of individual and cultural attitudes, but as central to the constitution of the social order: "Within such a framework, the construction of stigma (or, more simply, stigmatization) involves the marking of significant differences between categories of people, and through such marking, their insertion in systems or structures of power." This is precisely what Sahr does: he marks out categories and differences between Us and Them thereby operating the levers of power necessary to maintain the social order. This is also what we will see many people do in the course of this book. Now, Sahr may not recognize this and he may not "mean" it, but intentionality is irrelevant because discourse still has psychological and material impacts on those it marks.

In another letter, Sahr betrays his whiteness in a more compassionate manner, although here it is the anachronistic nature of his discourse that is disturbing. Sahr reminisces about a song he used to sing in Sunday school:

> Jesus loves the little children,
> All the children of the world.
> Red and yellow, black and white,
> They are precious in God's sight.
> Jesus loves the little children of the world.

Given his age, Sahr would have sung this song between Jim Crow and the civil rights era; however, to be still thinking this way implies that he has lived a racially segregated life and has never had to think about the meaning of his own racial identity in the world. This is clearly not the song "red and yellow, black and white" people sing today when talking of racial equity. What they say instead, standing in solidarity with people of color, is Black Lives Matter and Native Lives Matter. If one has genuine feelings of compassion for people of color and if one is truly committed to Black liberation, "a world free of anti-Blackness, where every Black person has the social, economic, and political power to thrive" (Black Lives Matter 2018), then one should take one's cues from those fighting for their lives. One should stand in solidarity with people of color in *their* movements, saying in unison with them, yes, Black Lives Matter. Sunday school ditties from the 1960s just do not cut it anymore and they never have except in white institutions.

Many liberals will shake their heads in disgust at Sahr's racism and oppressive interpretation of scripture yet might harbor similar ideological orientations in which they blame the poor for their situations. Typically in these instances, science, health, evidence-based medicine, and the economy are used eloquently to justify stricter controls over the poor. Dominant discourses are rife with journalists and health experts wielding prohealth, antipoor, neoliberal batons at food assistance programs. For example, an article on the front page of the *New York Times* (2017) titled "In the Shopping Cart of a Food Stamp Household: Lots of Soda," puts on display the stereotypes associated with people who are food insecure and use assistance programs. The article by Anahad O' Connor suggests that a disproportionate amount of food stamp money is going toward unhealthful foods such as junk foods, sodas, and sugar-sweetened beverages. This is despite the fact that the USDA report actually found little difference between purchases made by SNAP households and other households. In a similar vein, Ludwig, Blumenthal, and Willett (2012), in an article published in the *Journal of the American Medical Association*, argued that growing health care costs are reasons to warrant restructuring programs like SNAP. They applaud the WIC program, which already imposes severe restrictions on food purchases by mothers. Instead of advocating for broad-based structural solutions— increasing the minimum wage, entitlements, providing child care subsidies, and removing price supports for industrial agriculture—these professionals advocate for policies to further discipline the poor. The cold calculus of neoliberal stigma is seen in this clincher: "The public pays for sugary drinks, candy, and other junk foods included in SNAP benefits twice: once at the time of purchase, and later for the treatment of diet-induced disease through Medicaid and Medicare" (2568). In these two articles the ideological assumption that food insecure people have poor decision-making skills results in recommendations for harsher systems of poverty governance. This is typically the way in which neoliberal stigma expresses itself among liberals: it appears rational and balanced in the interests of science, logic, and the economy, but denigrates minoritized groups in the process and in so doing maintains the status quo.

It is not surprising that in each of these articles, the voices of privilege displace the voices of the oppressed. The voices of the hungry, food insecure, and SNAP recipients are neither present nor represented. Poor people, single mums, single dads, and children—those who suffer the disproportionate burden of hunger and food insecurity—are absent from the discourse. As a pattern, the voices of those we hear in the texts correspond to their systemic location. Sahr, O'Connor, and Ludwig, Blumenthal, and Willett: their words betray normative masculinity and whiteness, the connection between "property, privilege, and paler skin" (Slocum 2007, 521). They are on the top of the social ladder looking down. Their words perpetuate a narrative that legitimizes the social order, in which some people are on top and others below. This kind of elitism is similar to racism of which Bonilla-Silva (2010, 8) writes: "Those at the bottom of the racial barrel tend to hold oppositional views and those who receive the manifold wages of whiteness tend to hold views in support of the racial status quo." Amidst the clanging of industrial, entrepreneurial, and political interests, there is a complete erasure of those at the bottom of the food system—people living with hunger and food insecurity (Pine and de Souza 2013). It has become normal today to talk about the poor without consulting them. The tacit assumption is that poverty is normal, ordinary, and the poor have nothing of value to offer and do not deserve representation (DiFazio 2006). Their silence is accomplished through discourses that shame and blame food insecure people as well as discourses that appear rationale, logical, balanced, and scientific, but that are in fact permeated with neoliberal values and assumptions. Even as responsibility is continually shifted and refocused from macro to micro, from system to individual, from government to community, from oppressor to oppressed, the people most affected—symbolically and structurally—are silenced.

The next section provides an overview of the key conceptual themes interwoven throughout this book. These themes taken together answer a fundamental question: Where does the stigma of hunger and food insecurity come from?

Stigma and the Political Economy of Stigma

The term *stigma* in its Greek roots refers to marks on the skin or tattoos made by a pointed object; historically, it was a technique used to mark slaves, criminals, and prisoners of war so as to recognize them in case they escaped (Jones 1987). Since then, the phenomenon of stigma has come to encompass both visible and invisible marks on bodies, in bodies, or even near bodies, as in *stigma symbols*, which refers to the signs and symbols that associate an individual or a group with a particular debased identity (Goffman 1963). For instance, food pantries and food stamps may be seen as stigma symbols because they come to stand in for the conditions of hunger, poverty, and welfare. Erving Goffman (1963, 3), who pioneered the work on stigma, defined *stigma* as a "deeply discrediting" attribute, wherein stigmatized individuals are believed to possess a characteristic or a trait conveying a devalued social identity. Stigmatizing processes include labeling, stereotyping, and separation of people into Us and Them, the end result of which is discrimination (Link and Phelan 2001). Today stigma is seen as a multilevel concept, including *intrapersonal stigma*, which refers to the internalization of negative attitudes by the stigmatized; *interpersonal stigma*, or person-to-person discrimination; and *structural stigma*, which refers to societal-level conditions, cultural norms, and institutional policies that constrain the opportunities, resources, and well-being of the stigmatized (Corrigan, Markowitz, and Watson 2004).

Critical perspectives on stigma advance a broader historical and sociopolitical understanding of the nature of power and privilege interlocked with stigma. Theorists lament that over the past sixty years, the central thrust of stigma research has been at the individual level with a focus on stereotypes, negative perceptions, and consequences, often to the exclusion of broader societal patterns that create and reinforce stigma (Link and Phelan 2014; Parker and Aggleton 2003). Parker (2012, 166) invites stigma researchers to move beyond Goffman's initial model of stigma as a "mark" or negatively valued difference and toward thinking about "stigma as social process fundamentally linked to power and domination" or the "political economy of stigma." Stigma and stigmatization function at the point of intersection of culture, power, and difference—and it is only by exploring the relationships among these categories that we can understand stigma not as isolated phenomena, or expressions of individual or cultural attitudes, but as central to the constitution of the social order (Parker and Aggleton 2003). The political economy of stigma thus focuses on "how stigma is used by individuals, communities and the state to produce and reproduce structures of social inequality. It also pushes us to examine the political economy of stigmatization and its links to social exclusion and how historically constructed forms of stigma are strategically deployed to produce and reproduce social inequalities" (Parker 2012, 166). Stigma in essence then is as much a function of power and privilege as it is about disenfranchisement and marginalization: stigma is tied to history, politics, and injustice at every level.

Ideological Formations, Discursive Practices, and Discursive Erasures

Ideology and ideological formations play a pivotal role in social processes such as stigma. According to van Dijk (1990, 1995, 2001), ideologies are similar to social cognitions in that they are shared by members of a group, abstracted from personal knowledge and experiences, and have undergone a process of generalization and normalization. However, ideologies are more fundamental social cognitions in that they reflect more basic aims, interests, and values of groups. Ideologies may be thought of as underlying presuppositions, basic convictions, and axiomatic or elemental beliefs that are the basis of sociopolitical cognitions of groups. Because of its elemental nature, ideology is able to bring together and "make sense" of a variety of different issues. For example, people's specific attitudes about welfare, immigration, business outsourcing, and patriotism may all be based on a basic racist ideology. It is important to point out that unlike beliefs, where people are able to articulate "what they believe in," individuals are usually unaware of the ideological dimensions of their positions and therefore are not committed to them. This is why to see Sahr articulate the ideological dimensions of his beliefs so explicitly is both surprising and helpful. It helps to make sense of his view on hunger and food insecurity—as well as the route he takes to solve the problem. Dominant ideologies are often accepted as nonideological commonsense assumptions about the world and may be used by groups to disenfranchise other groups. Dominant ideologies demonstrate a very typical strategic pattern of flattering the in-group, while derogating the out-group. They exhibit positive self-representation and negative other-representation and an opposition between Us and Them (van Dijk 1995, 2001).

Ideology, discourse, and practice are inextricably linked together. The term *ideological formation* or *ideological discursive formation* (IDF) denotes the collapsing of the plane of ideology into that of discourse (Fairclough 1989). Ideologies find expression in discourse—the realm of cultural meanings, messages, knowledge, and knowledge systems that human beings operate within—or more simply in social practices, talk, and text (Fiske 1991). The mutual influence of (discursive) representation and (material) reality has been long and well-established across disciplines, a notion central to Giddens's (1984) structuration theory. Ideological formations influence practices, procedures, structures, and institutions in the material world. Stigma is rooted in ideology, and thus the same interaction holds true. Microlevel occurrences of stigma do not exist in isolation but are continuous with the macrolevel context of politics and culture. Stigma is enacted, mediated, and managed through discourse, and discourse in turn influences material realties that create conditions for disenfranchisement (Fiske 1991). Indeed,

Harter et al. (2005, 312) define *stigma* as the "structuring of social relations that reproduces definitions of outsider and other."

In this book, I use terms such as *absence, silence,* and *erasure* to signal the fact that it is not just visible practices that should be interrogated, but also *discursive erasures*—those practices that have been rendered invisible and are hidden or absent from discourse. In so doing, I am drawing specifically on the *culture-centered approach* (CCA) to communication, in which communication scholar Mohan Dutta (2007) argues that it is the absence and erasure of voices from dominant epistemic structures that produces material disenfranchisement. The CCA is grounded in a body of scholarship called *subaltern studies,* of which Dutta writes: "Subaltern refers to the condition of 'being under.' The subaltern voice is marked by its absence, by not having been noticed. Therefore, subaltern studies scholarship interrogates the ellipses, absences, and silences that are marked in the dominant writings of knowledge. Through the articulation of these absences, subaltern studies seek to create alternative ways of knowing the world, opening up discursive spaces to marginalized voices" (310). Because the subaltern is in a positon of having been erased, the goal of the research is to identify absences and erasures, as well as to recover voices, by asking questions such as: Whose voice is missing? Who is unheard? Who is not speaking? What is absent or missing from the story? Who is not in the picture? Who is not at the table? Who is trying to get a seat at the table, but cannot?

Neoliberalism

Neoliberalism can be understood in at least three ways: political economic doctrine, subjectivities, and governmentality (Larner 2000). As a political economic project, a core belief of neoliberalism is that an unfettered market with less government will provide more efficient services and jobs. Neoliberalization involves the privatization of public resources and spaces, the minimization of labor costs, reductions in public expenditures, and elimination of regulations for private corporations. Neoliberalization also involves the devolution of responsibility from the state to private actors and entities—a primary reason we have seen a growth in charitable food assistance over the last thirty years (Rose and Miller 1992).

In terms of subjectivities, neoliberalism influences personal identity and relationships through the creation of *neoliberal subjectivities*, a term denoting the ways in which market logic increasingly pervades the thoughts and practices of individuals (Rose 1989). The ideals of individualism, efficiency, profit, and self-help have become internalized within individuals, to the exclusion of other social determinants of well-being. Massey (2015, 26) argues that "vocabularies of the economy" have altered ourselves and our everyday social relationships; "this vocabulary of customer, consumer, choice, markets and self interest moulds both our conception of ourselves and our understanding of and relationship to the world." There has been a "semantic stretching" of market terminology from the realm of business and economics to other spheres of social life (Holborow 2015). Social relationships are defined by monetary transactions. Terms such as *equality*, *social justice*, and *public* are displaced by the language of self-interest and competition (Massey 2015). Holborow (2015) notes that the cluster of neoliberal keywords such as *output, entrepreneur*, and *choice* are part of the ideological glue that hold the neoliberal narrative together. She writes: "It redefines the relationship between the individual and society with social behavior being guided not by collective institutions and interaction, but by supply and demand, by entrepreneurs and consumer choice, by individual companies and individual people. Social activity and exchange becomes judged on their degree of conformity to market culture" (34). Neoliberalism offers a social order in which equality, collectivism, social justice, and public good are dismissed in favor of an individualistic bootstraps ideology.

Thirdly, neoliberalism can be viewed in terms of *governmentality*, a Foucauldian concept, implying "a set of practices that facilitate the governing of individuals from a distance" (Larner 2000, 6). For Foucault ([1963] 1994), in the modern era, social control or governance was exerted not by direct coercion, but through the process of creating *docile bodies*—individuals who knew the parameters for self-regulation, parameters that were reinforced by procedures that acted as regulatory measures or "disciplines." A key characteristic of neoliberal governmentality lies in the process of creating citizens capable of self-regulation. Larner argues that though neoliberalism may mean less government, it does not mean less governance. Indeed, there is more governance today than ever before, but today regulation occurs through practices designed to govern individuals from afar. Welfare agencies, for instance, are managed through technologies of governance such as budgeting, accounting, and outcome metrics (Bondi 2005). This is also seen in Sahr's letter, in which he invites a kind of self-monitoring by creating three categories of people by which we can surveil ourselves and others.

The Stigma of Poverty and Welfare

The condition of poverty has, since the beginning of modern Western society, carried an array of negative meanings. Chaim Waxman (1983), in *The Stigma of Poverty*, observes that the stigma of poverty attributes to the poor a status of being "less than human." The poor are thought of as having a weak character, lazy, irresponsible, and not interested in educating or improving themselves. Judgments about the poor include the belief that the poor have no morality and engage in stealing, mugging, and sexual promiscuity. The question of who is poor and to which group of people stigma attaches is a subject of debate. In 1966, sociologist David Matza argued that it was almost impossible to define precisely which segment of the poor population constituted the "disreputable poor"; however the condition of pauperism came closest to it, including people such as the "dregs," "newcomers," "skidders," and the "infirm." Although paupers— including beggars, tramps, criminals, and prostitutes—form the core of the stigmatized group, stigma and its effects can be found throughout the lower class. Stigma occurs with decreasing severity, such that the further removed one is from the core, the less severe the stigma—but in general, lower-class culture is seen as pathological, abnormal, and contradictory to an acceptable way of living. The experience of stigma is also shaped by how visible a particular "mark" is. For instance, homelessness is often more visible and disruptive than other forms of poverty because people lack homes and are therefore subject to the gaze of others. Because people without homes also experience challenges with cleaning and grooming, their impoverishment is more discernible (Waxman 1983).

In the West, the stigma of poverty is thoroughly intertwined with the stigma of welfare, going all the way back to the Middle Ages, when English Poor Laws enforced a variety of harsh measures intended to stigmatize the poor (Waxman 1983). The laws started a several-hundred-year trend in which poverty became a problem of the individual, rather than a social or structural problem. This is also when poverty governance as a system of social control was instituted. Poverty was considered a negative condition and a result of idleness and moral failure, and welfare policy was primarily concerned with maintaining public order rather than care of the poor on their own account. Repressive policies during the Middle Ages were intended to stigmatize or set poor people apart from others; for instance, those receiving public assistance were required to wear distinctive clothing and badges. These policies were legitimized by the belief that only the process of rigid resocialization could eliminate the moral defects of poverty. Later reforms to the Poor Laws separated the "deserving poor" from the "undeserving poor" based on the perceived health and ability of individuals—a distinction that goes all the way back to Calvinism, which saw work as an absolute duty and the best way to please God (Waxman 1983).

During the eighteenth century, under the guise of science, the theory of social Darwinism led to increasing antipathy toward welfare and increased poverty governance (Waxman 1983). The "survival of the fittest" theory led to many reforms of the Poor Laws, including the doctrine of less eligibility, which stated that persons on assistance had to be kept in a condition worse than that of the lowest-paid worker so as to provide a strong incentive to work. This was based on the suspicion that poor people would avoid work if there was no incentive to do it—a suspicion that is alive and well today, as seen in Sahr's letter.

Over the last three decades, discourses of suspicion surrounding the poor and those on welfare have been taken up, perfected, and unleashed in full force, coinciding with neoliberal and conservative values. In 1984, Charles Murray, an American libertarian social scientist, published *Losing Ground*, a book that was the seminal statement of the conservative position on poverty and social welfare and an influential text during the Reagan, Bush, and Clinton eras (Elisha 2011; FitzGerald 2017). This text was crucial to setting the stage for a disciplinary and punitive public assistance system and ushered in a more muscular form of poverty governance. Murray's main thesis was that social welfare programs increased poverty rather than eliminated it by creating incentives that rewarded short-sighted behavior. Murray argued that the behavior of the poor was shaped by economically rational choices; welfare programs created a context in which the rational choice was *not* to be independent and *not* to get ahead in the world. Simply put, according to Murray, it had become profitable to be poor. The solution then was to implement a system that asserted a tricky balance between rights and duties linked to work, moral values, and family values, all of which would reduce the evils of welfare dependency. This is the ideology behind poverty governance even today: receiving public assistance must be made difficult—to the point of being unbearable—such that only those who "genuinely need" the support will seek it out.

Intersectionality: Race, Gender, and Whiteness

The feminist concept of *intersectionality* refers to the interactivity of social structures of race, class, and gender in the experience of oppression and privilege (Crenshaw 1991). In her work on identity politics and violence against women of color, Crenshaw argues that the experiences of Black women are frequently the product of intersecting patterns of racism and sexism; however, these experiences tend not to be represented within the discourses of either feminism or antiracism. In other words, discourses are either about gender or race, but never about both; as such, Black women are marginalized within both spheres. Intersectionality addresses the life experiences of individuals and communities that are *multiplicatively oppressed*— whose lives are structured by two or more disadvantageous categories. Conversely, intersectionality also implicates those who are *multiplicatively privileged*—who experience multiple systemic privileges. For instance, in the context of stigma, this means that individuals whose identities cut across a variety of stigmatized social categories such as poor/brown/female will experience stigma more severely than those who are poor/white/female. The next section unpacks the stigma of race, gender, and whiteness as they relate to systems of disenfranchisement and privilege.

With regards to race, in many ways, Fanon's (1967, 172; emphasis in original) bleak words—"Wherever he goes, the Negro remains a Negro"— are still relevant today and applicable to an ever-broadening group of racial and ethnic minorities. Race is not a fixed or natural category; it does not have a biological essence but is a result of discursive, material, and social processes. Racial groups are social creations and reflect a process of both affiliation and external ascription that are constituted in structures and everyday practices (Bonilla-Silva 2010; Doane and Bonilla-Silva 2003). Racial stigma is the tacit association of "Blackness" with "unworthiness"; within this mindset, social disparities become sites for the production of stigma, particularly when there is the belief that the disparity is the fault of those who lag behind. Historically, the focus of the antiblack frame was on physical and moral attributes of Black Americans (color, hair, lips, apelike, smell, immoral, criminal, dangerous, lazy, oversexed, ungrateful, rebellious, and disorganized families). These stereotypes were geared toward ensuring white settlers as the true and rightful owners of land and resources. Referred to as *inherited racial stigma*, the root cause of racial stigma can be traced back to the institution of chattel slavery and the associated rituals and customs that supported the master-slave hierarchy (Feagin 2013). Feagin observes that racism and capitalism "emerged together as part of the *same* political economic system that took root in European countries and their colonies in North America. In this early period, thus, modern capitalism *was* systemic racism, and systemic racism *was* modern capitalism" (25; emphasis in original). Proslavery writing emphasized the savagery, cannibalism, devil worship, and licentiousness of Africans; at the time, scientific arguments—such as those grounded in craniometry—were used to explain the alleged mental and physical inferiority of Blacks (Feagin 2013; Washington 2006).

Today, race is marked by an active suppression of "race" as a legitimate topic in public discourse. In the Jim Crow era, the social standing of Blacks was explained in terms of biological and moral inferiority, but in a neoliberal era, the social standing of Blacks is explained in terms of market dynamics and cultural limitations, such as a poor work ethic or lack of personal responsibility (Goldberg 2009). Racial stigma flourishes because of the "collective forgetting" that has occurred via the sanitizing of collective memories and national narratives (Bonilla-Silva 2010; Feagin 2013). These discursive erasures have resulted in the weakening of collective memories of oppression while constructing and reinforcing positive, often fictional memories of history. For example, the story of genocide, slavery, theft, and colonization is reframed as a story about modernization, industrialization, urbanization, and wealth (Feagin 2013). Because this bloody past is suppressed, downplayed, or mythologized, even reasonable white Americans have difficulty recognizing present-day racial realities accurately.

In addition to race, the stigma of welfare is deeply contoured by its association with women, poor women, and unwed mothers, tied to notions of irresponsibility, illegitimacy, and promiscuity (Fraser and Gordon 1994). Seccombe (2011) argues that the welfare debates of the 1990s hinged on changing assumptions about the role of women in the marketplace and the family, where a patriarchal dictum about women being under the control and supervision of men was prominent. An analysis of newspaper articles published in the years before welfare reform (1995–1996) showed several references to the (incorrect) fact that women on welfare "don't work"; they were described as "teen mothers," "overly fertile," or "drug users" (Hancock 2004). During this time, the tropes of the "poor black woman," "welfare mother," and "welfare queen" took center stage. Feminist scholars Fraser and Gordon (1994, 311) write: "The expression *welfare dependency* evokes the image of 'the welfare mother,' [who] often figures as a young, unmarried black woman (perhaps even a teenager) of uncontrolled sexuality." These patriarchal notions continue to be structured into the welfare system itself. Fraser and Gordon observe that governmental entitlement programs are deeply gendered, such that the more "feminine"-track programs of SNAP and Medicaid are deemed "welfare," while other, more "masculine" programs of social security and unemployment benefits are deemed legal entitlements and therefore not stigmatized. Thus, even though both tracks are dependent on government support, the "masculine" programs posit recipients as "rights-bearers" and "purchasing consumers," whereas the feminine track continues "the private charity tradition of searching out the deserving few among the many chiselers" (321).

In thinking about race, there is a tendency to focus on people of color while overlooking whites as a racial group implicated in racial issues. The study of whiteness reflects a new approach to understanding the continuing dominance of whites today (Frankenberg 1993; Kobayashi and Peake 2000; Nakayama and Martin 1999). It is based on the recognition that in a racialized social system, all actors are raced, and race has implications for all actors because it disenfranchises some and privileges others. The late Ruth Frankenberg, a white woman and a pioneer of the field, observed in *White Women, Race Matters* (1993) that whiteness has at least three dimensions to it: "First, it is a position of structural advantage, associated with 'privileges' of the most basic kind, including for example, higher wages, reduced chances of being impoverished, longer life, better access to health care, better treatment by the legal system, and so on. ... Second, whiteness is a 'standpoint' or place from which to look at oneself, others and society. Thirdly, it carries with it a set of ways of being in the world, a set of cultural practices, often not named as 'white' by white folks, but looked upon instead as 'American' or 'normal'" (54). Similarly, Kobayashi and Peake (2000, 394) observe that whiteness is a position of normalcy and moral superiority "from which to construct a landscape of what is same and what is different," and it allows other places such as foreign tourist sites to be subjected to a white gaze. Whiteness is the ordinary power that white people have. It is the hiddenness of whiteness that allows for its conflation with existing social norms, values, and institutions such that white cultural interests are often confounded with national interests—and meanings of citizenship. Conversely, nonwhite cultures are seen as deviating from the norm and are thus inferior to white cultures.

Participating in whiteness means continuing to see the world through a "white racial frame," which is ubiquitous and operates at multiple levels (Feagin 2013). Feagin observes that the white racial fame has a strong positive orientation to whites, highlighting white superiority, virtue, moral goodness, and action, and a strong negative orientation to racial "others." He writes in the preface: "The white racial frame includes a broad and persisting *set of racial stereotypes, prejudices, ideologies, interlinked interpretations and narratives, and visual images*. It also includes *racialized emotions* and *racialized reactions to language accents* and *imbeds inclinations to discriminate*. This white racial frame, like most social frames, operates to assist people in defining, interpreting, conforming to, and acting in their everyday social worlds" (xi; emphasis in original). People are socialized into whiteness and the white racial frame in multiple arenas—at home, at school, through the media, work, politics, and corporate decisions. Importantly, whiteness studies recognizes that though racism is easily identified in its more vulgar forms, more often than not it occurs today insidiously through ellipses, defensiveness, microaggressions, and in the machinations of policy—in ways that cannot easily be detected as "racist." Simply put, the "crazy right-wing" person flying the confederate flag and the white liberal with the Black Lives Matter sticker may have similar responses in their everyday lives to situations about race: they may both live racially segregated lives, cross the street when they see a person of color, volunteer at food pantries and homeless shelters, and be against affirmative action policies, although for allegedly different reasons.

Religion and Faith-Based Organizing

Despite declining patterns of formal religious adherence, faith-based organizations (FBOs) are a dominant source of community engagement and service provision today. FBOs employ a wide range of political theories, ideologies, and practices, ranging from "faith-permeated" organizations, in which there are explicit references to faith, to more secular or postsecular organizations, in which humanistic values are prioritized (Adkins, Occhipinti, and Hefferan 2012). A key distinction between evangelical and liberal positions found in the West is in their attitudes toward social action, which cut right through denominations (Beaumont and Cloke 2012). The more liberal theology accepts a less dogmatic understanding of God by interpreting scripture through critical and literary analysis, in which human reason, tradition and cultural and political climate are applied to Biblical interpretation. On the other side, the evangelical position has four main priorities: the need for personal conversion, a belief in the Bible as the infallible word of God, the centrality of the cross at the heart of the salvation message, and the need for evangelism. These distinctions delineate two very separate territories of Christianity with regard to attitudes toward social action (Beaumont and Cloke 2012).

Scriptures are multivocal as such different communities end up emphasizing different voices in Scripture depending on their ideological orientations. A key distinction between evangelical and liberal positions can be found in the *gospel of prosperity* and *liberation theology* perspectives. The gospel of prosperity has a long history of stigmatizing the poor (intentionally and unintentionally) by proposing a direct relationship among the attainment of one's goals, material success, and belief in Christ. Quite simply, those who are rich are blessed by God and, by implication, those who are poor are not. Waxman (1983, 80) explains: "Just as the Lutheran and Calvinist Protestant tenets of the calling and predestination led to a view of work as inherently positive and material rewards a sign of chosenness and virtue, they unintentionally provided a new religious legitimation for the perception of the poor as immoral. If material rewards for hard work as taken as a sign of moral worth, then wealth tends to become identified with worth and the absence of wealth with the absence of moral worth. ... Thus, the Protestant ethic provided a new theological legitimation for repressive policies towards the underserving poor."

The gospel of prosperity is still preached today around the world. In the Zimbabwean context, Bornstein (2005) has shown that Christian organizations such as World Vision construct development as something that can be crafted from "within" individuals. These discourses mask the economic and political forces beyond community control and instead locate responsibility for development among the poor. In the United States, Sager and Stephens (2005) found a tendency in their analysis of sermons to blame the homeless for their problems; the message was that poverty was a result of spiritual failing and that with proper religious commitment, the homeless too could experience material rewards. In short, if the homeless just "got religion," they would not be homeless.

The prosperity gospel finds its counter in the *liberation theology* and *Black liberation theology* perspectives, in which God is identified not as a God of the rich and powerful, but as the "God of the oppressed"—also the title of a seminal book by the late Black theologian James Cone (1997). For Cone, eschatological freedom or a vision of a new heaven and earth was essential and fundamental to the survival of oppressed groups. For people oppressed by physical and material enslavement and with little wealth to show, power came via the presence and Spirit of God. God did not provide an abundance of wealth but an abundance of spirit. Paulo Freire (1970), a forerunner of the liberation theology movement in South America, interpreted the gospels of Christ as a call for social justice. Asserting the interconnection between spiritual and political freedoms, Freire underscored that inequalities among human beings were not the result of God's will but of conditions perpetrated by human action.

More recently, scholarship has interrogated the convergences (and divergences) between faith and neoliberalism in the context of social action. Mona Atia (2012, 809) refers to the melding of religiosity and neoliberal economic rationales in Islamic FBOs as "pious neoliberalism," which she defines as the "discursive combination of religion and economic rationale in a manner that encourages individuals to be proactive and entrepreneurial in the interest of furthering their relationship with God." Atia examined how Khaled, a well-known transnational Islamic revival and development effort in the Middle East, calls on Muslims to become pious and entrepreneurial subjects. Rather than drawing on discourses of social justice and equity, organizational narratives draw on self-help and management science in service to faith doctrines. The discourses are designed to cultivate neoliberal subjects who work toward financial investments, self-improvement, productivity, and entrepreneurship. Atia shows how piety and neoliberalism intermingle while highlighting the contradictory aspects of neoliberalism. Here religious and economic rationale do not compete or contradict each other but, similar to conservative Christian discourses, blend seamlessly together.

These fundamental differences in faith beliefs have enormous implications for how social action is practiced. For conservatives, individual conversion is the means to overcome personal failure; as such, their social action work focuses on individual reform and empowerment. This can be seen in Sahr's letter, in which the implicit recommendation for the third group of people he mentions is a change of heart and a change of their lazy ways; there is no Biblical responsibility toward this group of people. For liberals, poverty is seen as unjustly caused by social, economic, and political structures, so social action involves providing support to individuals, but also getting involved in resistance movements, advocacy, and policy work (Occhipinti 2005). However, here efforts are constrained by the problematic tensions embedded in whiteness, which wants to reach out to the Other, but at the same time maintain the wages of whiteness. Contrary to Sahr's position, a vastly different framing of hunger can be seen in more liberal Christian and Jewish traditions, as explicated by the Religious Action Center of Reform Judaism (RAC, n.d.):

> The Talmud explains that each Jewish community must establish a public fund to provide food for the hungry, and our sages explain that feeding the hungry is one of our most important responsibilities on earth: "When you are asked in the world to come, 'What was your work?' and you answer: 'I fed the hungry,' you will be told: 'This is the gate of the Lord, enter into it, you who have fed the hungry'" (Midrash to Psalm 118:17).

Providing several scriptural references to reinforce its position, RAC advocates for better public policy—policies that increase SNAP benefits and funding for antihunger programs.

Conclusion

The problem at the heart of this book has to do with the belief circulating in American society that laziness and irresponsibility are the true causes of poverty—a belief codified in Sahr's description of a category of people who "do not want to work and will not work." Age-old welfare discourses combine with new meanings in a neoliberal era to unleash a more subtle and nuanced antagonism toward the poor and minoritized groups, captured in the term *neoliberal stigma*. The loci of these ideological formations are complex and intertwined, coming from religious, economic, and political domains. Neoliberal stigma relies on an incessant refocusing of narratives from the macro to the micro, from the system to the individual, from whiteness to brownness, from socioeconomic conditions to problems of morality, spirituality, and character. Neoliberal stigma is flexible and though it is more obvious in conservative discourse, it can also be found among folks across the political spectrum.

Neoliberal stigma has important implications for practice and policy; it has the effect of reinforcing individual-level solutions to poverty and enforcing harsher systems of poverty governance. Studies in political science show that Americans tend to attribute poverty to individual shortcomings and a "lack of effort" on the part of poor people (Feagin 1975; Kluegel and Smith 1986). In evaluating the causes of poverty, people place more importance on poor people's behavioral characteristics—such as the lack of thrift, poor money management, and lack of effort, ability, and talent, as well as loose morals and drunkenness—rather than on structural reasons such as low wages, scarcity of jobs, poor schools, and racial discrimination (Feagin 1975). The failure of whites to see the systematic connections between history and the present results in people being blamed for disparities and for "reaping what they have sown." These beliefs have important consequences for policy, such that Americans typically express greater support for the principle of helping disadvantaged groups than for actual policies aimed at enacting those principles (Kluegel and Smith 1986). Contrary to what many theorists believed, racism and racialized thinking have not been annihilated with industrialization and modernization. In fact, racism has already been linked to neoliberal policies that negatively impact the livelihood, health, and opportunities for people in the African and Caribbean regions, as well as within the United States (Giroux 2014;

Goldberg 2009; Klein 2007). There is little disagreement today that racial ideologies played heavily into welfare reform and workfarist policies; the Welfare Reform Act of 1996 disproportionately affected African Americans and communities of color (Soss et al. 2004).

In the end, we might say, "Well, Sahr did not mean it like that," "he is ignorant and unaware," or that "he is politically incorrect" and "he really cares about helping people," or that I, the researcher, am reading too deeply into it. However, Sahr's letter and the other texts depicted in this chapter are part of the massive deluge of discourses circulating in American society that reinforce stigma against the poor and minoritized groups and carve out demarcations between Us and Them. Regardless of intention, these narratives directly impact the health, well-being, food security, and livelihoods of citizens and play a role in maintaining the social order.

3 Voices of Hunger: Making the Invisible Visible

John: If I have money I go down to, what's it called, *Coney Island*, and get a plate of fries. Do you ever go there?
Interviewer: I've been there once.
John: They give you a plate of fries as big as your arm. It's a huge portion. It's like fries for a family. I get a glass of water and come back and have a cup of coffee at the shelter.
Interviewer: That's kind of your meal?
John: Yeah.
—John, white male, Chum client

John: The Environmental Chemist

John is a frequent client of the Chum food shelf. He is an elderly white man approximately sixty years of age. At one point in his life, John enjoyed an illustrious career working at the Honeywell and Pillsbury corporations as an environmental chemist; his job focused on looking for contaminants in the water. Perhaps from my accent or the way that I look, visible markers of my identity, he realizes that I am not from Duluth, maybe not from the United States. He tells me that he is a global citizen. "I live in a global world," he says, "I want to know what's going on around the world. I want to know the weather nationwide. I want to know what's going on in Duluth. I can't get the news so I'll sometimes buy a newspaper. Sunday paper is in my bag." He reaches to show me. John was married twice; he lost one wife to cancer and was a caregiver for her until she passed away. His faith is strong. He says: "A lot of people I loved. I had a former wife that died of cancer and the biggest lesson I learned was it's not what you lost, it's what you had. You're gifted by God. He gives and he takes away. It's his to do. Someday I'll see her again."

John utilizes government and charitable food assistance, but is far from being food secure. If hunger policies were working well, then these sources of food would work to alleviate John's food insecurity. However, this is far from the truth; these channels stave off hunger but do not create a food-secure situation for John. As noted in the opening, crackers, water, and French fries are how he fills up—and that's on a good day. John receives a small amount in SNAP benefits each month, which he uses to purchase items at the grocery store. John is appreciative of the food from the Chum food shelf. He usually gets food he can store in his locker at the Chum homeless shelter: industrial food like precooked meats, canned vegetables, and soup. When he has money to spare, his favorite place to go is Coney Island, a diner in downtown Duluth, where he gets a plate of fries to fill his stomach. At Chum, 51 percent of participants interviewed were like John, with a high level of food insecurity; 41 percent had low to medium food insecurity; and only 4 percent were food secure. At RP, food insecurity was prevalent as well, but less extreme: 13 percent of participants experienced high food insecurity, 53 percent experienced low to medium food insecurity, and 31 percent were food secure.

John lives at the Chum homeless shelter. A series of health events eventually led to his unemployment, food insecurity, homelessness, and subsequent depression. He was in two car accidents, but the accident that dealt the biggest blow came from a horse! He was administering deworming medicine to a colt when it bolted ten feet off the ground, dislocating John's shoulder. He says: "I could feel the muscles rip all the way down to my waist. It was real sore for a couple of weeks. I couldn't drive. I was so weak. It healed up and then thirty years later, I'm tired. I'm in pain." He could no longer work because of his disabilities and soon began to have severe bouts of depression. The homeless shelter is a hard place to be. "It's a terrible place," John says. "I'm a deep Christian with a college education and I don't fit over there at all. There are some nice people but there are some really, really bad people. It's kind of a cross section of humanity." John compares living at the shelter with his experience a few months ago living in a beautiful cottage on the shores of Lake Superior. "You can get up in the morning and look at the sunrise and it was gorgeous." He was asked to leave the house at the start of the tourist season in Duluth but was grateful for the time he got to spend there. John comes to Chum because it is a place where people like him go to in Duluth. As Lee Stuart, the director of Chum, says of the homeless shelter: "Yeah, this is a throwaway people place."

Accessing food is a struggle, but it is not the only struggle in John's life. A lack of resources means a shortage of other basic needs, like housing, health care, transport, education, and even taken-for-granted personal hygiene products. In the United States, a lack of resources and job opportunities, poverty, and inadequate social safety nets are key drivers of food insecurity (Coleman-Jensen, Gregory, and Singh 2014; Nord et al. 2010). There are strong relationships among food insecurity, income, housing, fuel prices, and the economy, so when fuel and housing costs increase, food insecurity among families also increases (Gundersen et al. 2003; Kirkpatrick and Tarasuk 2011; Webber and Rojhani 2010). John copes with hunger by utilizing food shelves and soup kitchens and eating cheap food at gas stations. However, living in poverty means that danger is always imminent: fighting and bullying at the homeless shelter, the pain of untreated illness—physical and mental—unexpected life events, and terror at the hands of bureaucratic systems and officers. John is stressed today because of an incident with his car. John lost his license a year ago and because he does not have a home, he parks his car on the street even as he is trying to sell it. The previous day, a man had come to him, interested in buying the car. John told the man to take it for a test drive, but the customer ended up taking it for a joy ride. The cops got involved and John spent all day trying to sort out the mess with the police, paying for a parking ticket, and trying to find a locksmith to open the car. The stress of the incident and the additional expenditure has him wired today. The food pantry cannot manage John's immediate problem of hunger and does little to solve the problem of poverty that is at the root of it all.

In this snapshot of John's world, there are broader issues of livelihood at stake, of which food is only one. The problem of hunger and food insecurity is deeply intertwined with other stressors that come with poverty: homelessness, mental illness, disability, unemployment, and lack of access to good schools and education, to name a few. Food insecurity is intertwined with stress, anxiety, feelings of powerlessness, violence, and trauma, but the magnitude of these nonfood issues is not captured in the food-insecurity data (Chilton and Booth 2007). The idea of intersecting or interconnected needs is not a new one. The right to adequate food frame-work (United Nations Human Rights 2010) observes that "human rights are interdependent, indivisible and interrelated"—so violating the right to food can interfere with the fulfillment of human rights, such as the right to health, education, or life, and vice versa. The livelihood perspective of food similarly points out that though food is a basic need, it is only *one* of several objectives that people pursue (Yaro 2004). Food scholar Simon Maxwell (1996) argues that people employ complex coping strategies when faced with multiple deficiencies, threats, and uncertainties—as seen in a study conducted during the Darfur famine in Sudan, which found that people chose to go hungry in the present to preserve assets and future livelihood. Simply put, "people go hungry now, in order to avoid going (more) hun-gry later" (158). This type of coping was true not just for people in Sudan three decades ago but also is true for food insecure people in the United States today. Individuals and families cope by reducing or manipulating food intake so as to spend resources on other basic needs, such as housing and transportation and, when possible, phones, television, and cable TV—communication technologies necessary for social and economic survival in the United States today.

Goal of the Chapter

Neoliberal stigma is a type of political economic stigma that distinguishes between Us and Them based on values of individualism, hard work, and personal responsibility. The tension at the heart of neoliberal stigma is cap-tured in the belief that there is a category of people who "do not want to work and will not work." Set against these stigmatizing discourses, the goal of this chapter is to recover, make visible, and foreground the voices of the hungry, the "throwaway people," the food insecure, the welfare recipi-ents, voices that are typically neither present nor represented in hunger dis-courses: the people who have been made invisible in the discursive sphere. In this chapter, in the voices of clients of Chum and RP, we hear about the complex struggles that poor people, people of color, and mothers and fathers face. In these stories, the multiplicative burden of oppression that people of color face is palpable. This chapter also contextualizes hunger and food insecurity in the larger framework of people's lives, showing *entitle-ment failure* to be the root of the problem—that is, how public institutions fail to buffer citizens from economic collapse and tragic life events; further-more, consistent with systems of poverty governance, the state (and arms of the state) sets up profound barriers that limit the self-determination of citizens. The chapter shows how citizens internalize neoliberal stigma. Even amid the most grueling of life circumstances, individuals highlight their hard work and their personal responsibility, and in the most sorrowful of stories, people blame themselves for missing the economic mark.

The Livelihood Toggle: "You Can't Really Survive on Minimum Wage"

Clients of Chum and RP are continuously in a process of balancing their needs with limited resources, as well as weighing their immediate needs against future needs. Many Chum clients I interviewed were employed but did not earn enough to pay for their basic needs. John's story was not an uncommon one. There was palpable anxiety about the economy, the rising cost of living, and the future. When asked how the food pantry benefitted him, Victor, a Native man who is employed and receives SNAP benefits, said rather plainly: "It feeds me. It helps feed me. Especially when I run out of money and everything. It's very hard to pay for everything. You really can't survive on a minimum-wage salary." Renee, a thirtysomething Native woman, similarly explained that Chum helped her family: "Because we can eat a meal, a good meal. It helps out a lot." She gets $200 in monthly SNAP benefits, but noted, "It's hard to stretch with me and the family. You really can't survive on a minimum-wage salary." For Renee, an increased mini-mum wage would decrease her level of food insecurity and even possibly make her food secure.

Clients juggled their SNAP benefits and food pantry assistance in enter-prising ways. Some would first "shop" at food pantries, then use precious food stamps to buy items from the grocery store. Others would first use SNAP, then go to the food pantry at the end of the month, when SNAP benefits ran out. Isaiah, an older Black man and a client of Chum, said: "Well, it helps me to make ends meet. You know, I tend to run out of food right around the last week of the month. So then I use the food shelf to last me until I obtain my social securities." Consistent with the livelihood perspective, Isaiah explained that he gets $710 per month on social security and uses it to pay for rent, gas, and electricity; when he is through paying for everything, he barely has any money left. He spends approximately one hundred dollars per month on food, usually to purchase meat; the rest of his food he gets from the food shelf. Clayton, a fortysomething African American man, has two children to feed. The price of food and the cost of living has gone up, so he is always juggling resources. He explained: "I know, this is kind of unfair, but let's say my rent goes up or I have to pay for tuition. You know, I got to put some money aside and I know I need food in my house, so that's why I come here, to see how I can improvise."

Interviewer: Sure. So it's not really about not having money for food, it's because the price of something else goes up.

Clayton: Yes.

Clients from RP expressed similar concerns about the economy and their reasons for using RP. They had deep anxieties about the cost of living and frequently noted that their salaries and wages had not kept up. Clients also used RP to "stretch their food budgets" and to "make ends meet." Participants talked about wanting to buy homes, get married, and have kids, but they knew that even those who were able-bodied and employed might not achieve their most basic goals. Chris, a young white man, explained: "It's a good value to help out. Groceries are getting expensive and ... we are scared, it's a big expense." RP helps families save on groceries so that they can have some extras at times. "Just buying, I don't know what you would call, I guess it's not necessities, but I don't know, just buying extra things, not food, but like to go to a movie with the kids or something like that or buying something they want ... So it helps that way by saving, you have to spend money on other things." In Chris's world, going to the movies with the kids once in a while was a luxury—a way to bring a little normalcy to their lives. Rick, a white school teacher, said that since he started using RP he has seen his savings grow. For him, RP was a blessing because it allowed him to save for the future: "We would love to have kids, but right now, it's not reality because we are able to save couple of hundred bucks, and how do we take care of a kid? So we are trying to be responsible with everything, but like I said, if it weren't for Ruby's Pantry, most of that money would go towards grocery costs, and so it's been a blessing to be able to have some money set aside. Right now, we are depending on our emergency fund; that's life."

Clients at RP also received welfare in some form—disability, unemployment, and/or SNAP benefits—but these entitlements were insufficient to make ends meet. Bill and Evelyn, a husband and wife couple, both white, came to the interview together and explained that they used RP two years ago when they were low on income. "The cost of food and food stamps don't stretch that far. It's beneficial. It stretches out the food budget." They discussed their horror at the grocery store each month, where filler foods have become the main course. Evelyn exclaimed: "I've seen almost every item, since the first of the year, has gone up anywhere from ten cents to a quarter. And some items even more. And the meat is outrageous now. It's just ... It used to be that hamburger was a stretcher. Well, not anymore. That's a main ingredient." Bill reinforced her point, adding: "Yes, $3.25, $4.00 a pound some places. It's ridiculous. We've kind of figured, for the $20 we spend at Ruby's Pantry, we're averaging about $75 or $80 worth of groceries."

Across racial groups, clients at Chum and RP said that they could not imagine a time when they would not use food pantries. Even though they had jobs and worked hard, completely contrary to the American dream, winning the lottery was the only way they could imagine not going to food shelves and pantries.

Interviewer: Can you imagine a time when you'll stop using Ruby's Pantry?

Evelyn: With the economy, no. I can't see it.

Bill: Not unless we win the lottery. And that's probably not going to happen, because—

Evelyn: (laughs)—we don't buy tickets.

Paula, a white woman who worked at a motel, but was laid off, said: "Yeah. When I hit the lottery. Then I donate to the food shelf because I won't forget where I come from." Antoine, an African American man and a client of Chum, said that he could not imagine not using the food shelf: "I could say if I get halfway rich or whatever, I'd stop using it. I'd probably give to the food shelf ... I don't want to use them just because it's there; I use it because I have to. Otherwise, I would just fade away."

Caring for Children and Grandchildren

Food security data show that households with children tend to be the most food insecure (e.g., Coleman-Jensen, Gregory, and Singh 2014), and this certainly played out at Chum and RP. Participants talked at great length about their food needs relative to caring for children. Parents with young children were anxious because, "kids eat a lot." Ashley, a young white mum, explained that she has used the Chum food shelf off and on for the last ten years. She initially started using it because she did not have a job and food stamps were not enough, but she now does janitorial work at the university, so she has not been in for a while. She started coming to the food shelf earlier in the summer because school was not in session, so her daughter did not have access to the government free and reduced lunch program. Paula, a white woman, was in a similar situation. She has six birth children and four adopted kids. They are all grown up now, and "the grandbabies are rolling in." Paula saves a lot of money on canned foods—probably around seventy-five dollars a month—by using the food pantry. Her food stamps don't stretch for the whole month because her children and grandchildren are often over at her place to eat. She says, "You know how it goes. They leave the nest but they never leave the nest. They come over when they are hungry and all that goes. That's the same thing I do to my mom; I stay too."

Securing the long-term stability, security, health, and well-being of children is at the center of the struggle parents and caregivers are engaged in. Xavier, a middle-aged African American man, said that the first time he used the Chum food pantry was when he was living at the homeless shelter in 1999. He is now back at the shelter. Xavier used to have a decent-paying job, but he got injured on the job and found himself divorced and without a home. He did not grow up in a family in which money was an issue, so the livelihood toggle is new to him. He says, "Yeah, I'm at the shelter because I need help." Xavier has five children, all boys, of whom he shares custody with their mother. He said that at one point he had all five boys with him at the shelter, which was "kind of really rough. Being in and out of the shelter and trying to feed the kids, it's like, it was kind of hard. Yeah, it was kind of hard." He enjoys having his kids with him; they hang out and play basketball at the community center. He uses all of his creative energy to figure out how to make a better life for his kids. Sometimes when his kids visit him, he saves up so that he can rent a motel room for a weekend, so they can be together in a better environment. To do this, he compromises on food: he eats what he can find at the food shelf or the soup kitchen.

Gabrielle, an African American woman in her mid-fifties, was once employed in a service profession, but physical and mental health issues sent her into a downward spiral: she lost her vehicle and her job and nearly ended up homeless. She said, "I help people with their problems, but I had my own problem and didn't know what to do." Gabrielle values education and encourages her kids to work hard in school, but the financial burden is overwhelming. Gabrielle exclaimed: "I wish so hard that they could have a free education because they're going out to do something so great in the world." Her son is twenty-nine and $140,000 in debt, with a master's in musical theater; her older daughter is about $50,000 in debt, with a BA in sociology; and her younger daughter just graduated high school in May. For Gabrielle, a policy solution that would help her alleviate some of life's struggles is free or subsidized college education for her kids, education that could tap their full potential. Her younger daughter called her last night, crying because she wants to go to college so badly but the family cannot afford it. Gabrielle comforted her, saying, "God's going to make a way. He's going to make a way ... put it down, leave it alone, and go back to it. Leave it a day. Go have some tea, relax, do something fun." For Gabrielle, her faith is what keeps her going. She worries about the immense stress and pressure her children are under and fears that they may also be susceptible to depression and suicide. "I mean, I know my kids are strong and not suicidal like that, but she needed me right then, and we talked for two hours, and by the end of the conversation I had her laughing. So, praise God, and I haven't talked to her yet today, so after this I'm going to call her."

In the end, for all the precious, talented, and precocious children and grandchildren being taken care of with the help of Chum and RP, one cannot help but wonder what the future holds for them in terms of financial security, health, and mental well-being. The impact of hunger and food insecurity on children is particularly profound. Food insecurity has a negative impact on the physical, mental, and psychosocial development of children (Casey et al. 2004; Cutts et al. 2011; Metallinos-Katsaras et al. 2011; Whitaker and Orzol 2006). Malnourishment negatively effects the cognitive development of children, resulting in loss of knowledge, brainpower, and productivity, and iron-deficiency anemia in children can lead to developmental and behavioral disturbances. Studies have found links between food insecurity and poorer academic performance, school absences, suspension from school, involvement in fights, headaches, depression, and other physical, emotional, and behavioral concerns. Furthermore, when children live in food insecure households, their health status may be impaired, making them less able to resist illness and more likely to become hospitalized. For children at Chum and RP, physiological hunger is staved off momentarily by a pack of noodles and a can of beans, but these minimal offerings do little to eliminate structural barriers that keep them from advancing. From a rights-based perspective, violating the right to food can interfere with the fulfillment of other human rights—such as the right to health and right to education and violating the right to education can in the long run interfere with financial security and the right to food and health. This is clearly the case here for children dealing with multiple livelihood insecurities.

Hunger Is Not Just about Nutrition

I was surprised to learn that Chum, a food pantry, distributed nonfood items as well. Clients can make requests for special household items or hygiene products, such as toilet paper, soap, toothpaste and toothbrushes, baby diapers, and feminine hygiene products. Distributing these "extras" is one way in which Chum is responsive to the fact that on most days people who visit the food shelf live in a "tangled web of unmet needs," a phrase borrowed from Poppendieck (1999). A research project conducted by Feeding America (2013) found that in addition to lacking food, many American families struggled to afford basic nonfood household goods, including products related to personal care, household care, and baby care. They often made trade-offs with other living expenses so as to access essential household goods. Families coped by stretching, substituting, borrowing, and doing without food when they were unable to afford necessary household items such as soap and toilet paper.

At Chum, almost all clients made requests for the toilet paper and received two small rolls of it. Toothpaste and deodorant were also fast-moving items. Women sometimes requested feminine hygiene products like tampons or sanitary pads, which Chum stocks in small quantities. Young families appreciated the baby diapers, which were unaffordable to them in stores. Leslie, an older retired white woman who has volunteered at the food shelf for a while, knows the clients well. She knows, for instance, that Liz loves to paint her nails, so when she arrives, Leslie will bring out all the nail polish from the back and invite her to choose one. She also knows that when Haji comes in, she should have salad dressing available for him because "he loves his salad dressing." In all of these requests, the notion of interconnected needs and the livelihood perspective are brought to the forefront. People need food, but they need other things as well, including the occasional luxury to allow them to feel like human beings—complex, contradictory, and full of meaning.

Requests for special food items highlight the fact that food is more than nutrition; it is about culture, emotion, and social well-being. Food comes first—the central idea behind the "food-first" principle that progressive food policy is built on. Without food, life deviates from the norm. The absence of food changes the way in which we live and our very being in the world. Food is an expression of family, love, care, and identity. Chum stocks salad dressing, cake mixes for special occasions, condiments, spices, salt, sugar and flour, and taco shells and fixings in the back. It is in these "extra items" that the complex personhoods of individuals are most illuminated. Gordon (1997, 5) describes *complex personhood* as "conferring the respect on others that comes from presuming that life and people's lives are simultaneously straightforward and full of enormously subtle meaning." Amid the most difficult of situations, we hear lives full of meaning and possibility. For instance, on one of the days that I was volunteering, a mom, her daughter, and grandma came in to get food; it was the little girl's birthday and they asked if they could also get a cake mix, frosting, and party supplies to celebrate. Before I went off to find the items, her grandma advised me that they only wanted a cake mix that had not passed the expiration date. She said, "It doesn't rise after the expiration date"—the kind of knowledge that only comes from deep experience living with poverty. As I rummaged in the back, I realized that most of the cake mixes had expired. I wondered how many parents and children had been disappointed by sunken birthday cakes. With great elation, I managed to find a cake mix and frosting, which still had a year left on it. I brought it back to the family, where the grandma dutifully checked the dates and thanked me. There were no party supplies; I wondered what creative solution the family would come up with to solve that problem.

It was not uncommon to have people stop by Chum and make requests for pet food. They would poke their heads in the window and ask for a can or two of cat food. Usually, the staff and volunteers complied readily—no paperwork required. Other times, while picking up food for themselves, people would catch a glimpse of the pet food lying under the counter. Their eyes would well up with tears, and they'd exclaim unbelievingly, "You have pet food?" and then hesitantly ask, "May I take some for my dog?" Chum always has wet and dry cat food, dry dog food and treats, and cat litter on hand. Clients talked lovingly about their pets, saying things like, "Well, Rosco has to have his treat every day!" This kindness flies in the face of ideological formations that frame hungry and poor people as irresponsible and lacking in accountability. As an outsider to poverty, I myself could not imagine how they found the time and the emotional resources to care so deeply for their animals. I also found it ironic that in the system of poverty governance, animals are shown more respect than people with regard to their right to food.

Jumping through Hoops

Clients at Chum and RP were caught in the oppressive forces of poverty governance, which constantly required them to prove their need for assistance and jump through hoops. The government played a huge role in the lives of clients at Chum and RP, with 85 percent utilizing some form of government food support, 65 percent receiving economic support, and 77 percent receiving Medicare or Medicaid. Through the voices of the hungry and food insecure, it became clear that the real problem was not personal or moral defect, but entitlement failure: a lack of adequate political and legal systems that allow individuals to meet their basic needs (Sen 1983). The US welfare system is an apt example of structural stigma, in which stigmatizing ideologies are embedded in programs and policies that serve to "keep people away, keep people in, and keep people down" (Link and Phelan 2014). SNAP has one of the lowest fraud rates for federal programs (approximately one cent on the dollar in 2006–2008; Dean 2016), yet participants are treated with suspicion, as though everyone is out to scam the system. Potential SNAP beneficiaries are subjected to rigorous screening procedures. The quality-control process involves analyzing cases for accuracy; for example, at the certification interview, SNAP recipients have to explain how they make ends meet. If a recipient reports very low income but pays bills each month, this could be an indicator of unreported income and a red flag. Each state SNAP agency uses a computer program to determine eligibility. This program interfaces with other databases, such as the unemployment office, child support office, and even prison systems. When a client's situation changes, the SNAP agency gets a match alert. All of these procedures are in place to extract proof of worthiness from poor citizens rooted in neoliberal stigma—the idea that the poor are lazy, do not want to work, and are out to scam the system.

Janet, an older white woman, spends her life caught up in a web of patchy governance, or what Pine (2016) refers to as "the porous continuum of care," in which maneuvering around benefits is a time-consuming yet necessary part of her life. Janet is caught up in juggling food stamps, social security, and disability but does not experience any real change in the quality of her life; in fact, navigating these benefits has led to increased anxiety and depression for her. The red tape and bureaucracy of the convoluted system tear her apart. She says: "I understand there should be some hoops to jump through, but it is endless; seems like it is never done." She explained that when she had her own apartment, she used to get $137 dollars a month in SNAP benefits, which was great, but when she moved to her friend's house, she started getting only sixteen dollars. She said, puzzled, "I don't know what they think, if we are all sharing medical bills and food bills or whatever else." Janet is not sure what she would do without RP. "We need a lot of food. So I will either have to stop taking medication and buy food or stop buying food and buy medication. With Ruby's Pantry I don't need to make that decision, I don't have to, I can just come here and have something to eat and be able to pay for my medications." Janet is particularly frustrated on the day of the interview because she recently found out that she makes twelve dollars more than she should to get pharmaceutical medical assistance. She exclaims, "Just tell me I don't qualify! Twelve dollars, it's so frustrating." It seems like every month she deals with some problem with social security, Medicare, food stamps, or medical assistance. Filling out forms has become a full-time job for her—and a distressing one at that. "This is my full-time job; it is what I do for a living. I fill up forms and I try to get questions answered. I am still confused that I just sit and cry, and then I call my sister and she will try and help me. It's just hard, it's really hard." Janet is bewildered by a system that will not allow her to advance—a system that restricts and restrains her talents, entrepreneurship, and skills based on a calculus rooted in stigma.

Bernadette and her husband, Richard a retired veteran, both white, attended the interview together. Bernadette clarified how picking up food at RP gave her peace of mind. "It's in the middle of the month, so it helps just relieve that stress of what's next?" She and her husband cannot imagine a time that they will stop using RP. They explain that they pay $650 in rent, which is half of their income. Although they receive food stamps, they are inadequate given rising costs. Bernadette exclaimed: "Oh, it's outrageous ... Every time you went to the store it was going up, and the hamburger—that alone in two years to what—three dollars a pound right now! It's outrageous. Do you get more compensation from food stamps? We get the same amount of food stamps in the last three years, and that price of a hamburger has gone up almost two dollars. When that was part of your staples for the month as far as for stretching your budget, hamburger is one of the biggies. What do you do?" Richard, her husband, noted that he would like to do some part-time work to supplement their social security income but would be penalized if he did. Isaiah, an older African American man and a client of Chum, similarly explained the irony of his situation: when he was homeless, he was not hungry because he received $200 worth of food stamps, but now that he has a home, he is short of food. "You know, but now I'm paying rent and gas and electric. And then they took it away and I don't understand that at all." So the choice is either "you can eat but you don't have a place to live, or you get a place to live and you can't eat." Isaiah's articulations capture the convoluted logic of poverty governance in a neoliberal era: governance driven not by evidence, but by assumptions going all the way back to the English Poor Laws of the Middle Ages and to the belief that entitlements incentivize poverty (Waxman 1983). The policy recommendations that emerge from these articulations are clear: devise a more humane system of governance that eliminates complex paperwork and takes into account the whole individual and her interconnected needs, a system that provides a seamless continuum of care such that citizens can actually thrive and fulfill their aspirations.

Physical Health Issues, Anxiety, and Depression

Several participants from both Chum and RP experienced ongoing physical and mental health problems. Their illness narratives resonated with the words of medical anthropologist and public health expert Paul Farmer (2005), who argued quite simply that "poverty makes you sick." In his seminal book, *Pathologies of Power: Health, Human Rights, and the New War on the Poor*, Farmer argued that many health problems were in fact problems of *structural violence*—that is, the large-scale forces of violence, poverty, and

other social inequalities rooted in historical, political, and economic processes. These structural violences shape the distribution and outcome of disease and contribute to national and global health disparities.

In the United States, there is a large body of research on *health disparities*
or the differences in health determinants and outcomes among populations (CDC 2013). Populations affected by health disparities include low-
and no-income citizens, racial and ethnic minorities, women, children, the
elderly, and people with disabilities. These disparities can be attributed to
the "social determinants of health," defined as "the conditions in which
people are born, grow, live, work and age. These circumstances are shaped
by the distribution of money, power and resources at global, national and
local levels" (WHO 2018).

Consistent with broader national patterns, race and class-based disparities are long-standing issues in the city of Duluth. The 2010 census data
showed that 18 percent of whites live in poverty compared to 67 percent of
Blacks and 56 percent of Native Americans. A St. Louis County (SLC) Health
Status Report (2013) shows that the mortality rate for people of color in
Duluth is 19.29 compared to 15.09 for whites. The projected life expectancy
in Duluth's 55812 zip code was the highest at 84.65 years, while the lowest
projected life expectancy was 73.44 years found in Zone D, which is comprised of zip codes 55802 and 55806—a difference of 11.2 years. The Central Hillside neighborhood falls within zip code 55802, and this is where
Chum is located and many of Chum's clients live as well. The SLC report
further observes that the Central Hillside neighborhood has many conditions that negatively impact life expectancy such as older dilapidated housing with substandard conditions, limited or no access to affordable healthy
food choices, and limited or no access to safe places for exercise. (St. Louis
County Public Health and Human Services 2013).

These health disparities come to life in this study. Poor whites struggled with physical and mental health issues, but these experiences were
intensified for people of color. In clients' illness narratives, the interactions
among food insecurity, physical disability, and mental health—in particular, depression—were noticeable. What started out as physical pain led people down a path of anxiety and depression. Janet, an older white woman,
suffers from physical and mental health issues. She has Crohn's disease,
which attacks her digestive system and her joints so that she cannot stand
for more than ten minutes at a time; even sitting is painful. She has tried

a lot of different treatments, but with no luck so far. She says: "There are days I will eat nothing but cheese because I cannot stand to eat anything else. Everything else just makes me sick to my stomach and I feel weak. The most common scenario for me is I won't eat anything all day until I get home and then I get sick." Janet's debilitating illness, the worry of not being able to pay bills, her food insecurity, and isolation have all contributed to depression. She sleeps a lot—fifteen hours on some days. "Yeah, I would stay in bed everyday if I could. I mean, when you dream your dreams are awesome, and when you are awake you are like, oh God, not again." Her roommate keeps her on task and pounds on her room door to get her out. When she lies in bed at night, all sorts of things run through her head, like whether she will ever be able to own her own apartment or even afford to rent a place herself. What will happen if she fails? She says, "I do it over, over, over, and over until it is four in the morning and I haven't slept and then I am sick … It is very, very frustrating. You can shut it out during the day through distractions, but you don't have those distractions at night." Desire, loss, fear, and hope are intertwined with her experience of hunger. In stark contrast to how public discourses portray the hungry, Janet is far from lazy. To be sure, there are some who will use the example of Janet sleeping for fifteen hours as an indicator of her laziness, but chronic fatigue is in fact a symptom of her illness, an illness exacerbated by the stress of dealing with the public assistance system. There are some who will want to medicate her for depression, when what she more fundamentally needs is access to basic needs and for government policies to stop treating her so suspiciously.

Antoine, an African American man, is careful about what he eats because he is diabetic. He disclosed that he was very tempted by the doughnuts put out at the Chum food shelf that morning but did not touch them. He talked about the importance of self-control and discipline. "That's tempting, you know? We all got some kind of demon in us that makes us want to do something and eat overboard. The main thing is trying to control it. If it's in control, you're good, a plus for everything." Antoine is a thin man but says the problem is not his weight. His grandmother had diabetes and so did his father and mother, although he did not find out he had it until he was forty-seven years old. Antoine talks about how he grew depressed when his body became messed up. "That's my main thing, getting depressed real bad. I go into a shell. I don't want to talk to nobody, and that's when I need to get up and go to church, go talk to somebody." When I ask him why so many people are depressed, he says it could be from "not having what you need": "It could be a lot of things that make you depressed, mainly just not having what you need. It don't have to be a lot, just have a decent home and decent food to eat and knowing that you got a roof over your head. That's not a lot to ask for, it's not. It shouldn't be that way. We got so much in this world. We got so many great people." The lack of access to food and resources takes a toll on the mental health of clients.

James, a middle-aged Black man, attributed his depression to physical injuries and racial oppression. He had total knee-replacement surgery some years ago, which resulted in him losing his job. Interrupting the white working-class imaginary so prominent in dominant discourses today, he talked about how much he loved his work and how this work was integral to his identity. He says: "I'm a worker, but when I became homeless, depression issues kicked in, and oppression issues came about, and wow!"

Interviewer: What do you mean by that, oppression?

James: Oppression. In our society, people tend to look at you by the color of your skin. For that person who is getting that kind of heat from people like that, it tends to discourage them to go out and try and be a part of society. They require so much of you to be a part of society. Everybody's not equipped to absorb all that the world has to offer or even be a part of it. There's a lot of things that a human being can do out here as far as professions, but if you don't have it in you to pursue it, even though they're good, you've got to find out where your place is in life. I'm a laborer by my nature. I just work ... I'm tool-orientated and machine-orientated, so I like machines and tools. I'm a guy.

James has experienced a lot of rejection in his life; nevertheless, manual labor is a part of his identity, and hard work and discipline are values he holds dearly. Countering the neoliberal stigma that circulates around him, he says: "All my aunts and uncles, they all work. Working has been a part of my upbringing. It wasn't street hustling, if I may say so. I grew up with some good values, very, very good parents, the best that they could be in this world today." His parents passed away a while ago, and James is sad that he cannot call them to let them know he's okay.

Trauma

Even as individuals struggled with hunger and food insecurity, they experienced unexpected life calamities: intense trauma, violence, adverse childhood experiences, loss of loved ones, and chaos. This profound trauma was
the backdrop to their lives. Clayton, an African American client at Chum,
stood out because of his deep grief at the death of his daughter. When I
asked Clayton how many kids he had, he said, "Well I did have four, but
now it's three for my daughter passed away." There it was: the few words
that structured the rest of our conversation; a life event that structured the
rest of his life. He said in a quiet voice that his daughter died a few years ago
from a cancer called *neurofibromatosis*, a genetic disorder that causes tumors
to form on nerve tissue. She was only fourteen. "She would have been sixteen, March 13 of this year. She died on my dad's birthday." It was a disease
she had since birth, but Clayton says that it was his fault they did not detect
it earlier. He lives with the guilt, the grief, the sadness of believing every day
that he is to blame for her death. He continued: "The only thing I could
do now is pray that she is within God's fences and I will see her again,
and I try to keep that in mind, but it's like a pressure cooker; the pain is
so big it's like it's just piling up under so much pressure, and I still haven't
stopped crying."

Bereaved individuals are similar to "wounded storytellers," as described
by Arthur Frank (1995), whose bodies, minds, and emotions exhibit signs of
the "illness" of bereavement. When I asked Clayton about how he manages
the grief, he is precise, methodical, and almost clinical in his description,
like a wounded storyteller who has thought about this every single day:

> So I do four things: I take long walks in Canal Park and I sit there and just listen to
> the water and think. Number two I listen to some music. They say music soothes
> the savage beast, so certain things that I hear not only does it remind me of my
> daughter, but it reminds me of my childhood, the things that I had that I want
> to grab ahold to once again. The third thing I do is I put my feelings on a piece
> of paper and write poetry or I draw it out, and fourth and the final thing that I
> do, I pray and I ask the Lord, forgive me of my transgressions, for if I want you
> to forgive me, I have to forgive others as well. It's a good thing my daughter said,
> "Dad, whatever you did wrong in your past, God forgave you." It's not easy seeing
> a daughter die in your arms, for as long as I have my son and two daughters by
> my side, my stress level is still high, but they help me to manage it so I won't do
> something crazy like I almost did. Yes, I almost committed suicide, but I know it's
> not going to help. My children still need me.

Duluth with its Great Lake, Lake Superior, provides a way for residents to experience peace, even if only for a moment. Clayton's deep loss has forced him to examine how he lives in the world and has made him more deliberate and purposeful in life. When a child dies, a family is left to revise the meanings it has constructed for itself as part of the unending grieving process (Arnold and Gemma 1983). For Clayton, his other children are the only reason he is still alive today. When we juxtapose Clayton's story, his discipline, his poetry, his way of being in the world, the guilt that he feels, alongside the politicized narratives that demonize the hungry and food insecure, we are left wondering who exactly the demon is.

Michele, a middle-aged Native woman and client of Chum, described herself as a "city native" because she has never been to a reservation or a powwow. Michele has spent much of her adult life dealing with problems of addiction. Not too long ago, she was using crack cocaine and abusing pain medication; she ended up using one drug to overcome another, and finally began to sell drugs to maintain the habit. Now these are the stories—stories of alcohol, drugs, and addiction—of people of color that typically enjoy circulation in the public sphere. These are the news pegs that dull reporters love to hang on to. These singular stories will be circulated in the media over and over again, then used as evidence to validate harsher penalties and restrictions for welfare recipients. However, we would be wise to remember the words of Lee here, the director of Chum: "Poverty, it's brutal, it's hard, it's systemic, it's rarely a choice, and if it looks like a choice, it's because the chooser is broken." Michele has been diagnosed with depression, bipolar disorder, and PTSD. She has suffered adverse childhood experiences of sexual abuse and domestic violence, an epidemic among Native women in her social location. The historical trauma of belonging to a community nearly wiped out by genocide, genocide perpetrated by white people, has an ongoing impact on her social and mental well-being. Michele takes a variety of pills but has an astute critique of doctors who try to medicate her all the time. She says, "Every time you turn around, the doctor wants to give you medication. I'm not going to be a guinea pig. 'Let's try these to see what happens.' 'No, let's not.'" When I ask her how she copes with stress, she says:

> Sometimes I just get irritated and snap on people, even though that doesn't solve anything. It gets it out a little bit. I was keeping in the back of my mind that everything happens for a reason and God has plans for you. It's called life. It goes

with ... the cards you're dealt ... The cards you're dealt is what you made it. Should I have raised myself better, maybe I wouldn't go through that. If I had paid my rent instead of paying for this, that and the other, I wouldn't be behind. The legal issues, if I wasn't doing drugs, I wouldn't be charged with drug sales ... I learned in life, people can only do to you what you let them do. That takes care of it sometimes. It's just all the stuff that goes through my head. If I take my medication, it's not as stressful.

Consistent with the neoliberal narrative, Michele holds herself completely responsible for the circumstances in her life. For Michele, physical, mental, and behavioral problems are all interpreted as a matter of choice. Michele even thinks that as a child she was responsible for her own upbringing. There was something she should have learned when she was a child that could have prevented where she is today. She has been sober for twenty-seven months.

Morgan tells a narrative of betrayal, without revealing too much. Morgan picks up food from the Chum food shelf and currently lives at the homeless shelter. Morgan is gay. Like many others at the food pantry, Morgan used to be a working professional. She was the chef at a country club for fifteen years before she went on disability. She and her same-sex partner made good money but then found themselves out of work, and their relationship splintered. Much of Morgan's trauma has been inflicted upon her by her immediate family. Even though she has family in the region, she stays at the homeless shelter. The eldest of six kids, Morgan has always taken care of everybody else but never gotten any care in return. Her brother and his wife make good money but spend it all on drugs. Morgan has given her mom several thousand dollars, which she has siphoned off to her brother and siblings. The lack of concern and care for her was made clear in one event, which was a turning point in her life:

Morgan: I came down for a knee-replacement surgery and I was in for five days and I called my mom and I said, "Who is picking me up?" Nobody, nobody. Things like that.

Interviewer: How did you get back home?

Morgan: A cab. It was 185 dollars. So, lucky I had it. You can see it is much more preferable to be here. At least I know who I am dealing with.

Morgan is currently at the shelter to escape the abuse of her family. She says, "My family is very, very bad for me." It is clear that she is holding back in the interview. She does not tell me how her gender and sexual identity are intertwined with the hunger experience. Indeed, there are many things she does not say; there are gaps and ellipses in her story, but in how she moves, in her stutter, in her silence, desire, loss, chaos, sorrow, and grief are made clear.

Violet: "I Don't Know What Kind of Disorder I've Got"

Violet is an older Black woman, extremely thin and frail; she does not weigh more than a hundred pounds. Violet has worked in construction her whole life—a Black working-class woman. During the interview, she was friendly, full of life, and described herself as a "jokester." Violet says her biggest struggle is remembering to take her cholesterol medication. But as the interview goes on, cholesterol seems to be the least of it. Violet discloses that she quit drinking three years and six months ago to the date. She talks about her four children and nine grandchildren. Her older son is on disability, so she uses her food stamps and the Chum food shelf to get groceries for him and her grandchildren. Violet then talks about a past abusive relationship and how this brought her to Christ. "I didn't really start getting religious until I got into an abusive relationship. Out of all my relationships this was the worst. I come to call on Christ to get me to hopefully see Him every day, and not *him*. If you get what I mean. I remember one day I was cooking something, and around him I always felt like I had to walk on eggshells. You look at him wrong, he's going to argue. I just prayed to God, "God, please let me get out of this mess." Every time I would get out, I would find myself back in. This was the last straw. I cried, I prayed so hard. A few days later ... we had just started arguing and I left and I woke up and it was like, woohoo, it was lifted off me."

Violet's story is reminiscent of the research conducted by Chilton and Booth (2007), who found two kinds of hunger among African American women who used food pantries in Philadelphia: hunger of the body and hunger of the mind. *Hunger of the body* is the outright painful sensation of hunger caused by insufficient food, the physical impact of hunger on the body, and the way hunger interrupts sleep and daily activities. *Hunger of the mind* is related to trauma, feelings of depression and hopelessness, stress, deliberate (self-inflicted) hunger, abuse and violence, and the inability to eat. The researchers suggest that both types of hunger are manifestations of structural violence, and they recommend a broader framework to examine the health effects of food insecurity—one that addresses women's safety, economic independence, and physical and emotional well-being.

Similar to the women in Chilton and Booth's study, Violet does not eat either. She explains: "I'm sort of good at stretching until I can actually go to the grocery store or whatever. I'm pretty good. I don't really have an appetite. Why, I don't know. People say I'm getting fat. How, I don't know. I eat like a bird, put it that way. If I don't eat for about a day or so and I wake up the next day, drink me some water, take my vitamins, might drink me milk, which I can't drink any milk anymore. It's that age ... To me, I eat like a bird. When I say I eat like a bird, I eat like a bird. A saucer full will fill me up." I am shocked and stunned by how little Violet eats. This is not the story of anorexia or bulimia that I typically hear from my female students. This is not the story of starvation caused because of famine or the complete lack of food. It is far beyond the realm of my experience and the literature, and I have no follow-up questions. Later, I come back to her with a question about why she doesn't eat, and then it becomes clear. She says she doesn't eat because when she was young, her mother never forced them to eat. She added, "Of course, she never cooked. Of course, *there was never food in the house.*" She explained that even now when her stomach is growling, her mind tells her that she is not hungry. "If I do go eat something, it's not because I want to eat it. It's because my mind is saying 'eat.' I might eat two, three tablespoons of whatever and I'll be full ... I don't know what kind of disorder I've got." Her disorder is the hunger of the mind related to trauma, depression, a life of deprivation, and violence. For Violet, growing up with hunger, living though an abusive relationship, and caring for adult children all reveal a life full of challenges, but also one motivated by human agency. Despite her hunger, she joked around with me even as she demonstrated an incisive critical consciousness about her class and racial position in society.

The "Buffering Effect" of Social Support

Folks who had family in the region, who had good relationships with their family, and who were integrated in the community fared better compared to those who did not have close ties in the community. The emotional and instrumental support that family provided protected or "buffered" people from the negative effects of stress—consistent with the existing literature (e.g., Kollannoor-Samuel et al. 2011). Claire, a young white woman and a client of RP said, "My parents are pretty good to me if I need money for something." She added, "Yeah. I'm not that poor yet. If I really needed a dollar ... I'd probably call my sister up and say, 'Hey, I really need some money.' She would help me a lot, I know she would." Penelope, a middle-aged white woman, noted that her mother-in-law and sister-in-law helped her out. For instance, when her husband was in surgery, her mom-in-law helped bring him home and do the grocery shopping. Just knowing that family was around to help if needed was an important source of security. Rick explained that he and his wife managed on their own as far as finances were concerned, but if they both lost their jobs, then both sets of parents would accept them into their homes. He observed: "So it's nice to know that, that network is there."

The folks who did not have family or friends in the region had the most difficulty coping with the multiple insecurities of poverty. Migration of family members to other parts of the country for work often led to this isolation. These participants lacked the protective buffer of social support to shield them from stress and anxiety. John, whose story was told in the opening of the chapter, is one such example. Katherine, an older white woman, has friends in Duluth, but cannot depend on them because they are older like her and cannot drive anymore because of bad eyesight and arthritis. Her daughters live in Minneapolis and do not come up very often. Chris and his family moved to Duluth to be with his wife's family, but his in-laws passed away some years ago, and now they have no one in Duluth who can support them. He added, "If I was in the Twin Cities, I would have lots of people for my kids."

Many participants—in particular, those without family nearby, those estranged from their families, or those whose families were in similar financial situations—identified paid professionals as central to their support system. These included caseworkers, case managers, counselors, psychiatrists, therapists, and even probation officers. These were the people my participants talked to, those who listened to their stories and provided feedback and evaluation. In *The Careless Society*, John McKnight (1995) critiqued the care industry, calling it "counterfeit care." He observed: "Care cannot be produced, provided, managed, organized, administered, or commodified. Care is the only thing a system cannot produce. Every institutional effort to replace the real thing is a counterfeit" (x). This argument rings true, but it was also true that for my participants, primarily people of color, these paid professionals were an important source of support in their lives, as seen in a quote from Michele, the Native woman whose story appeared earlier: "I've got a good support system. I've got social workers, case workers, in the midst of looking for a different therapist. I've got my probation officer." Antoine's family lives all over the country. His mother lives in Chicago, his dad passed away a year ago, he has some family that lives in Georgia, and his kids live in Wisconsin. Antoine, who suffers from physical health issues and depression, understands the importance of talking with someone and has a case manager who fulfils that role: "I might call her a friend; we're real tight. She's just like a mother. She talks to me, you know, and she might pray for me. I found that when you get really depressed you've got to talk to somebody else. You're going through that dark shit. I think a lot of people in this town are really depressed."

Volunteerism, Not Activism

William DiFazio (2006) argues that poverty has become "ordinary" today. Whereas a vocabulary of social change once was used to talk about poverty, this is no longer the case; poverty is seen as permanent and immovable, ordinary. The language of possibility, social action, and activism prevalent in the 1960s has been replaced by the more conservative language of individual achievement and personal responsibility. An important consequence of normalizing poverty is that the poor no longer speak for themselves and they are no longer invited to participate in social movements.

This was certainly the case with participants in this study. Poor clients volunteered as a way to give back to the community and in some cases to meet the demands of workfarist policies. Volunteer activities ranged from working with churches and nonprofits to volunteering at schools and community centers. Isaiah, an African American man and a client of Chum, enjoys working with kids. He explained: "I've done some things here, teaching kids how to play drums and starting a drill team. And I opened up an ice house for them to go skating. You know, it's kind of like giving back, you know, so I do that." At the Chum homeless shelter, clients are expected to do chores, so here Isaiah volunteers to clean the bathrooms. "Because I use them, I was using them myself, and I wanted them to be clean. So that was my volunteering." Xavier has also volunteered quite a bit. He did not grow up struggling for basic needs but found himself more interested in helping others as he grew older: "I mean, I didn't grow up struggling, you know. I didn't come from a family where we had to get out and look for food and that kind of stuff. Then after I got older I became interested in people and I worked for Salvation Army in Atlanta, Georgia, so I used to see destitute people, and you know I promised myself that if there was anything in life that I could ever do, you know, help somebody else out of the woods. So, that's why I try to do what I can and try to volunteer." For participants, volunteering was a way in which to give back to society and show gratitude for what they had received. For them, volunteer work did not ensue from a place of privilege but rather from empathy that comes with lived experience.

There was much interest among participants in sharing their personal stories with the public to bring about broader political change, but they had never been asked or invited to do so. Gary has volunteered quite a bit but has not been involved with advocacy for political change. Participants are caught in a web of political discourses that make claims about who they (the hungry) are, what the solution to hunger is, and how it should be managed, yet they had never been asked to participate in finding solutions for what is allegedly "their" problem. Although they were asked to volunteer, the same was not true of political advocacy. This is seen in Isaiah's interview.

Interviewer: Would you be interested in changing something in the system? Would you be interested, for instance, to sign a petition to say we need more access or to even sometimes share your story?

Isaiah: Sure, I would do that, I would really do that.

Interviewer: Have you ever been asked to participate in any kind of political activity?

Isaiah: As far as food goes?

Interviewer: Yeah.

Isaiah: No.

Isaiah worked at a call center campaigning for President Obama twice, but he has not been involved with advocacy for his own specific needs. Jermain had a similar response:

Interviewer: How about this ... Would you be interested in being more involved in political activities to get more access to food?

Jermain: Yeah, I would, that is worthwhile. Because, it's people, it's families that need places like this ... You don't just ask somebody do you have facilities to cook and give them food stamps. Half of them don't know how to use them. With the food stamps, you know, you can't buy things like toothpaste, toilet paper, you know, and I don't see why not. That should be included with food.

In this instance, Jermain provides a simple solution to the intersecting needs of people experiencing deprivation: reducing restrictions on what can be purchased with SNAP.

There were only a few folks who were not interested in telling their stories in public, for fear of being hurt—for example, Violet:

Interviewer: Would you be interested in being more involved with political activities ...

Violet: Nope, because they throw shit too.

Interviewer: Okay. What about to get better access to food? Activities like signing a petition or sharing your story?

Violet: I don't know. I have never actually thought of something like that ... I don't know. I'd have to think about that one.

Similarly, Rochelle was happy to sign a petition but was not interested in telling her story, as she noted: "My first instinct. I'm not going to tell nobody nothing." Overall, these findings provide a glimpse into how hunger is depoliticized today. Poor citizens volunteer in their communities but do not have access to mainstream spaces of politics and decision-making that have a direct impact on their lives and livelihoods.

Conclusion

In this chapter, I highlight that independence, self-reliance, and self-sufficiency are not individual at all but rather forged within a complex network of private and public institutions: family and friends, employers, counselors, social workers, and government offices. The chapter shows that by the time people have reached the food pantry, they have already confronted several human rights abuses: lack of employment or a decent living wage, lack of education, affordable housing, violence, and hunger, to name a few. Contrary to neoliberal stigma circulating around them, participants are constantly engaged in a livelihood juggle, using vast amounts of creative energy to take care of their families. A few decades ago, Poppendieck (1999, 315) pointed out that people need so much more than food: "Although poor people in our society are sometimes hungry, they live most days in a tangled web of unmet needs and unrealized hopes. ... A program or policy that tried only to prevent acute hunger is aiming too low. It is not acceptable to have people in our society too poor to participate and contribute, too poor to provide a decent chance in life for their children, too poor to pursue happiness. We need to aim for the creation of a just and inclusive society that taps everyone's potential and makes us all better off in the long run, not just a society where no one starves."

Institutions, laws, and policies have stigma embedded within them, which otherize, exclude, and negatively impact the lives of people. The welfare system is an apt example of structural stigma that serves to keep people "down, in, and away," even in the absence of person-to-person stigma (Link and Phelan 2014). This was the case in this study, in which participant after participant talked about the incessant juggling they were involved in to navigate the restrictive and punitive welfare system. Amid challenging life situations, participants were bewildered by the inadequacy of food stamps, social security, and disability benefits, as well as the amount of labor, stress, and anxiety that went into receiving entitlements. The system actively disempowered them, restricting self-determination. Hunger has profound physical consequences, but there are also social and psychological burdens that come with the experience of hunger. The stigma of hunger produces a double burden: the economic burden of trying to put food on the table, and the social burden of stigma. Indeed, there is nothing ordinary about the experience of poverty. There is no normalizing poverty. Poverty is always stressful. It always requires vigilance, hard work, and being always "on" just to stay afloat.

Sadly, John's story presented at the beginning of this chapter is not a rags-to-riches story, but a riches-to-rags one. In fact, it was a story that many food pantry participants told and one that is indicative of entitlement failure. Even as the American dream continues to be propagated in the public imaginary, the reality is quite the opposite: people are more likely to fall down the socioeconomic ladder of success than climb up. People are more likely to stay within a particular class location than have economic mobility. People who have a decent education, people who are employed, people who are capable, ambitious, with goals and hopes for the future, find themselves stuck. This phenomenon is reminiscent of the words of Dr. Bhimrao Ramji Ambedkar (2014), a member of the untouchable Hindu caste and framer of the Indian constitution—who said, "Caste is like a multistoried building with no exit and no staircase. You live and die in the same floor you were born into." There is a similar reality in the United States today. Although, unlike India, the United States is one of the richest, most industrially advanced, and powerful economies in the world, with a GDP of $18 trillion per year and a per capita GDP of $57,300 (almost fourteen times that of the Indian GDP).

Field Note: Desire and the "Third Space"

As I write this chapter from my own position of material privilege, I recognize that for people, including my students, in situations of poverty, these stories are disheartening because they showcase hard work, pain, struggle, health issues, depression, and anxiety, amid bleak shimmers of hope. These stories are frightening because they show that the American dream is just that—a dream. There is no way up and no way out as governance structures work to keep the social order intact. From a research point of view, this is the primary dilemma of what Native scholar Eve Tuck (2009) refers to as "damage-centered research." My research focuses on the problem of hunger; therefore, the questions I asked focused on problems. In this chapter, I documented the pain, the loss, and the struggles of individuals and communities and contextualized these issues amid forces of oppression.

Although this makes sense in terms of research that seeks to illuminate social realities, the question Tuck poses is this: What are the hidden costs and long-term repercussions for communities thinking of themselves as broken? Tuck argues for a shift toward desire-based research frameworks when studying indigenous communities, in which desire is concerned with understanding plurality and contradiction. She observes: "Desire-based research frameworks are concerned with understanding complexity, contradiction, and the self-determination of lived lives. ... Such an axiology is intent on depathologizing the experiences of dispossessed and disenfranchised communities so that people are seen as more than broken and conquered. That is to say that even when communities are broken and conquered, they are so much more than that-so much more that this incomplete story is an act of aggression" (416).

Interrupting the social scientific binary between structure and agency, desire frameworks call into recognition a "third space." Tuck writes: "This is more important because it more closely matches the experiences of people who, at different points in a single day, reproduce, resist, are complicit in, rage against, celebrate, throw up hands/fists/ towels, and withdraw and participate in uneven social structures—that is, everybody" (420). Desire disrupts the structure/agency binary to reveal "people layered in composition and meaning." In this framework, desire accounts for loss and despair, but also hope, vision, and "the wisdom of lived lives and communities" (417).

Drawing on this notion of desire, I would like to illuminate some key moments in the discourse that speak to desire. In this chapter, we see citizens rich in their complexity, intellect, and spirit as central to the hunger story in America. We hear stories of college degrees, work, volunteerism, giving back to the community, making contributions to society, contributing to the workplace, the love of nature, bold decision-making in the face of trouble, mindfulness, quirkiness, prayer and spirituality, and, in the case of John, global citizenship. These citizens, forced into the margins, have a heightened consciousness about the world around them and a vision for what things should be like. These citizens, amid the crushing burden of economic oppression, racial oppression, and structural violence, give us a very clear sense of what the problem is and offer rational, political solutions grounded in their lived realities. Many were eager to engage in activism and tell their stories to make a difference—for themselves and society. These were individuals who experienced the fragility of life and who in response sometimes stayed in bed, sometimes cried it out, sometimes pushed back against the forces keeping them down, but most often kept the wheels churning and went about their daily lives, caring for themselves and being cared for. Even amid the loss depicted in these stories, people talked on the phone and laughed. They held on to their aspirations. They told jokes, took walks by Lake Superior, and remembered their work lives fondly. It is my hope that in the gaping holes of these still partial and incomplete stories, one hears people layered in composition and meaning.

Policy and Practical Implications

The policy implications from this chapter are clear: there is a clear mandate to increase minimum wage, increase SNAP benefits, and reduce restrictive and punitive processes that drive the public assistance system. A fair public assistance system should enable households to maintain stability and security and at the same time provide them with a launching pad to realize their hopes, dreams, and aspirations. There should be logical systems of governance based on scientific evidence rather than on age-old myths and stereotypes that have traveled to us from the Middle Ages. Political narratives regularly threaten increasing restrictions on SNAP, even when all evidence points in the other direction. The evidence reinforces the livelihood and human rights perspective, which argues that people's rights are "interdependent, indivisible and interrelated"; therefore, making legal entitlements less restrictive and more flexible is extremely logical. Policy in the United States, one of the wealthiest nations on earth, should at least come close to guaranteeing its citizens basic human rights—human rights based on the principle of respect for every individual, grounded in the fundamental assumption that each person is a moral and rational being who deserves to be treated with dignity.

Achieving political goals requires shifting the narratives surrounding the hungry and food insecure through the creation of participatory forums, in which marginalized citizens can speak and be heard. Forty million citizens and more have been made invisible in the discursive and political arena. There is a need to foreground the voices of the poor as sites of knowledge production and political action. The goals of these participatory spaces are to recover voices that have been erased from the discursive sphere, to bring these voices back into focus, and to channel these voices into the realm of policy. Dutta (2008) points out that the absence of the poor from mainstream spaces of policy-making is linked to their material disenfranchisement; in other words, communities that are materially disenfranchised are also disenfranchised communicatively by the absence of venues for participation, recognition, and representation. It is becoming increasingly clear today that the hungry are allowed to speak, but only through food drives, fundraising campaigns, corporate responsibility campaigns, and public relations efforts for food banks. Here the poor may talk about their pain, damage, and pathology, but never safely articulate a political consciousness—never safely demand their basic human rights to adequate food. There is an urgent need to create spaces where citizens can contribute to policy—where citizens can tell their stories and advocate for their rights. Facilitating these participatory forums and spaces is necessary to reframe hunger, to reposition the hungry, to disrupt neoliberal stigma, and to move toward more progressive political solutions.

4 The "Good White Women" at the Chum Food Shelf

I make her do the interviews with me when I interview folks, and then she really gets the point that they are no different than her, they are no different than anybody else in the world. They just don't have as much money. So it takes away the stigma that so many people, especially kids that grow up surrounded by wealth, have that *those* people are so different. You know, "I am not going to deal with those people, they have got their problems and I have got nothing to do with them, and they are nothing like me." I think that she has really come to realize that they are absolutely no different than her and I. We have just been lucky enough to keep our jobs for years and there is no other difference. So those conversations have come up a lot or she has commented that, "Wow, mom, if dad lost his job we would be at the food shelf." Oh yeah, we would. "Oh well, that's really scary, mom." It is. Yeah, so it comes up, all of it, and a lot just to do with the fact that everyone's really not that different and yet we are always one step away from being in one or the other category or camp, so to speak.
—Lisa, white female, volunteer at Chum

Lisa and Her Daughter

Lisa is a long-term volunteer at the Chum food shelf, and a regular one at that. For the past five years, she has packed food for clients every Wednesday evening—the evening assigned to working families. A highly educated white-collar professional, Lisa works long hours each day in a high-stress job and then, once a month, gives up a precious Wednesday evening to volunteer with her eight-year-old daughter at the Chum food shelf. Lisa says her reason for volunteering at Chum is a selfish one. Her family lives in a rich neighborhood, all their friends are wealthy, and her daughter goes to the best school in the city. Volunteering at Chum is a way to expose her daughter to people who are not wealthy and do not live like they do. The pedagogical goal is to show her daughter that They are just like Us and that moving between one "category or camp" and another is simply a matter of employment and who gets to keep their jobs. From Lisa's perspective, this kind of exposure takes away the stigma that rich kids who grow up in wealthy neighborhoods have about poor people. For Lisa, the Chum food shelf has opened up a rewarding dialogue with her daughter. They can talk about how fortunate their family is to be employed and how thankful the families are who come to the food pantry.

Lisa's lesson plan is incomplete, however, for two reasons: (1) she overlooks the history of white domination that continues to privilege whites and (2) she frames charity as a fruitful way to help people in need—overlooking systemic interconnections and the need for more empowering, rights-based approaches. Lisa adopts a color-blind discourse to talk about difference, stating that people who use the food shelf are "absolutely no different than her and I" and that "there is no other difference." But there is a difference. Most Chum clients identify as Native or African American; in the interviews, approximately 60 percent of clients identified as people of color and about 50 percent suffered from high food insecurity. In a city like Duluth with extreme racialized poverty, there are indeed stark differences between Lisa's family and the clients at Chum. Even if we sidestep slavery and genocide, in more recent history discriminatory housing policies ensure that Lisa lives a racially segregated life with other well-to-do white folks just like her. Lisa's daughter goes to the "good school" in the city, lives in a home that her parents own, and has the benefit of watching successful white role models represented in the media. Lisa's daughter will never be gunned down by police officers for hanging out in her grandma's backyard; she will never watch from the backseat as her mom's boyfriend is shot seven times by a police officer. Even as communities of color prepare their three- and four-year-olds for the white terror that will be unleashed upon their bodies, Lisa's daughter is spared an education in systemic racism because it does not affect her.

Is Lisa ignorant? Is Lisa a racist? Does she think her daughter is too young to understand racial issues? Is she being politically correct? There are many ways to rationalize Lisa's discourse, but even so we must at least recognize two key points. First, Lisa speaks from a racialized position of whiteness. Perched high up on the rungs of the social system, being charitable is central to her identity and a fundamental way she knows how to "do good." The particularities of her worldview correspond to her systemic location, which simply means that as a pattern one would expect white women in the United States to use this kind of color-blind yet compassionate and charitable language. Ruth Frankenberg (1993), in her groundbreaking work on the racialized identity of white women, described whiteness as both a position of structural advantage and a "standpoint" or place from which to look at oneself, others, and society. Whiteness has "everything to do with not being black, with living in privileged and virtually all-white neighborhoods, with 'good' schools, safe streets, and moral values to match" (Kobayashi and Peake 2000, 394).

For white middle-class women in a post–civil-rights era, doing good works and self-sacrifice are central to their identities (Fothergill 2003). Behaviors of reaching out, caring for others, and "doing good" are the result of socializing females into caregiving roles but are also intertwined with class status. As members of the middle class, women like Lisa are able to give time and resources toward charitable causes. Lisa is not simply a good woman, she is a good *white* woman. A small difference in words, but one that will grate at her and cause much discomfort to her and women like her who are not accustomed to being viewed as raced. As a white person, she has only ever seen herself as normal, a human being, a good person, and a good woman. Identifying her as "white" makes visible her racial identity and marks her with color, history, and all sorts of racial baggage linked to white supremacy and the colonial doctrine of manifest destiny.

A key problem with charity is that it results in outpourings of gratitude on the part of givers, but never quite moves in the direction of food justice. Charity allows white middle-class women to reach out to the Other and to feel sadness for the Other, while also summoning up intense emotions linked to personal gratitude—as heard in the oft-repeated refrain: "I am just so grateful for what I have." Lisa is a good person. Lisa is a good mother. Lisa is a good woman. Lisa is grateful and thankful. Lisa is performing the role of the "good white woman" in American society. Through a three-hour weekly exposure in a highly regulated environment, she socializes her daughter into doing the same—to do good, to give back to society, to learn how to connect with Others, and to recognize her personal good luck and fortune. This discourse of gratitude occurs in the absence of any consciousness that the same system that accrues benefits to white people marginalizes communities of color. Lisa and her daughter are privy to the multiple wages of whiteness, wages that are the result of historical and ongoing exploitation of communities of color, but these facts remains unacknowledged.

This brings us to the second point that begs our recognition—the gaps and discursive erasures in Lisa's pedagogical activities, whether intentional or not, undermine the role of structural racism in society. In an environment in which all the volunteers are white and most of the clients are people of color, these discursive erasures reinforce white superiority, virtue, and moral goodness while continuing to otherize people of color, albeit in compassionate ways. In what she says and does not say, Lisa sidesteps the racial organization of society that holds whites and people of color in place. Lisa's charity does not extend beyond doling out food to actually invert the axis of oppression. Indeed, if it came to it, she may even vote against policies that do so in the interests of keeping things "fair" and "balanced." Simply put, Lisa does not ask *why*: Why is there food at the food shelves but not in people's homes? Why do we distribute food we would not eat ourselves? Why are there so many people of color here as clients but not as volunteers? And, a question closer to home: Why do I (Lisa) get such great satisfaction bringing you (my daughter) to the food shelf, while for clients who come here with their kids, it is a shameful experience? Lisa does not talk about the capitalist food system that creates hunger and then redistributes surplus food to remedy physiological pangs. She does not discuss food sovereignty and how communities of color have been denied their rights to grow, produce, fish, and hunt for food—even in Minnesota. She does not talk about the fact that even hungry people yearn for fresh food and whole foods and worry intensely about there being too much sodium in canned corn. She does not talk about women like Trinity, the African American woman for whom racism gets in the way of her employment. Instead, she talks about how clients are so thankful for the food they get at Chum and how they— the volunteers—should be so grateful for what they have.

Poverty and racialized poverty are endemic to Duluth. Here, white residents tend to have few interactions with people of color. As Lee Stuart, executive director of Chum, observes, these interactions are limited to situations in which whites are almost always in positions of power. The power, privilege, and unspoken norms associated with whiteness are intensified in this region, as are experiences of stigma for people of color. Some might argue that whiteness is inevitable in a setting in which there are so many white people, but as food scholar Rachel Slocum (2007) notes, this runs counter to the idea that whiteness is hegemonic in the United States, regardless of the number of bodies in a certain place. She notes: "Studying whiteness ... is not about counting all the whites and arguing that whiteness is 'more' or 'less' in places with greater or fewer of them" (521). Whiteness is part of race and central to theorizing race, racism, and antiracism, and studying whiteness helps us understand how race operates in the United States, regardless of numbers.

The study of whiteness problematizes whiteness by turning the research gaze from its traditional, exclusive focus on the racialized Other to those at the center—those on the top rungs of the racial system: white people. The title of this chapter purposefully identifies "good white women" to shift the lens on issues of hunger and food insecurity; the overarching argument is that hunger (like racism) is less about those who are marked and more about those who participate in assigning marks. Furthermore, food pantries obscure the fact that the hunger industrial complex is built on the good intentions of a lot of good white people- mostly women. Lisa may be a good woman, but, as John Biwen (2017) puts it plainly in the final episode of the award-winning *Seeing White* series: "So all white supremacy needs to keep chugging along, even here in the twenty-first century, is for most white people to go about our lives being nice and being good nonracists. ... So, and that includes people working, you know, doing the good work of working in the caring professions and social services and even charity work, right? If we just go about our lives, we can have a white supremacist society without individual racists. As it happens, we have individual racists, too." Moving toward a place of food justice beyond oppressive forms of charity necessarily requires food pantries to engage in antiracism work— not by problematizing brownness, but by interrogating whiteness. In the absence of critical thinking into the types of good works that whiteness brings, food pantries are just another vestige of structural racism in the United States today.

Goal of the Chapter

The goal of this chapter is to unpack neoliberal stigma as it emerges in the context of whiteness and doing good. *Neoliberal stigma* refers to the ideological formations in which parameters of hard work, accountability, and individualism are used to mark people as inferior or superior. Importantly, the chapter situates whiteness in relation to organizational discourses and larger systems of neoliberal governance that extract discipline from clients and volunteers alike; in other words, whiteness is not just evident in individual people like Lisa but at organizational and institutional levels. The questions posed by this chapter are: How do Chum's mainly white volunteers construct, reinforce, and disrupt neoliberal stigma through discourse and practice? How is whiteness reflected in organizational discourses and structures? With regard to practice, I am particularly interested in how whiteness wields its power through policies and procedures that discipline poor citizens and people of color. The chapter also highlights moments of possibility scattered throughout, possibilities for food pantries and good whites to join in the long march toward food justice and rights-based approaches.

Contradictory Discourses at Chum

Although Chum tends to be more politically liberal and strives toward a vision of social justice (i.e., a state of equality, equity, and redistributive justice), its official discourses are mixed in terms of ideological orientation. Waxman (1983) notes that over the last fifty years at least two major explanations have been offered for the existence of poverty; in the cultural argument, poverty exists because the lives of the poor are different from the nonpoor both economically and in "cultural" respects, including patterns of behavior and values. In the structural argument, patterns of behavior that manifest in the poor are not the result of unique values of the poor but instead the consequence of the poor occupying an unfavorable position in the social structure. The latter argument tends to be less stigmatizing, although, as we will discuss, Chum employs both arguments in its official discourses.

Chum produces several public relations materials, such as brochures, annual reports, newsletters, and emails sent to donors and community members, which identify the various social and economic factors that bring people to use their services. The structural or basic needs of clients are foregrounded in this excerpt: "The Food Shelf operates with the philosophy that people in need of food should have **access to this most fundamental of human needs.**" Justice and compassion are important to the work of

Chum, as is clear in its vision statement. Chum is "People of faith working together to provide basic necessities, foster stable lives and organize for a just and compassionate community." In official discourses, Chum uses faith-based arguments to encourage a particular response to poverty rooted in social justice, as highlighted in an excerpt from an annual report: "Supported by at least 10,000 faithful people, from 38 diverse congregations from neighborhoods 'east, west, downtown and over the hill,' the staff at Chum is guided by the question: *Given this unique and God-given person in front of me at this moment, how can I respond with the most love, the most generosity, the most compassion, and the greatest mercy? How can our work together help heal the broken world and bend the moral arc of the universe a little bit more toward justice?*" This excerpt invokes Rev. Martin Luther King's (1965) sermon at Temple Israel, in which he examined the "mountain of racial injustice."

Although the language of structures is sometimes employed in official publications, a neoliberal, market-driven language of self-sufficiency, independence, and personal responsibility is also found in the discourse. For example, organizational materials clarify that Chum's focus is on moving families from dependence to independence. The title for a brochure announces, "Help us to help others help themselves," and another commentary reads, "Chum maintains these food programs with the goal of guiding people toward self-sufficiency, to a place where they no longer need assistance." Another brochure presents a profile of an employee, Richard, who has served as a housing advocate for more than a decade. Richard's role is described as that of a "part parent," reinforcing a paternalistic relationship between Chum and its clients. The theme of dignity is central in the writing; Richard is quoted as saying, "Dignity is a personal thing ... You cannot make someone have dignity. You can treat them with dignity, and that helps, but real dignity is something that operates from the inside out. You have to create it for yourself." Later in the article, Richard emphasizes the importance of humility and inner worth: "If I can get someone to understand humility where they can become somewhat humbled by the service they're receiving, they can then start to go, 'Wow, I can do it.' That's when the esteem building starts. That's where the self-respect starts to germinate. That's when you start to see some kind of self-worth, not outer worth. And I'll tell you there have been some significant experiences here with people who have absolutely done some 180s, and that's what keeps me in the business." The notion that poor citizens, people who are at the bottom of the social hierarchy, need to learn humility is unsettling to say the least.

Lauding Richard for this work, the brochure states, "More specifically, he's helped a lot of people to help themselves. He shows love, respect and compassion, while at the same time calling for accountability. It's an important balance designed to help individuals discover something precious— their dignity." The individualization of poverty is clear across these official discourses, in which even when structural factors are presented as the cause of the problem, solutions are framed in individual and moral terms, captured in the words *dignity*, *humility*, and *inner worth*. Consistent with neoliberal logic, the focus is on the individual—the individual's character, independence, accountability, and self-sufficiency—and the solution is framed therapeutically using the language of personal healing and restoration. Instead of revealing the complexity of poverty and poverty governance today, these discourses validate suspicions people hold with respect to the motives, intentions, and moral character of those who are poor and food insecure. These stories erase the complexity of human beings who walk through Chum—how they give back to their communities, their aspirations, their heightened sense of consciousness about the world around them, and their visions.

Official discourses demonstrate painstaking discursive erasures with regards to historically patterned racial inequities. Mirroring Lisa's colorblind discourse earlier, racial inequity remains the unarticulated subtext in official discourses as well. Between the years 2009 and 2013, I found only one annual report with references to minoritized groups, albeit in colorblind language: "But increasingly, Chum will be seeking new ways to break through the barriers that marginalize and isolate so many of those we serve. This cannot happen without your initiative, prayers, and involvement." The barriers alluded to here are racism and structural racism. Explicit language about the problem of racial inequity was absent, but the accompanying imagery clarified the meaning. A cursory glance provides an immediate sense of which social groups are being served and which groups do the serving. The annual report zooms in on volunteers, staff, and board members who are white, whereas clients are represented by a mix made mostly of African Americans and Native Americans, plus a few white men and women. These images of people of color are beset with paternalistic taglines such as "Offering a hand to those in need," "Supporting friends from crisis to need," and "Food, shelter, dignity, hope." In one of the main brochures, there were six images of clients either alone or in groups, of which four images noticeably depicted people of color. Thus, like Lisa, who failed to draw the connections between race and class, official discourses also do not articulate these intersections. Race, though visible, has been made irrelevant, relegating the systematic oppression of minoritized communities to the backdrop.

Institutional Pressures

For Chum's executive director, Lee Stuart—a scholar who has spent her life in activism and organizing—these contradictions are reflective of the complexity of the organization itself. Lee started at Chum after spending nearly two decades as lead organizer of the South Bronx Churches, where she directed large-scale community-rebuilding projects. Chum does not have its roots in radical social action, however, but in traditional top-down service delivery. Chum has only recently begun to move into advocacy work. Chum is what might be referred to as a "corporatist welfare organization" because of its hierarchical structure and formal separations between managers, volunteers, and clients (Adkins, Occhipinti, and Hefferan 2012). Chum began in 1973, when ten Central Hillside (Duluth's inner city) congregations pooled resources to assist low-income people in Duluth during a regional recession. Chum today is made of about forty member congregations with a range of denominations and political leanings. Organizational decisions are influenced by member congregations, which can be limiting. Lee notes: "I mean there are liberal, conservative, Catholic, Methodist, Lutheran, Baptist ... Lutherans see the world quite differently than the world of Gloria Dei, and St. John's is very different from a place like St. Ben's, both theologically and ritually." Lee is engaged in antiracist work herself, but talks about how difficult it is to get the so-called good white folks in member congregations to get on board. Even as Chum creates spaces for ecumenical dialogue and provides for the needs of the poorest in Duluth, the "throwaway" people, recognizing and intervening in whiteness is an uphill battle. Lee observes that rarely has the work of member congregations gone beyond the realm of charity, which she argues is the downfall of faith institutions overall: "I think that the declining reliance on faith institutions in our country is partly because people stopped at charity, and weren't given the tools to express those values and those visions, you know, make straight the highway, make the rough places smooth, make the valleys gentle, make the mountains ... make the obstacles low. Those are powerful, powerful images. Now, how do we do that?"

Broader food system arrangements inform how Chum runs its food shelf. Chum receives grants from the federal and state government and is engaged in private-public sector collaborations to deliver services. In addition to procuring food through the Feeding America network, Chum receives food through personal donations and food drives held by various organizations in the city of Duluth, including the university where I work, the local co-op, and schools. A variable amount of food stocked at Chum is USDA commodity food that comes via the federal TEFAP program. Because Chum distributes TEFAP food, clients must go through intake procedures mandated by government policies to ensure eligibility and prevent overutilization of services. Chum only allows one visit per month, although this rule is sometimes broken on a case-by-case basis by volunteers.

Every time I talk to food shelf directors, my head hurts. The job is incredibly tough. It is intense and different every day. There is always a freezer that needs fixing, food that is rotting somewhere, a new procedure to follow, new volunteers to deal with, fluctuations in food prices, something that needs to be ordered, a problem that needs to be solved. They sit for hours with lists of food sent to them by the food bank and then try to determine the cost-effectiveness of buying products from the food bank versus directly from a retailer. The food shelf at Chum is no different. It has only one paid staff position and relies mostly on volunteer labor. The food shelf director at Chum is Frank; his days are spent dealing with either a shortage of food or an abundance of food, both of which require crisis management. He has to find a way to distribute food that was dumped on him, manage the food needs of his clients, and get rid of expired food. Frank often went into lengthy diatribes about food waste in the system, the emotional connection that donors have with food shelves, and micropolitics that occur between Chum, Second Harvest, and corporate donors. Food shelf directors are caught up in the business of moving vast quantities of surplus food while also being plagued by uncertainties about supply. Frank feels that he has little control in the hunger industrial complex—that the system benefits too many people for anyone to want it to change. It is in this context of managed chaos that whiteness and neoliberalism wield their power.

"Good (White) Women, Basically"

Unlike clients, the Chum food shelf volunteers all identified as white and from a middle-class background—typically older, retired, or semiretired women, and none had experienced hunger or food insecurity in their lifetimes. One of the volunteers described it in this way: "We are pretty much the same. I think we come from similar backgrounds. We have had opportunities in life which other people haven't." This is consistent with research that shows that volunteering is typically a middle-class activity because these individuals are able to give time, energy, and other resources (e.g., travel to the location) toward charitable causes (Fothergill 2003).

These white women showed great insight when talking about the connections between the economy and food insecurity. When asked about what brings people to the food shelves, volunteers like Lisa talked in great length about the struggles that families go through—homelessness, unemployment, retirement, health issues, divorce, and even the single calamitous event that brings families down. Linda, a retired social worker, who was a regular volunteer at the food shelf, talked about how the steel plant brought manufacturing jobs to Duluth, but when that left there were only professional and service jobs available. The lack of jobs training meant that people could not get those jobs. "So, then what is the solution? We sent them home, we gave them a check." She added astutely: "So then you say, okay on the ladder of life you are the type that goes to the food shelf, you are the type that gives to the food shelf. You know, I mean, is that how we rate ourselves, you know?" A few volunteers, in particular the older women who had been at the food shelf for a long time, articulated critiques about the institutionalization of food banks. Linda, referring to Chum, said, "I mean, they were just in a little corner; I mean, they were never a building!" Another, an elderly octogenarian, Joanne, who used to be a teacher, elaborated upon the risks of charity: "That's a risk of providing any charity; it becomes institutionalized, if you will. I have been here twenty years and, you know, our goal always was to be redundant and I have not seen much progress in that direction. There are some people who would say that just by the very nature of our politics in this country that we need an underclass to make the system work. I think it's horrible. I mean, I am a very liberal person politically and I am probably close to being a social democrat."

For all these women, volunteering at the Chum food pantry was a way for them to do good in the world. For some, volunteering was driven by faith beliefs; they used Biblical parables of the Good Samaritan and "loaves and fishes" to support their volunteerism. For others, it was more about social engagement, citizenship, and postsecular ethics. For Tracy, "deeds are more important than creeds," so making a better world by feeding the hungry, housing the homeless, working for immigrant rights, and supporting gay, lesbian, and transsexual people were all part of her spiritual growth and progress. Good citizenship meant giving back to the community. It also meant passing on values and life lessons to children, as in Lisa's story.

Volunteering also comes with advantages. The fact that volunteers do not get paid means a lot of flexibility in terms of schedules and job expectations. Volunteering allows these white women in Duluth to live their middle-class lifestyles and give back; as Cindy observed: "I don't have a paid job and I just wanted to be a volunteer as I wanted to find useful things to do. My husband is a doctor. I don't need the money and so I wanted to contribute and do something. Also, when you are a volunteer you have flexibility, because when you cannot come, you cannot come, and so I don't have to worry about travel plans." Volunteering was a way for these white women to socialize and bond with each other. Volunteers may not initially feel a sense of belonging to each other, but after seeing each other on a regular basis, they form a social collective of sorts—a collective formed not necessarily based on phenotypical characteristics but because of the seriality of their interactions, interactions afforded to them because of white economic privilege. By engaging in the task of distributing food to others, volunteers spend time with each other, enjoy meaningful social interactions, and become friends. Penny, a retired librarian, explained that distributing food to people in need was indeed only part of her motivation for volunteering: "I do enjoy the group of people that I am volunteering with. You know, we have [the] opportunity to converse and check in with each other, and joke and laugh and tell stories and stuff like that. You know, that's really good and it does feel good that you are putting food into people's mouth, that's part of it." Consistent with the white racial frame, volunteers held each other in high regard, referring to each other as kind, generous, courteous, respectful, and faithful. Penny ended the interview by saying, "I just stand in awe of the people that work in these organizations and their dedication. They are saints and they are just basically such good people and I just feel so honored to have been part of that in my time here."

Reaching Out and Breaking the Rules

Although volunteers bonded easily with each other, forging genuine connections with clients was a challenge at the food shelf, where interactions took place in a highly regimented manner. Charity reinforces social distance, hierarchy, and asymmetry; social theorist Pierre Bourdieu (1990) averred that it is through the act of giving that relations of power and domination are metamorphosed into legitimate and moral relations. Before the food shelf opens, there is typically a line of people waiting, a line that winds along the sidewalk outside. When the doors open, clients wait in the waiting area until their intake interview, after which they are taken back to the "shopping area" to pick out food. This is a small room with shelves of canned food, a table of fresh food, and a freezer of meat. The interviewer is the first person the client interacts with at the food shelf. If there are many clients that day, then numbers are given out to keep track of who should be served first. In keeping with poverty governance procedures, at the intake interview clients are asked about their income, types of federal or state assistance received, number of members in their households, and if they need referrals for anything else. This is the time to ascertain the person's income and eligibility for using the food shelf. If the individual has been to the food shelf before, their card will be on file, and the interviewer will cross-check it against what the client is saying, updating details as needed. Within the enclosure of the Chum food shelf, both clients and volunteers obeyed the arrangements of space and time, each following their roles precisely. On a busy day, the process of receiving food could take between two and three hours.

Volunteers acknowledge that the administrative procedures at the food shelf can feel demeaning to the client, but they do their best to forge connections and make the process more amenable. Poverty governance procedures demand that a particular intake interview question be asked: "Why are you at the food shelf?" A volunteer explained that people typically will say something like, "you know, I have no food" or "I am hungry." Once in a while people may go into more detail, saying things like "I just moved," "I have to come up with a rent deposit," "my food stamps got lowered," or "I have children coming into my household." These questions can sound judgmental, so volunteers make adjustments. Linda, for instance, does not question clients' responses, even when there is a discrepancy. "I just kind of leave that as, you know, whatever they say is the truth, maybe they forgot to write something ... Well, it isn't really for us to pry or to make people feel uncomfortable."

Volunteers reached out to clients with kindness and compassion by way of empathic conversation. In the context of alternative food movements, Slocum (2007, 524) writes that whiteness builds its own closed, cordoned arena, yet there are many instances in which whites come into close proximity with non-white others and reach out in "appreciation, curiosity and hopefulness." This "desirous proximity" was certainly true at the food shelf, where volunteers tried to forge connections. For instance, Lisa, the mom introduced in the opening of the chapter, talked about striking up a conversation with a client—asking them how they were doing or inquiring about a new job. Cindy pointed out that there were clients who came in on particular days because they knew a particular volunteer was going to be there. "At this time, you remember that the client has a sick child or someone had a surgery, you can say, 'Oh, how is your mom, last weekend you were here you were upset because she was in the hospital.'" Cindy characterized these incidents as moments of friendship.

Another way in which volunteers showed empathy was by breaking the rules and procedures. In these instances, volunteers challenged the neoliberal governance structures that disciplined their interactions and behaviors. The amount of food distributed at the food shelf is set by food shelf policies, government regulations, and the amount of food the food shelf has to offer at any time, which circumscribes the autonomy of volunteers. Volunteers broke the rules by handing out more food than allowed or giving something extra. Gayle, the former food shelf director, explained that if a family needed assistance more than once in a month, they would try to see if they could skip the following month's supply, but this negotiation was up to whoever was there at the time. Pamela, a retired nurse, talked about why she might hand out extra food: "I have nursing as my background, so somebody will come through and say that their child has a cold and I suggest extra fluids. They are not going to go to the doctor because there is no way to afford that. You know volunteers, we are kind of savvy that way, sticking an extra thing, you need more juice this week for your child, that kind of stuff."

Previously, the packers would go to the pantry to pack up the food for the client, but a few years ago, a new "client choice model" was put in place. Clients are now escorted around to choose their own food; this has helped build connections between volunteers and clients. Pamela explained: "In some ways there used to be more of a disconnect between us because we would only literally pack stuff. The person interviewing the clients would give us the packing stuff and we would go back and pack it up ... we would really be simply assuming what other people wanted. But that changed. The new process now involves clients coming back and choosing what they want off the shelf according to certain guidelines and limits." Linda noted that there is dignity in "making your own choices" and not having anyone looking over your shoulder. On a more pragmatic note, with this new system, clients go home with what they want to eat and will eat. Pamela continues: "Yeah, we try to give somebody an apple that doesn't have any teeth—I mean, come on, let's make apple sauce or let them juice their apple—and that was the stuff we did not see before."

Volunteers were excited to offer options and influence clients to make healthier choices. On many occasions, I heard volunteers encourage clients to take the fresh vegetables and fruits when available. The food itself provided an entry point for volunteers to build relationships with clients. One day, I observed Leslie, a long-time volunteer and a retired health care worker taking a man of African descent, a recent Somali immigrant, around the food shelf. He came to the food shelf every month, so she knew him from before. Even as he went through the intake procedures, Leslie carefully got double bags ready in the shopping cart for him, because she knew that he would be walking home. They went around picking out food, all the while engaged in friendly banter. Leslie encouraged him to take vegetables, saying, "You don't eat enough of your vegetables!" or "Why don't you try this, I know you like to cook! Come on, take something besides your ramen." There was such a pleasant quality to their conversation. I could not quite hear what the man was saying because he was soft-spoken, but there was a warm tone to their interaction, a bit like a bossy grandma conversing with an over-accommodating grandson.

White Fragility

Although there were moments of friendship and desirous proximity between volunteers and clients, the structure of the food shelf meant that this was a fragile space rife with conflict, both hidden and expressed. The interactions between volunteers and clients were structured by class, race, and organizational policies, and procedures. The numerous restrictions in place regarding the amount of food distributed was the common cause of conflict between volunteers and clients. During the intake interview, a small sheet of paper was filled out by the interviewer, which let the packer know how much food the client was allowed based on household size. This "slip" was usually at the center of the conflict. Clients felt that they were not getting enough food to feed their households and at times expressed this in ways deemed inappropriate by volunteers. In these situations, the white female volunteers were forced to come to terms with their own limitations for "doing good."

It was illuminating to see just how hard it was for these white women to negotiate these contentious interactions. Cindy recognized the unequal material relations that existed between clients and volunteers and worked hard to alleviate this dynamic. She explained: "Well, ideally, and I work very hard at this, I try to make it a friendly comfortable experience for people, like we are more coequals. I mean I know we can't be coequals but that I am a sympathetic listener and I can give them the time to tell me what their issues are, I can affirm them, I can give them a referral if I think that's appropriate, because most people don't want to be there." Penny described a conflict-ridden experience, which for her has been a turning point in her life.

> Well, there was actually one client, a lady in particular who was a little more prickly. Another packer had come in at noon and she had not gotten the information that I had, so as the two of them were going through the room, picking out the food, they got to the dairy items. The packer was going to let this person take something that she was not supposed to, you know it's supposed to be two points rather than one, so I said to her "you know we are supposed to limit this to larger families." The person actually intimated or inferred that I was being racist because she was Black. You know, I was like really shocked and anyways I just walked

away and then I continued to help the other packer. I was really offended and she came around and she said, you know, "I am sorry," and I said, "you know, I wouldn't be here if I have an issue," I mean, "I'm not, I wouldn't be here," and she said, "you know, I'm just having a bad day."

In the following paragraphs, I analyze this incident in more detail to show how racial and neoliberal ideologies cohere in this interaction.

Significantly, Penny starts out the story *without* identifying the lady as African American. However, in her use of the term *prickly lady*, I was already primed for the race of the client, because in this context, the term prickly fit precisely within the trope of the "Angry Black Woman" (ABW). The ABW stereotype is one that characterizes Black women as aggressive, ill-tempered, illogical, overbearing, hostile, and ignorant without provocation (Walley-Jean 2009). Professors of Law Jones and Norwood (2017, 2049) point out that the ABW, a combination of Blackness and nonconforming femininity, is innately intersectional: "This so-called 'Angry Black Woman' is the physical embodiment of some of the worst negative stereotypes of Black women—she is out of control, disagreeable, overly aggressive, physically threatening, loud (even when she speaks softly), and to be feared. She will not stay in her 'place.' She is not human" (2049). They observe that Black women in the United States are the frequent targets of bias-filled interactions in which aggressors both denigrate Black women and also blame women who elect to challenge the aggressor's acts. When Black women challenge assumptions about their second-class status, they disrupt the racial and gender comfort in which their white aggressors exist and upset notions of racial and gender superiority. The exercise of voice provokes a range of emotions including anger and argumentation from the aggressor. Aggressors respond by shifting attention from their acts and deflecting blame to Black women.

Also relevant to this discussion is the notion of *white fragility*. White fragility is defined as "a state in which even a minimum amount of racial stress becomes intolerable, triggering a range of defensive moves. These moves include the outward display of emotions such as anger, fear, and guilt, and behaviors such as argumentation, silence, and leaving the stress-inducing situation. These behaviors, in turn, function to reinstate white racial equilibrium" (DiAngelo 2011, 54). DiAngelo observes that because whites live in a racially insular environment, it creates expectations for racial comfort while simultaneously lowering their ability to tolerate racial stress.

This is certainly the case here. Penny, instead of working out her own privilege, adopted a defensive, power-laden attitude showcasing white fragility. Consistent with the aforementioned definition, she demonstrated "emotions such as anger, fear, and guilt, and behaviors such as argumentation, silence, and leaving the stress-inducing situation." For Penny—a good white woman, a white liberal—to be called a racist was the worst possible insult she could have received; it disrupted her racial and gender comfort and she became defensive. Penny then proceeded to tell the Black woman who exercised her voice: "I'm not a racist ... I wouldn't be here if I had an issue." More precisely, what Penny is saying is that there are so many clients of color at the Chum food shelf that she could not be a racist and continue to work there. This of course is not true and is exactly the way in which institutional and structural racism operates. It is quite possible to work and volunteer in a variety of state and nonstate institutions that "serve" people of color and still hold racial ideologies.

Critical race scholars point out that it is especially hard for whites—in particular, whites who think of themselves as good people doing good work—to reconcile themselves to the idea that implicit bias, stereotypes, and messages about race are part of their thinking, even when they do not recognize it (Bonilla-Silva 2010; Doane and Bonilla-Silva 2003). It is also difficult for whites to be able to see the interconnections between individual- and structural-level racism. They tend to agree that racism exists "out there," but not with regard to themselves. The fact that Penny can tell this story and use the words *race* and *racist* is a positive step toward a power-sensitive discourse; however, her defensive response minimizes the depth and scope of structural racism. Penny has not been socialized into developing the kind of empathy necessary to step across the perception gap, to adopt an antiracist position, or to stand in solidarity with this woman of color. Penny fails to recognize that the woman in front of her has experienced the crushing burden of racism in so many ways and so many times that she is in a very good position to recognize and name the source of her oppression. Penny juxtaposes her own calm and nonconfrontational behavior of "walking away" with that of the so-called prickly lady. In Penny's racial comfort zone, she views it as taking the higher ground, but from the vantage point of those on the receiving end, it is not. This was whiteness at its worst: silent, innocent, fragile, powerful, and oppressive. The better course of action for Penny would have been to stay, to talk, to break the rules immediately, and to recognize the thousands of years of white supremacy that in this moment they are both caught up in.

Although Penny is unable to come to terms with being called a racist, she does recognize the fallibility of neoliberal forms of governance. Initially, she dons the mantle of the neoliberal regime and uses its rules to wield power over the Black woman, but after the interaction she begins to think about ways in which to modify and reinterpret the rules: "I realized what I needed to do was to be not the person who was saying no, to be the person who was saying 'you can choose this and, you know, this is the way you can work around our system' or that getting to the slip and saying, you know, 'I didn't decide this, I am not the decider,' so this is just the way it is and if you want to talk to someone else about that, you can. That helped, that helped a lot." Here Penny is able to blame the system for its rules, but yet not recognize how her whiteness and racial comfort are also part of that same system. The difficulty Penny shows in accepting her own whiteness is telling. We are left to imagine the impact this interaction had on the life and livelihood of the "prickly lady," whose name we do not know and who is only spoken about. We are left to wonder about that moment in which this Black woman decided to speak out and the courage she would have needed to brace herself for the consequences of white fragility, knowing full well that she would be categorized as the "Angry Black Woman playing the race card."

At Chum (and most food shelves) the needs, voices, and complaints of clients were silenced both by the presence *and* absence of administrative procedures. Because food distribution occurs within a framework of charity, clients cannot complain about what they receive or how they receive the food; they must show gratitude (Tarasuk and Eakin 2003). There were no suggestion boxes at Chum in which clients could leave feedback about the food or service they received. There was a dilapidated notice hanging on the wall that explained how to file a grievance about Chum's programs, the first step being face-to-face communication with the program coordinator, and the final step being a written appeal to the Chum Grievance Committee—either of which would be threatening to any individual, let alone a vulnerable and food insecure individual. Even if the so-called prickly lady wanted to lodge a complaint about her experiences at the food shelf, there was no entity that she could turn to for a fair and empathic hearing. In sum, though the desire to reach out to clients was strong among volunteers, they did so from a position of privilege as white women in the in-group, and the structure of the food shelf supported this inequity.

The Hardworking, the Regulars, and Discourses of Suspicion

The language that stigma employs to demarcate the worthy and unworthy is constantly shifting. Across history, "stigma theories" have been used to justify the inferiority of the stigmatized, control meaning about groups of people, and warrant discrimination against the poor and racial groups. One such ideological formation has been the Calvinist distinction made between the "deserving and underserving poor." In the case of the Chum food shelf, volunteers did not use the terms *deserving* or *underserving*, but they came up with new language to draw distinctions. Volunteers used the terms *hardworking* and *regulars* to categorize clients, terms that move us from a morality grounded in spirituality to a morality grounded in neoliberal logic. Even as these mostly politically liberal volunteers were adept in the logics of economic injustice, they reinforced more conservative ways of thinking on the subject. Volunteers in one breath expressed compassion for clients but also discursively reinforced social distance, otherization, and the Us and Them phenomenon.

The hardworking group of people was constructed as comprising those who you would never "expect to see" at the food shelf, whereas the regulars were clients for whom using the food shelf was "a way of life." Sight, sound, smell, and the way in which bodies moved in this space played an important role in volunteer perceptions and expectations. Volunteers expected to see people who looked poor; when clients did not meet this expectation, they were surprised. Scholars note that the stigma of poverty is shaped by how visible a particular mark is; for instance, homelessness is often more visible and disruptive (Phelan et al. 1997). This was true at the food shelf. Tracy recounts the experience of having a well-dressed gentleman come into the food shelf, who surprised them by writing his income as "60,000." After talking with him, she learned that he had made that money the previous year working two jobs and that his wife had just had their eighth child, so he gave up one of his jobs to be home more. She cannot remember ever seeing them again. Pamela had a similar experience:

You know, sometimes when you do this volunteer work it seems a little frustrating because you do it day after day and you still see people coming in or some
of the same people or the same type of person with the same problem. But I
remember this, it was two o'clock, it was time to close shop, we had been busy
and everybody was let's get out of here, and this guy walked in and he was dressed
very well and he had a slip for seven people, five children in the family, and we
were looking at each other and we roll our eyes, why is this guy here? Then when
I went home I thought I know why, he was just so embarrassed. I knew that he
had probably either lost his job or something was going on in the family because
he certainly didn't look like a regular.

An important difference between the hardworking and regulars was in
the amount of shame and embarrassment volunteers attributed to them.
To the hardworking group were attributed feelings of shame, humiliation,
and indignity for using the food shelf—and these were seen as good things.
These attributions were not made of the regulars. People within the hardworking category were portrayed in a positive light and seen with hope and
optimism; external factors, such as the recession, were usually identified
as their main reasons for using assistance. The hardworking people were
seen as taking pride in their ability to be independent and support themselves, but this was not a feeling or intention attributed to the regulars.
Tracy described the difference between the hardworking and regulars in
this way: "There certainly are some regular clientele that show up, yeah,
pretty much once a month. Then there are the folks who've just found
themselves in such dire straits and those are the folks who are most reluctant to come ... sometimes they tell me the story of you know I donated
to this food shelf for years and now I have to use you, but when I'm back
on my feet I'll donate again. You know, people who've got lot of pride in
being able to support themselves and now can't so are really very embarrassed to be there." Volunteers found the shame expressed by these clients as refreshing; as such, this group of people drew more attention,
goodwill, and care from the volunteers. Cindy observed that these were
folks who all of a sudden found themselves at the food shelf and were
ashamed, and so "you just need the time to be kind to them and help them
understand that it's okay and that it won't be forever, without giving them
false hope."

Conversely, a "discourse of suspicion" was used to talk about the regulars. Here, the doctrine of compassionate conservatism and "benign suspicion" typically associated with conservative ideology were found, in which

compassion refers to unconditional love and care of those in need, whereas *conservatism* is a reference to the personal accountability and responsibility required for compassion to work (Elisha 2011). Evangelical author Marvin Olasky used the term *benign suspicion* as a recommendation for how charitable organizations could protect themselves from fraudulent assistance seekers (as cited in Elisha 2011). In the present study, there were several ways in which the regulars were constructed as "scamming the system." People scammed the system, volunteers said, by expanding or "embroidering" the size of the family so as to access more food. Cindy told a story that has become somewhat of a legend at the Chum food shelf. A family had come in and said that their family included a husband, a wife, and eight children and that they were temporarily staying at the drop-in center. Cindy went to the former food shelf director, who checked across the street at the homeless shelter and found that there was no such family there. Instead, they learned that only the mother and father were there; the children were in a different state. I heard this story told in a variety of contexts and by different people with the terms *sneaky, misconstrue, misrepresent, embroidering,* and *lying* used frequently to describe the event—all indicating a complex form of neoliberal stigma.

Another scam, volunteers explained, was people selling or trading the food they received. Lisa took great pride in her ability to verify this deception, although she too bookended her explanation with compassion:

Lisa: My shift is only with the working families, so the vast majority of the folks are very hardworking, making ends meet that aren't quite meeting, very hardworking, extremely appreciative, very appreciative; there are always a few scammers that I personally enjoy because they can't out-scam me.

Interviewer: How do they try to scam, though?

Lisa: I had a client come in and claimed that she needs diapers for her baby, and I said, "Really, your baby, your baby is in foster care and you're not getting diapers for that." "How do you know?" Because I know, I know what happened to your baby, you are not getting diapers. What she would do is, she would get diapers and she would sell them on the street or trade it to somebody for some other stuff, so people certainly will push no sooner you start giving, they are gonna push and take as much as they can.

Interviewer: They do that with food as well?

Lisa: They do, I mean to a degree. "Oh, this is 3 points, I only have 2 points left. Can I please, can I please please have it?"

Thus poor citizens, already inundated with the checks and cross-checks of poverty governance procedures, are subjected to even more checks at the food pantry by enterprising volunteers. Ironically, Lisa is at the food shelf to teach her daughter what it means to be poor and to destigmatize poverty; unfortunately, she is also teaching her daughter what it means to be recruited into neoliberal governmentality and exercise surveillance over the Other. Lisa is the gatekeeper, policy enforcer, and food shelf police unleashing jurisprudence on clients based on a neoliberal calculus. She is more interested in being right and in condemning this woman, who for whatever reason has lost her child, rather than allowing her to access what she should be legally entitled to. Steeped in her whiteness, she does not find the loving kindness, the *caritas*, the *agape*, the vision of justice necessary to resist, bend, and break the rules. Indeed, she practices a harsh form of charity.

It soon became clear that the term *regulars* was populated by gendered and racialized assumptions. Families that were not traditional nuclear families and families without homes were at the center of the regulars: "For the most part we certainly will have some other relatives, adults living there, or sometimes it will be more than two adults but we certainly have the families that have two adults and then four, five, six kids, things like, we do have the uncles, aunts, brothers, sisters living with the adults and then the various kids so, we get all different living arrangements and all different family sizes." The discourse surrounding regulars focused on single women with their multiple children and their disordered lives. Feminist scholars Fraser and Gordon (1994) argue that discourses of welfare are contoured by their association with women, poor women, and unwed mothers, as well as notions of irresponsibility, illegitimacy, and promiscuity. Even at Chum, an organization with a social justice orientation, discourses surrounding female clients encapsulated these tensions, as seen in Tracy's observation: "Sometimes you do see the same type of people and you think, will they ever get out of here? You will see a young woman in her twenties with three kids and you think, when will they get out of this cycle? and you try not to judge, but you know how difficult that is."

In this space, race was a physical mark that carried meanings, meanings associated with poverty and filtered through neoliberal logic. Geographer

Arun Saldanha (2006) argues that movement, smell, phenotype, and practices within particular spaces, in combination with certain material objects,
separate and connect bodies and create race and racism. He writes, "Race is
a whole event, much more than just a statement, important though that
statement may be in the emergence of the event" (12). This was true of
the Chum food shelf, where rich and poor bodies, calm and stressed bodies, healthy and unhealthy bodies, thin and overweight bodies, and white,
Black, and brown bodies were separated by the architecture and disciplines
of the food shelf. Because Black and brown bodies are not linked with all
sorts of wealth and ways of life in the same way that white bodies are,
expectations were met and ruptured based on phenotypical traits. This
is the same reason why I, despite my education, income, and inherited
wealth, expressed in good clothes and jewelry, was often mistaken for a
client in my early days of volunteering at the food shelf. In this setting,
when the body did not perform to the stereotype of who is poor based on
markers of class-based identity—dress, manner, language, behaviors, and
body type—expectations were ruptured.

A Discourse of Hopelessness

Although the hardworking group of people inspired hope and optimism
in the volunteers, a "discourse of hopelessness" was typically used to talk
about the regulars. Pamela, for instance, talked about a sense of hopelessness she felt because of the increase in numbers of people, children, and
entire families at the food shelf. Previously, the volunteers would have a
chance to sit down and chat around the table. But these days when she
goes to the food shelf, she is ready for the day because she knows she is
going to be busy. Linda described a similar sense of hopelessness: "It's actually more depressing now because you know when you start off you are
oh, I will help and I will do all this, but then after many years you will
look at it and say, well how much longer are we going to do this? So then
it's depressing from the standpoint of 'Is this all it's going to be?'" The
discourse of hopelessness, though seemingly benign, hides an ideological
formation about the poor that can be far more distancing, otherizing, and
demeaning than direct aspersions. Although compassionate, these articulations imply that poor individuals have become dependent on the system, are unable to transform their circumstances even when given the right

opportunities, and, in effect, have completely lost their ability to be fully human. The following articulation by Linda reinforces the culture of poverty argument:

> I would say probably the hardest for me to see is the survival mode that some peo-
> ple are in and that they are fine with that. You know that's what life has become
> for them. I will go over to the food shelf and go get my food, I will go over here
> and get this, and I will go and do this and I can get that and that's how I exist. I
> am not saying they shouldn't have these things, though that they are okay with
> that, that they have gotten to the point that they can't push themselves past that,
> they probably can't. I mean a lot of people we have in here probably wouldn't be
> employable, for a number of factors probably wouldn't be employable. So this is
> it. This is where they are at and that's kind of depressing to imagine well, this is
> what life is for these people. And it is for a lot them.

A little later, Linda reinforced the same point, saying: "Yeah, there is lot of people that come in regularly because like I say, this is how they live, this is what they are doing now, so okay it's time to go to the food shelf and get my packet of food and at Christmas time I go to the Salvation Army. I will get my Christmas presents and I will go to the free dinner you know at Thanksgiving. I mean they know how to go and how to do it and that's how they live." It is not hard to see that Linda speaks from a position of privilege. Poverty is never convenient, ordinary, or easy. In my interviews, there were no poor people who were "fine with" or "okay with" their poverty. Poor citizens "know how to go and how to do it" because their lives depend on it. What is also relevant here is how the policy environment strategically makes the poor hyper-visible. Rather than allowing people access to legal entitlements, public policy is set up in such a way that the poor have to beg at multiple charitable spaces to fulfill their basic needs. In doing so, they become visible and marked as people who "enjoy" getting handouts.

In some instances, even when volunteers articulated structural arguments as the cause of poverty, these structural arguments very quickly morphed into cultural arguments situated within a discourse of hopelessness. This sudden, almost imperceptible mutation from structure to culture was vivid across the volunteer interviews. Here is how Cindy put it:

> There is a lot of multigenerational poverty. There are a lot of people who were
> there because they are not easily employed because they don't have an adequate
> education. Duluth has an awful lot of entry-level jobs and sometimes there are
> people who are working but not earning enough, and there are some people for
> whom again it's that multigenerational thing, where it's almost a culture that is

passed on from one generation to the next, so you might have a mother who is welfare dependent and whose children are raised to anticipate a similar life, and so it becomes a cycle. Those cultures are very hard to change because the children seldom get praised for academic success. There is no role model, no wanting to get a high school diploma or go to college, so then it can be really very tough on them. There are also people who are there because they are actively alcohol or drug abusers or they have a disability, either physical or psychological or intellectual, that prevents them from being employable and they are dependent on society taking care of them.

This morphing from structure to culture resonates with Waxman's (1983) thesis about the stigma of poverty. Waxman observes that the structural argument is not that different from the cultural argument because when a pattern that began as a situational adaptation is transmitted over generations, it becomes a cultural pattern. This means that even many situational or structural arguments inevitably end up blaming or attributing the cause of the problem to the individual or community. Waxman's larger argument is that neither cultural nor situational theories are sufficient to explain the stigma of poverty; what is needed instead is a relational perspective that accounts for both the intra-action and the interaction of the poor and the nonpoor. In other words, stigma is not about a mark or devalued trait but about how particular bodies and attributes are given meaning in the service of power.

Brazilian adult educator Paulo Freire (1970) argued that discourses of hopeless, disillusionment, and grief are unfortunately quite common among people of privilege, who have little to gain by systemic change. Freire criticized the kind of hopelessness expressed here by the volunteers— the idea that conditions in the world were static and immutable—and urged people not to be pragmatic and adapt to the reality but to dream, to envision, and to imagine a new and different world. This imagination was a necessary condition for activism and social justice. He wrote in no uncertain terms about the fundamental role of elites in joining the struggle for justice. For true solidarity and liberation, the oppressors must be willing to rethink their way of life and to examine their own roles in the oppression: "Those who authentically commit themselves to the people must re-examine themselves constantly" (60).

Conclusion

In this chapter, we have seen that though white volunteers have the right political stances, social distance coupled with institutional pressures mean that they are easily recruited into neoliberal logics. In the space of the Chum food pantry, neoliberal stigma flourished because of discursive practices, as well as discursive erasures, silences, and absences. The racial and economic distances between volunteers and clients meant that organizational narratives responsibilized clients while remaining silent on issues of racial and economic advantage. Race was eclipsed in the discourse while at the same time providing the subtext for claims. Volunteers did not understand their power, privilige, and positionality in relationship to clients. They were able to articulate social justice concerns in the abstract, but in the everyday turmoil of the food pantry with its processes and procedures, they were recruited into the neoliberal juridical rationalities of discipline and punishment. Volunteers were charitable in donating their time and energy to distributing food, but less charitable in making sense of and normalizing the behaviors of food insecure people. This paradox is exemplified in the fact that Lisa on the one hand brings her child to the food shelf to teach her about the poor but on the other takes great pride in rooting out the scammers. This chapter also shows that whiteness wields its power through innocence, fragility, and passivity. When white innocence encounters systems, rules, and procedures, it assumes them to be fair and therefore enforces them, all the while failing to work out how privileged individuals participate in oppressive systems and structures. With the best of intentions, volunteers expressed personal gratitude for their own circumstances and pity for the Other, but also ended up surveilling and policing poor citizens and creating new languages to demarcate the so-called deserving and undeserving poor. The subversion necessary to advance equity and justice was for the most part absent.

It is my argument that the food shelf, in its everydayness, obscures the racialized poverty that is at the heart of the unjust food system. In one of the richest countries in the world, food shelves are humdrum, normal, and routine; however, they remain unquestioned because they distribute food and have good people working within them. These enclosures hide the fact that the food pantry system, and the hunger industrial complex overall, is built on the good intentions of a lot of good white people. Amid all this goodness, the voices of poor citizens and people of color remain unheard. The Chum food shelf is an unremunerated teaching tool used to guide a vast variety of people on a variety of journeys to self-discovery, not unlike Lisa and her daughter. It is used by institutions such as churches and universities to promote the practice of citizenship, ethical engagement, and giving back to the community. In the city of Duluth, where 90 percent of the population is white and where there are gross racial inequities, volunteering at food pantries is yet another way in which white people and people of color live racially structured lives. In these spaces, white people and people of color come together to serve and be served, as independent and dependent, as rich and poor, as superior and inferior, as marked and unmarked. This is why Lee so aptly says, "Poverty breeds social isolation, but so does privilege."

Implications for Practice and Policy

From a policy perspective, it is clear that what is needed to end hunger is a radical transformation of the food system, increased entitlements, and increased opportunities for people to provide food for themselves (Allen 1999; Poppendieck 1999; Riches and Silvasti 2014). The food shelf is not a solution to end hunger but another structure that contributes to class, race, and food inequities. Food pantries legitimize and prop up the capitalist food system governed by the corporate food regime that serves powerful stakeholders while the needs of individuals and communities are ignored. Food pantries can play a vital role in the march toward a rights-based approach to food. Most food pantries see their job as primarily to distribute food—not necessarily to be involved in antiracist and gender work. This is problematic given the direct connections between race, gender, food insecurity, and health outcomes, as evidenced by statistics about who is hungry in the United States (Slocum 2006). In charitable settings, the problems of racism and gender equity are seen as peripheral to the technical problem of distributing food, when in fact they are at the heart of the unjust food system. Food pantries must be reminded that the food system in the United States was built on genocide and slavery and continues to be organized around racism: people of color disproportionately experience food insecurity, lose their farms, and face the dangerous work of food processing and agricultural labor (Slocum 2006). Food pantries need reminding that in the

United States, problems of poverty, illness, addiction, and mental illness in communities of color can be tied to historical traumas, more than two hundred years of slavery that brought African men and women in chains to serve a dominant white master and half a millennium of occupation of Native lands and genocide. Indeed, it is this kind of collective forgetting of history that facilitates the production of neoliberal stigma—and food pantries as a solution to hunger.

To be clear, the problem is not one that concerns only the Chum food pantry and the few white women depicted in this chapter. I use these women to showcase a much larger problem: the thousands of white men and women who serve in these roles across the length and breadth of this nation, who unintentionally come together to form the "food system." Indeed, 51 percent of Feeding America's sixty thousand food programs rely entirely on volunteers, and 62 percent of these programs are run by faith-based organizations (Feeding America 2014; United States Department of Health and Human Services 2014). I should also point out that this case study with its critique of volunteerism should not be used by those who stand on the sidelines, never having volunteered or lifted a finger in service, to justify their inaction; this would be antithetical to the spirit of this chapter. I use this particular case to point to future possibilities. Indeed, one can only imagine what would happen if all the white women serving in food pantries today put on their activist and advocate hats tomorrow. What walls of silence would crumble? White women are powerful, and given the way the electorate is set up they are powerful and necessary allies in dismantling the unjust food system.

Slocum (2007, 532) argues that whiteness should not be dismissed completely as ineffectual to bring about broader social change; she writes that whiteness "has progressive potential and can transform itself and change its tendency to produce and reinforce racial oppression." The volunteers all showed a desire to reach out and engage with the paradigmatic Other. They all brought with them good intentions: faith beliefs, ethical motivations, beliefs about citizenship and giving back, and a commitment to doing good. In rare moments, these "basically good white women," liberal and progressive and with faith beliefs, carved out spaces of resistance, subverting neoliberalism. They did so by interpreting and reinterpreting procedures and policies, renegotiating their own expectations and values, and balancing faith/ethical commitments with the rules. They sympathized with clients and reached out to them with kind words and actions. Even if they did not engage with whiteness, they engaged with neoliberal rationalities. All of this points to possibilities for transformation. The food pantry, a dead end of sorts, can be a site of possibility, of progressive potential—but for this, good white women (and men) will have to engage in the grueling task of reformulating their identities: from "saints" to belligerent citizens, advocates, and antiracists, who see themselves as raced and part of the unjust food system. Creating visionary counternarratives and transforming the identities of people who volunteer within these spaces will be required, as seen in the Chum annual report, to "bend the moral arc of the universe a little bit more toward justice."

5 Spiritual Entrepreneurs at Ruby's Pantry

A lot of people think that we just give out food. Nothing could be further from the truth. WE GIVE OUT HOPE! It has been said that you can live only so many days without food, so many days without water and so many minutes without air, but you can't live a second without hope! And that hope comes through the kind acts and words of our over 15,000 volunteers who are the hands and feet of Jesus bringing our guests the good news of eternal life through Christ.
—Lyn Sahr, white male, founder of Ruby's Pantry, "Store Up Treasures in Heaven," August 23, 2016

Introduction: Conservative Christian Entrepreneurialism

The Ruby's Pantry (RP) home office website proclaims: "Tasty food finds for frugal families." RP is the community outreach arm of Home and Away Ministries, the latter having recently been rebranded Ruby's Heart. The goal of RP is to salvage and redistribute corporate surplus food. RP was founded in 2003 by Lyn Sahr, a pastor of a small, nondenominational evangelical Christian church in central Minnesota. It was named Ruby's Pantry after Sahr's grandmother, Ruby, a kind-hearted and devout Christian woman. RP first began as a Christian mission to Mexico and then morphed into a charitable food distribution service for rural communities in the upper Midwest. With the tagline "America's Rural Foodbank," RP articulates its mission in this way: "To procure and distribute corporate surplus food and goods to help fight poverty, hunger and disease in rural communities in the United States for those with low resources and in crisis through churches, food shelves and other local civic organizations." In an interview with Sahr, he

observed: "In the United States, it is not so different. We have plenty of children going to bed at night hungry and spending the entire weekend going
without food anxiously waiting for breakfast before school on Monday
morning." As of August 2016, RP was serving approximately ten thousand
families with a million pounds of food via approximately fifty distribution
sites per year.

The conservative evangelical leanings of RP create a thorny space in
which politics, religion, and business come together to inform how hunger is constructed and how solutions to hunger are framed. RP employs a
model of what might be termed *spiritual entrepreneurship*, in which faith
beliefs are integrated with business or entrepreneurial practices (Gandy
2016; Holton, Farrell, and Fudge 2014). Entrepreneurialism, of course, is the
very foundation of capitalism. Entrepreneurs drive the creative-destruction
process of capitalism by producing a new commodity, by opening up a new
supply source, or by reorganizing an industry, among other things (Dees
1998). The core concepts of spiritual entrepreneurship are innovation, risk
taking, and awareness of opportunities, all of which are tied to religious
doctrine and faith beliefs. Marnie Holborow (2015, 72) argues that entrepreneurs are the "social icons of our neoliberal age." Being entrepreneurial,
she says, is "shorthand for having a positive approach to life and what it
means to be a modern person, its appeal lies in its beguiling 'can do-ism,'
with the promise of material benefit into the bargain" (77). Neoliberal ideology encourages self-determination, a "get up and go" attitude, having the
right attitude, and a "positive mindset." Mona Atia's (2012) theorization of
"pious neoliberalism" illuminates the tricky combination of religion and
economic rationale that encourages individuals to be entrepreneurial in the
interests of a better relationship with God. In these contexts, Atia observes
that religion and economic rationale do not compete or contradict each
other but rather are in sync with each other.

RP exemplifies spiritual entrepreneurialism and more specifically pious
neoliberalism because of the integration of religious and economic rationales in its solution to hunger. For Sahr, supply and demand come together
through God, who facilitates innovation, creative destruction, and opportunity. Sahr identifies himself as a "possibility thinker"—a quintessential
blending of entrepreneurialism and spirituality: "Without God's help we
could not get 17,500,000 pounds of food, we would not have 9 semi-trucks
and 20 some semi-trailers to haul and store food and we certainly couldn't

provide food for over 130,000 families a year. Without God, we can do nothing. But with God, all things are possible! He's the reason I am a 'possibility thinker'" (July 8, 2015).

RP is entrepreneurial to the extent that it offers a new way of operating charitable food assistance and provides a new outlet for surplus food. Calling itself a "pop-up" food pantry, RP operates like a business franchise. It bypasses the national Feeding America network and sources food directly from corporations. The food is then transported to local distribution sites, run by churches, which are also "entrepreneurs," taking the initiative to organize pop-up food distributions in their communities. At RP, clients make a "donation" of twenty dollars for food, of which eighteen dollars goes back to RP to support logistics; the remaining two dollars is kept by the local church to invest wherever they see fit. Consistent with the spirit of entrepreneurialism, RP has made massive investments in equipment, space, and procedures to run its operation, from a fleet of semitrailers to forty-thousand-square-foot facilities to professional marketing and branding expertise. The RP home office has also started a Facebook page through which people can get notifications about RP and preview the kinds of foods available at the next distribution. There is an online "guest registration system" through which clients can prepay and pick up food at a particular time. Clients are referred to as "guests" in an attempt to reduce stigma associated with food assistance. RP has a loyalty card program, in which clients get a stamp for each visit and receive an extra share after ten stamps, which they can either keep or donate. There is also a sprinkling of RP merchandise that people can buy from the online shop on RP's website.

RP's conservative ideology is signaled in its slogan: "RP is a hand up, not a hand out," a phrase that goes all the way back to the racialized and gendered welfare debates of the 1990s. In the United States, the term *handout* is code for what's given to welfare recipients—a stigmatizing term implying that the recipient lacks independence and agency, is getting something for nothing, has his or her arms permanently outstretched to take something from others, and has a defective moral character. RP calls itself a "hand up" because unlike traditional food pantries, at RP people pay twenty dollars to receive food; they are thus not getting "something for nothing." The twenty-dollar fee is important materially and symbolically: materially, it helps defray logistical costs for the operation, and symbolically, it justifies the worthiness and deservingness of clients.

The construction of RP's clientele is centered on this imaginary separation between Us and Them. RP is for the so-called hardworking, deserving, and good citizens, but not for the paradigmatic Other, people who in the public imaginary take advantage of public assistance programs. Sahr positions RP as distinct from public food assistance programs and shows a disdain for welfare and government restrictions. Because RP does not receive government support, there are no procedures related to poverty governance such as eligibility checks or income restrictions. To receive foods, clients show up on the third Thursday of the month and pay twenty dollars for a "share." There are no restrictions regarding how many shares an individual can purchase so long as clients pay twenty dollars per share.

Ruby's Pantry–Duluth

Any church in RP's area of distribution—the upper Midwest—can start its own distribution, or a *pop-up*. Local pop-ups follow food safety regulations and protocols set by the RP home office about how food should be stored, displayed, covered, sorted, or contained; however, when it comes to religiopolitical ideologies, there is much more variation. Evangelism is central to the RP home office mission, but local churches adopt flexibility in how much religious content they have at their sites. Pop-up churches vary considerably in political orientations, from more conservative evangelical right-wing churches to more liberal churches.

In Duluth, the First United Methodist Church (FUMC), also known as the Coppertop Church, was one of the first distribution sites in the city and is currently the only RP distribution site in the city. Although the RP home office articulates a fairly extreme, conservative evangelical position, the Coppertop Church is politically liberal and identifies as an "open and affirming" church. RP–Duluth at the Coppertop Church is run by an inter-congregational volunteer board, in which both liberalism and conservatism are present. Here, the RP operation represents the complexity and shiftiness of neoliberal ideology. Larner (2000, 12) argues that there are many configurations of neoliberalism, and "close inspection of particular neo-liberal political projects is more likely to reveal a complex and hybrid political imaginary, rather than the straight-forward implementation of a unified and coherent philosophy."

Goal of the Chapter

Grounded in the assumption that neoliberal projects are complex and not always ideologically coherent, the goal of the chapter is to show how spiritual entrepreneurialism and the politically conservative ideology from the RP home office get taken up at the local Duluth site. How do steering committee members and volunteers at the local distribution site in Duluth interpret the discourses, policies, and procedures of the RP home office? *Neoliberal stigma* refers to the social distancing and otherizing processes created through neoliberal political rationalities that operate at the levels of culture and institutions and play a role in subject and identity formation. This chapter shows how entrepreneurial food pantries like RP reinforce neoliberal stigma as well as the notion that social problems are the domain of individuals and can be solved through the marketplace. In this fun, festive, and entrepreneurial space filled with faith beliefs and good intentions, notions of food justice, entitlements, and food sovereignty are completely erased. The language of equality, equity, and social justice is displaced by the language of the economy, hard work, and self-reliance. The lack of critical thinking around neoliberalism and around issues of race, class, and gender reinforce the food gap, moving us further away from a rights-based approach to food security.

Hard Work at the Thursday Distribution

The Coppertop Church is a large, conspicuous, modern structure that sits atop a hill at one of the busier intersections in the city. Food distributions are held at this location on the third Thursday of every month. Like other food assistance programs, there is a vast amount of physical labor involved in organizing the food distribution. The labor is a coordinated effort of no less than fifty people working to distribute food to anywhere between two hundred and three hundred people in just a few hours. The semi-trailer carrying food from the warehouse in Pine City approximately 150 miles away from Duluth arrives at the Coppertop parking lot at around 3:00 p.m.—a massive truck filled to the brim with pallets. There are usually three or four steering committee members present on site, who run the operation with efficiency and managerial skills to match any chief executive of a multinational corporation. However, unlike typical charitable enterprises in which women predominate, there is an even breakdown of male and female volunteers. The female volunteers tend to stay indoors and perform tasks of repackaging, organizing, and arranging while the men unload the trucks, carry pallets in and out, help guests carry their food out, and break down cartons. Pat talked about how physically challenging the job is: "You are on your feet from start to finish, from 3:30 to 8:30 or 9 o'clock. So that's a long time. You are kind of running around, so, you know, I have a pedometer, and on Ruby's days I put in around twenty thousand steps."

Once the food is unloaded, the most labor-intensive portion of the operation begins: managing the quality of donations through packaging, repackaging, sorting, and cleaning. The optimism that permeates the space is reminiscent of the kind of esprit de corps that occurs amid a natural disaster, where differences are set aside and people pull together to get the job done. The volunteers do messy jobs like sorting through rotten potatoes and bagging loaves of bread. One time I volunteered, I was stuck emptying huge pallets of crackers into one-gallon Ziploc bags. It took twelve of us nearly two hours to fill about eight hundred bags of crackers. Another group of volunteers worked on emptying large sacks of oatmeal into smaller, one-gallon sacks, with still another group repackaging sweet potatoes. Some of the women who had been there before said, "Thank God we don't have to do the potatoes this month; you haven't lived until your finger has gone through a bad potato. These sweet potatoes are much better." That day, there was no repackaging of regular potatoes, because everyone was getting a twenty-pound bag! The volunteers were industrious, excited, and working hard in the basement to get it all done before the guests arrived. Some volunteers were setting up tables with plastic cloths and arranging them in two rows on either side of the church basement. At each of the little groups, everyone was deeply engrossed in their tasks; there was some chatting, but most were deeply focused on their work.

The committee typically does not know beforehand what food is coming on the truck, which can be a challenge. Celeste remembers a few occasions on which gigantic blocks of frozen fish and scrambled eggs made their tasks particularly hard:

Celeste: One day they sent fish. I think there was salmon and maybe something else. But it was in a big thing like this [holds hands far apart], and it was frozen solid together. You couldn't pry the fish.

Interviewer: Because they weren't even wrapped individually?

Celeste: No, no, they were sides of fish all frozen together in one big block. They tried to work on it and couldn't get anywhere. They ended up not being able to give it out, and they had ended up giving it to Damiano's.

Interviewer: Because it must be a food safety issue, too, everybody digging their hands into this block of fish. Did you tell them?

Celeste: I think they told them about it. We got another one that was quite special was scrambled eggs, and they were in another one of these things, and they were frozen. Now scrambled eggs aren't the same as fish, they're already scrambled and they're cooked. This stuff, if you heat it up in the microwave and put some ketchup on it, it's not too bad, you know. We ended up, we had to buy a pitchfork, a brand-new pitchfork to break it apart. Since then, they have not sent us that or it was bagged differently. It's like they must be from McDonald's, these scrambled egg rounds, you could count them out, but they weren't frozen into a solid block.

These examples of massive quantities of frozen raw fish and scrambled eggs provide vivid images of how socially and ethically engaged volunteers in Duluth, Minnesota—at the periphery of the world system—contribute free labor to the cleanup and redistribution of corporate capitalist waste linked to national and global food regimes.

RP: A Ministry for the Body and Soul

Lyn Sahr is a charismatic individual, a gifted writer and opinion leader who does the discursive work required to create and nurture his organization's identity. Sahr seamlessly narrates Christian doctrine in relation to neoliberal values of individualism, entrepreneurialism, freedom of choice, and minimal government. Similar to a televangelist, but on a smaller scale, every month for the last three years (and sometimes twice in the month) Sahr has published letters on the RP website, in which he brings together piety, neoliberalism, and the problems of hunger and food insecurity. These letters go out as emails to the organizing staff at RP and to various distribution sites. Using business language, the home office of RP is referred to as "corporate" by local distribution sites, and the letters are titled "From the Desk of Lyn Sahr." These letters articulate, interpret, and clarify the values and mission of RP. The letters make clear that RP is a Christ-centered ministry that provides "food for the body, but also spiritual food for the soul." Sahr labors this point in many of his letters, with statements such as "Food is only a small part of the importance of Ruby's Pantry," or statements like those in the opening excerpt. The volunteers of RP are referred to as the "lifeblood" of RP and compared to the "hands and feet" of Jesus. RP has twenty-five paid employees and approximately fifteen thousand volunteers. Speaking of the volunteers, Sahr invokes Christian imagery of the death and resurrection of Christ: "They lay down their life four or five hours for our guests at each distribution. Thank you for all you do! Volunteers are the life blood of our organization" (February 23, 2016). Sahr reinforces that volunteers are doing important work, even though it may not seem a lot and they may not receive recognition. The "loaves and fishes" story is a recurrent narrative used to point out that God can take a little and turn it into a lot.

Drawing on the prosperity gospel, Sahr frames abundance as the material expression of God's favor. Mona Atia (2012) notes that the linking of spiritual and material benefits is the hallmark of pious neoliberalism, and this is certainly a recurrent theme in Sahr's letters. The idea that giving begets success and prosperity is seen here: "Who is greater blessed, those receiving the food or those who bring it!" and "He loves to surprise us with more blessings than we expect or comprehend ... when we live generously! Be a giant of generosity" (September 22, 2016). Conversely, the lack of generosity is met with fire and brimstone: "A wise old pastor once said this; 'If you only have enough for yourself, you don't have enough!' He went on to explain that a person who is a thief must stop stealing, go to work, and share with those in need. He went on to say that 'A person who is not generous is basically a thief at heart!' I have never forgotten his words" (September 22, 2016). Sahr uses examples of famed Christian evangelists to show how important money is for spiritual ministry: "Billy Graham won millions of people to Christ all around the world. And God provided millions and millions of dollars to accomplish this calling" (August 23, 2016). Billy Graham was one of the main architects of the pull-yourself-up-by-your-bootstraps and religiomilitaristic ideology. Graham died on February 21, 2018, leaving in his wake all the discursive work necessary to bring together the militaristic, economic, and moral superiority of America. Graham brought patriotism and Christianity together and created the political voting bloc we know today as the "evangelicals" (FitzGerald 2017).

In contrast to the prosperity gospel, "spiritual poverty" is another recurrent theme. Spiritual poverty, for Sahr, is the main reason that people experience hunger. Sahr outlines the dual problem society faces here: "Society is in trouble both economically and spiritually. We want to help meet the needs of body and soul. If we fail to do what we can, then we fail. But we believe that God wants us to help more people or we wouldn't have the tremendous food supply that we currently have" (May 31, 2016). The cause and effect relationship between spirituality and material success is neatly tied together in Sahr's examination of the "poverty bandit" (September 26, 2015). The letter starts out with a verse from the Bible: "A little sleep, a little slumber, a little folding of the hands to rest—and poverty will come on you like a bandit" (Proverbs 6:10–11). In his analysis of this proverb, Sahr writes:

> As I read this scripture I can't help but think of those people who feel helpless and trapped in poverty. In these days of difficult economic times some people have actually given up the pursuit of their dreams for a better life. I know and understand what it is like to go without. But I never quit trying to find a way to improve my life and that of my family. When you make an honest effort to pursue your dreams of a better life, it is amazing what can happen. But again, don't give up! When people give up and just sit and watch life go by, "Poverty will come on you like a bandit." The "Poverty Bandit" will steal your joy and the scripture teaches us that the "Joy of the Lord is our strength." Proverbs 6 describes a person who is sleeping and laying around doing nothing. I encourage you to pray and ask God to show you what you can do to improve your life and ask Him to provide a way.

Here it is not historical and structural factors that shape poverty and a sense of powerlessness, but rather laziness and giving up. The age-old gospel of prosperity solidifies the view that the rich enjoy the bounty of God's blessing, while the poor are not blessed. In the image of the "poverty bandit," we see the seamless integration of political, religious, and economic ideologies used to encourage self-reliance and self-improvement. The path to a better life is not by way of structural and historical reparations, but through spiritual therapy. It is through the complex blending of faith and entrepreneurialism that individuals overcome their moral defects and learn how to be responsible citizens driven by a can-do attitude.

In Sahr's letter, race is concealed in the text but revealed in the imagery alongside it. The text has embedded within it an image of a Black man—the paradigmatic racial Other—with a shaved head. He is holding his head in his hands and leaning over a desk, with one arm extended into a clenched fist. It is one of only three images found across the sample of Sahr's letters. We cannot see the man's face or eyes. The only thing that is clear is that this is a Black man overcome with a sense of hopelessness, presumably because the poverty bandit has stolen his dignity and pride. The text super-imposed on the image reads: "I call to God and the Lord saves me." The explicit connection drawn is that spiritual poverty leads to physical lazi-ness, which leads to material poverty. The underlying interpretive context for this message is anti-Black racism. This individual presumably belongs to the category of people who "do not want to work and will not work"—a category Sahr outlined in chapter 2. This is a lazy person not taking respon-sibility for his life. Is it just coincidence that this picture was chosen to go with this particular text or does race truly lurk just beneath poverty dis-courses? All the social scientific evidence points to the latter (e.g., Feagin 2013; Gilens 1999). The white racial frame, which posits whites as supe-rior and Blacks as inferior, is reinforced here when Sahr compares himself favorably, saying "*I* never quit trying to find a way to improve my life" (emphasis added). All in all, this text now joins the deluge of discourses circulating in society that reinforce age-old racist assumptions and stereo-types about people of color being poor and lazy, while absolving the roles of capitalism, structural racism, and a whitened Christianity in producing racial disparities.

An explicit and crude form of mother blame emerges in Sahr's letters as well, demonstrating the gendered avatar of neoliberal stigma. Mothers are blamed for everything today—the size of their kids, allowing their chil-dren to watch too much television, not monitoring their eating habits, and relying on convenience food (Boero 2010; Kirkland 2011). Mothers of col-or—in particular, Hispanic American and African American mothers—are particular targets, and the culture of poverty argument is evident in these discourses. This kind of mother blame is on display in a letter from Sahr: "Then again we have some parents who do nothing to try to make a way for their children. Recently there was a mother who didn't have enough mother's milk to feed her baby, didn't have enough money to buy formula and didn't know about all the social programs. She mixed her milk with water, fed the baby and the baby died. The word tragedy does not begin to describe what has happened to her" (September 21, 2015). The analysis appears compassionate, but compassion here is used as a blunt instrument to beat the mother—a mother who did "nothing" to "make a way" for her child. Why did the mother not use the social programs? Why did she not know about the social programs? Absent from this discourse is any discussion of gender inequities, cuts to social programs, and the role of misogynistic systems of poverty governance that have made it a nightmare for women to get assistance.

In the following excerpt Sahr stirs up more suspicion about parents. Here Sahr's heart breaks for the children, who he frames as morally pure, innocent, and therefore deserving of sympathy and assistance, but parents are framed as guilty and suspicious:

> Recently we were asked to help a local backpack program in Minnesota. I am astounded that anyone would not have food for their children to eat on the weekends. Is it because their parents are using their money for other things and the children are going without? Or do the parents just don't have enough money to buy adequate food for the children? I don't know and it really doesn't matter. What matters is that these special, innocent gifts from God are taken care of, provided for, and fed. Frankly, I find it heartbreaking. I believe there are eternal consequences for those who neglect and abuse children, but not just for the parents. I believe that we have a responsibility to stand in the gap for these children and it also has eternal consequences for those who are called to help and say "No!" I believe that Ruby's Pantry has been called to help provide and feed those who cannot take care of themselves without judging or blaming the children for the neglect of the parents. (June 16, 2015)

In this excerpt, the voices of mothers and fathers who bear the burden of raising children amid unrelenting hardship and who struggle and need help themselves are overlooked. People like Ashley, a young white mother who started using the food pantry because she did not have a job and food stamps were not enough, or Paula, a white woman who has six birth children and four adopted kids, who she is still taking care of, or Clayton, an African American man who is still grieving the death of his daughter and blames himself for her cancer. Absent from this discourse are the many reasons parents fall short of the mark in caring for children: lack of job opportunities; underfunded schools; residential segregation; the high cost of college education; alcohol and addiction; lack of access to health care, treatment facilities, and mental health care; lack of child care; and a corporate food regime that creates hunger and food insecurity.

In one of the richest, most advanced industrialized nations in the world, the multiple reasons for hunger are sidestepped with Sahr's words "I don't know, and it really doesn't matter." The most important and critical connections between hunger and poverty, patterned along gender, class, and race lines, are glibly swept under the rug. Tellingly, in Sahr's analysis, Ruby's Pantry, a program that distributes surplus industrial food, is presented as the most effective solution not just to hunger, but to the problem of material and spiritual poverty. Sahr employs the Christian metaphor of "standing in the gap" to motivate people to donate to RP. People who give to RP have the opportunity to become saviors—white saviors—to poor children abandoned by their irresponsible and morally defective parents. Here whiteness lurks just beneath the surface of the term *savior*.

Fracturing of Conservative Christian Ideology at RP–Duluth

In Duluth, the initiative to start RP was taken by a woman named Bonnie. Bonnie was a member of the Coppertop Church. According to members of the steering committee—the group that came together to organize RP in Duluth—Bonnie's energy and excitement for the program was infectious. Celeste, another steering committee member, described how she was invited for a meeting by Bonnie one time and soon found herself in the thick of it. Multicongregational steering committees are not typical for RP distribution sites, so unique to RP–Duluth, Bonnie contacted other churches in the area to see if they would like to be involved. RP–Duluth today continues to be organized and run by this very same steering committee, the members of which come from a variety of denominational, class, and political backgrounds and have just stuck with it through the years. The committee did its research before contracting with RP. They vetoed one food distribution organization because it only distributed perishable food items; another program was vetoed because "it just did not fit." Rev. David Bard, the minister at Coppertop at the time, noted that this organization had Bible verses inserted into meal packages, which made some members uncomfortable. The committee decided instead to go with RP because it provided healthier food in larger quantities and was better managed, and though it was faith-based, it did not prescribe religious content for the distribution sites.

Steering committee members varied in their appreciation of the conservative evangelical orientation of the RP-home office. The two members at either ends of the political spectrum were poles apart in their thinking on this. Ellen, a middle-aged white woman, found the explicit Christian perspective of the RP home office problematic. She talked about how uncomfortable she felt after the initial presentation from RP, because it sounded quite religious. Ellen described her church as "socially active, very justice oriented where self-worth is important" and took offense that RP framed its work as Christian because, as she exclaimed, "I mean, it is more than the Christians that are doing this work." For another member, Nathan, the most conservative member of the steering committee, the fact that RP was attached to a Christian ministry made it more meaningful. He felt that the larger goal of RP was to bring people to church: "By having it at a church we might be getting people through the door that have never been in. Does that mean that they are going to have to come back? We hope so, but at least they have stepped in and they know that it is a faith-based program. Somehow I see it as if they are accepting that there is a God and that He is caring for them through us."

These two members also varied in how they thought about the problem of hunger; they both believed that hunger could not be eradicated, but for different reasons. For Ellen, who identified as extremely liberal, the problem could not be solved because of class struggle. As she noted: "I think there is always going to be people who have and people who don't have." On the other end, for Nathan, the problem of hunger could never be eradicated because people are too proud to help themselves: "Eradicate the food issue? No, I do not think it will ever go away because it is so much bigger than everyone realizes, and I say that because everyone has private issues. Everyone has 'I don't want anyone to know that I need it' and some people have been able to overcome and say yeah, 'I really need the help' and they go get it. Others never will and so there is always going to be the problem which may not be as visible. No, I don't think it will ever, not in this country where everybody has everything."

Despite religious and political differences, steering committee members felt they worked well together, referring to these differences as "nonfactors." Celeste explained: "That's never been an issue. It's, yeah, the faith backgrounds are different, but for some reason, it's kind of like, the moral values are consistent, the moral values, the right and wrong ... You're dealing with helping other people. People need to eat, and this is so basic that that kind of difference is a nonfactor." Their practices were motivated by religious, secular, and postsecular humanist beliefs, and in this space, they found common ground in being able to bring food to others. The fact that you could get so much food out to people for twenty dollars was the primary motivating force, as noted by Cynthia: "Most families are one hospital bill, one car breakdown from economic disaster, so if they can come up to the Coppertop and get twenty dollars' worth of food, that's worth so much more, holy moly, it's a lifesaver for them. It's a lifesaver."

Although faith was the motivation for their work, many committee members were rankled by the conservative evangelical approach of the RP home office. Their response was to ignore these aspects of the program, keeping their eyes on the more pragmatic goal of providing food. Cynthia, an older white woman on the committee, noted: "I think that the majority of people sitting at our steering committee, they're far more liberal in their theology and their thinking than Ruby's Pantry is. We just don't play that game." Celeste rolled her eyes. She said that she did receive the letters from Sahr, but said, "Do I read them?" and then loudly smacked her hand, evoking a parent admonishing a naughty child who has not done her homework. She added: "It's almost like we're not trying to sell faith here ... You know, I don't mean it to be a negative, but hey, we're working on food. We got to get the truck unloaded, and we got to get, and you know, try to be nice, try to be kind, say hello to the people, be nice, you know, all this kind of stuff. It's so basic. The faith is there but it's kind of underlying."

Twice a year, the RP home office has regional meetings, and local sites are invited to participate. RP sees it as a kind of religious revival, explained Cynthia. "They are trying to grow a community and bring everybody together in the space that is doing this great work." This is all very well and good, but it annoyed her that they push religion so much: "So we have very loose ties to Ruby's Pantry in Pine City. They'll do our annual meeting and we always send a couple of people down to it, but over the years, we've grown less and less interested in it, because it's very ... Their theology is very conservative and so, most of us are offended by it. We'll sit there and make these terrible comments to each other, which is really bad, but we do it because it's like 'don't call me down for a two-day conference and then spend hours of it with Christian music and that stuff.'" Cynthia noted that when the RP folks start to talk about the "evangelical stuff," that's "when we go to the bathroom or get a refill on our coffee because really, we're not interested."

The RP home office encourages local sites to have places where people can pray and receive prayer through the laying on of hands, but committee members felt this was not practical at Duluth. Unlike smaller rural towns in Minnesota and Wisconsin that are more homogenous in terms of religious and political beliefs, Duluth is a city with people from diverse backgrounds. The general feeling among steering committee members was that people came to get food, not religion. Celeste explained: "I think some of the folks here, if you were trying to sell religion to them, they would go right out the door. Our group, our people, it's a lot different from here." Rev. Bard typically offers a prayer with volunteers before the start of each distribution. Cynthia stated: "David is very good at walking that fine line of giving thanks for the food, giving thanks for the people who are volunteering. I'll say this ... it would be pretty hard to be offended by the prayer by almost anyone. You know what I mean? It's not like he's up there. 'Oh, Jesus,' he's not doing that, but he's being thankful. I think people appreciated that spiritual aspect to the work we were doing."

Rev. Bard, the pastor at the Coppertop Church when distributions began, was described as the "glue that holds it all together" and "a big cheerleader" for RP–Duluth. Rev. Bard, a mild-mannered and jovial man, identified as a progressive Christian, with a social justice orientation to his ministry. Born and brought up in Duluth, Rev. Bard was well-known in the community for his humility, generosity, and activism. For him, doing this food work was a direct outcome of being a person of faith, as he explained: "I mean, I really believe that as a follower of Jesus Christ I need to be doing things that reach out and help other people and help make the world a better place." Despite concern in his congregation about damage from food and drink to the sanctuary, Rev. Bard persuaded the congregation that it was an essential part of the church's ministry. To keep his congregation committed to hosting RP, on Sunday mornings before the RP distribution, he would say, "Remember folks, Ruby's Pantry is coming up. It's such a good program. We're so proud to have it here at the Coppertop," and the following Sunday he would let his congregation know how many people came to RP and how much food they distributed that day.

The steering committee has also organized initiatives to make RP more than just about distributing food. During 2012, at the time of the rollout of the Affordable Care Act, the committee used RP as a site to sign people up for insurance. Because two hundred to four hundred people show up at each distribution and most people wait at least an hour or two before they get their food, RP provided the perfect opportunity to provide other services. There were health care navigators on site for several months explaining options and eligibility to people on a case-by-case basis, and organizers created a confidential area where folks could have those discussions. This is another example of the fracturing of political ideologies at RP–Duluth. Opposition to the Affordable Care Act was the mainstay of conservative politics during the Obama years, and this kind of government "welfare" is something the RP home office would frown upon. However, this was a nonfactor for the organizing committee, who found it empowering. Pat noted: "So we were meeting other needs besides just the food access ... that was actually very, I guess, empowering you know to help people in those situations and there is a certain sense in Ruby's Pantry where everyone's in the same boat, so nobody feels like other people are watching them get their information."

Fun and Festive!

The atmosphere at RP is fun, festive, and welcoming. The distribution is punctuated by a sense of excitement and anticipation. The ideological strains of compassionate conservatism and benign suspicion are not discernible at all—in fact, all that comes through is the kindness and abundant generosity of strangers. On a typical Thursday, the registration and sign up begins at 4:00 p.m. as the volunteers are repackaging food and rearranging the tables in the distribution area. By 5:15, the food is repackaged, the pallets lined up, and people are all signed in and waiting in the large foyer and sanctuary until their numbers are called. Volunteers wait excitedly for clients to come through with their laundry baskets, eager to give out the food. RP usually has no trouble finding volunteers. They come from local churches and the broader community. RP attracts groups such

as school groups, cheerleaders, high school dance teams, and college organizations, all of which contribute to the fun and festive atmosphere. When
Rev. Bard was still at Coppertop, he played the host, as he liked to call it.
He stayed with guests in the sanctuary and spent his time explaining the
process to new people.

To reinforce the importance of dignity, particular communicative practices are adhered to at the distribution. For instance, terms such as *guest*
and *partner* are used to greet people, instead of *client*. Throughout the setup
period, committee members emphasize the importance of being friendly
and social. "It is important to smile at people, because we're here to help.
This is why we're doing this—to help others." Every time I volunteered, I
was constantly amazed at how, through the hustle and bustle, volunteers
continued to pay attention to the needs of individuals. For instance, one
time the line stopped moving and I was in a hurry to keep it going, but the
other volunteers waited patiently, offering to assist the elderly folks holding
up the line. For volunteers, interactions were brief but meaningful. Ellen
explained that if she sees people with canes or walkers, she will walk up
to them and say hi and see if they need help carrying out the boxes. She
knows a disabled couple that comes in, and she has formed a friendship
with them by always making sure she finds them a place they can sit down.
Nathan observed: "I guess when you are in a helping type of role like that
then you can feel like you have little more permission to say, really, how are
things going for you?"

For volunteers, getting food and the social aspect of volunteering were
important motivating factors. At least half or more of the volunteers were
also clients. While you still had to pay, a perk of volunteering was that
you could skip the line and pick up a share at your convenience. Jennifer, a client and volunteer, said: "I don't know, I must say, it's fun actually because we do really work hard but I appreciate getting the food too."
Nathan described the feeling of volunteering as "addictive". Katherine, an
RP client and volunteer, uses RP pretty consistently—not only for the food,
but also because it allows her to connect with other people. She stated: "To
tell you the truth, it's kind of a social thing. There's people that go there at
2:30 or 3:00 and it's the same people all the time. I really look forward to
going there and talking to these people."

"A Hand Up, Not a Hand Out"

A letter of Sahr states: "When we started Ruby's Pantry it was to be generous to all people who needed a hand up. After all these years I would like to think we have been doing that" (September 22, 2016). The phrase "a hand up, not a hand out" is a popular expression of neoconservative ideology that emerged from the doctrine of compassionate conservatism made famous during the welfare debates of the 1990s. *Compassionate conservatism* is a worldview that encourages reaching out and social engagement with those in need while simultaneously holding people accountable. In this framework, helping others means holding people to task—ensuring that they are good stewards of one's compassionate giving and that they do not become dependent on your compassion (Elisha 2011). RP is just one in a long line of conservative Christian organizations to use this complex blend of business and Christian doctrine in social engagement. For example, Heifer International, a US-based organization with a mission to "end world hunger and poverty," via entrepreneurial solutions, also describes its work as "a hand up, not a hand out."

Using compassionate conservatism, givers are asked to utilize discretion, discernment, and discrimination in their acts of charity, making distinctions between those who are "deserving" and "underserving." In an ethnographic study in Knoxville, Tennessee, Elisha (2011) explored the complex theology through which white, socially engaged evangelicals wrestled with the idea of compassionate conservatism. Elisha found that on the one hand, evangelicals desired to be selfless and gracious, to give with "no strings attached," but on the other hand, they also believed it was their mandate to instill godly virtues in others, particularly the virtues of moral, financial, and spiritual accountability, seen as lacking among the poor and indigent. The result was persistent fear among conservative churchgoers about the "hazards of entitlement" and "service-induced dependencies." This struggle resulted in the formulation of informal rules and guidelines through prayer and consultation with other volunteers to assess the sincerity of those seeking help and to prevent "indiscriminate charity."

Unlike traditional food pantries, which provide food free of charge, a defining organizational practice of RP involves a payment or a "donation" of twenty dollars for a share. This fee serves the dual purpose of helping RP defray operational costs and preventing indiscriminate charity and service-induced dependencies. This point is brought home in Nathan's words: "You need food for life and when we say that Ruby's Pantry is a hand up and not a hand out we are letting people know that we understand you need help and here is some food to help you, but *we are not just giving it to them*" (emphasis added). The statement "we are not just giving it to them" captures the essence of compassionate conservatism; simply put, RP is not free. The fee of twenty dollars is a way to distinguish RP from other forms of public assistance derogatorily termed *handouts*, by which people supposedly get something for nothing.

The "hand up, not a hand out" discourse constructs a clientele that is different from traditional food pantry users. In the political imaginary, RP clients comprise the Us (the hardworking individuals and families simply needing help to get by), whereas traditional food pantry users are Them (the lazy welfare recipients). In this otherizing framework, character and dignity are determined not by genuine character and dignity, but by one's ability to pay twenty dollars.

Interestingly, unlike the welfare discourses of the 1990s that persist today and can be found at places like Chum, RP offers a new entrepreneurial language of optimism linked to values of self-help, a can-do attitude, and personal accountability. The twenty-dollar payment, instead of being framed as a cost, fee, charge, or price, is framed as an "opportunity for dignity":

> Ruby's Pantry is "**a hand up, not a hand out.**" In reality, people feel good helping the organization with a small financial contribution. Participants receive an abundance of food. Often the families will leave with over $100 or more worth of groceries. ... When attending one of our distributions you are truly a guest and partner in this ministry. A guest because our volunteers are there to serve you with enthusiasm and partner because you are given an "opportunity for dignity" by donating $20 to help cover the operational costs.

Paying this money is not a burden here, but rather an invitation to citizenship and a more dignified way of being. In using the phrase *opportunity for dignity*, RP effectively produces a space where food assistance can be doled out and received in a nonstigmatizing manner. Paying twenty dollars leads to the perception that clients are contributing members of society, deserving and responsible citizens who are not taking something for nothing.

Valid citizenship in the eyes of RP accrues from the marketplace. Citizenship is reduced to economic citizenship; clients earn their dignity by paying twenty dollars for their food. Twenty dollars transforms the identities of people within the RP space from stigmatized welfare recipients to fully human beings worthy of respect and dignity. Simply put, paying the $20 humanizes and dignifies individuals.

The racialization of welfare recipients lurks right beneath RP's discursive practices. The RP home office website states that a large part of its mission is "to activate people in being alert to the needs of others ... regardless of race, religion or ethnicity." Even as a routine color-blind clause is used here, the white racial frame persists. In an interview, Sahr described RP as providing an "opportunity for dignity, so people did not have to feel like they are on welfare." He compared RP to other food assistance programs in the "inner cities of Milwaukee and Minneapolis" by referring to people in "those communities" as "poor people who are used to hand outs." In the United States, the phrase *inner city* typically implies disinvested neighborhoods populated by poor people and communities of color, people who are also usually stereotyped as lazy welfare recipients. The designation "hand up, not a hand out" in this context is a racially coded one. So when Lyn Sahr writes: "When we started Ruby's Pantry it was to be generous to all people who needed a *hand up*" (emphasis added), he is indeed qualifying that RP is not for "all people" but rather a particular segment of the population *who need a hand up*. RP is not for "those people" in the inner cities who are used to handouts; instead, RP is for financially, morally, and spiritually accountable people—racial codes used to imply white people.

Nathan verbalizes the intention of the RP program by saying that RP is meant not for welfare recipients but for a "different type of people":

> You need food for life and when we say that Ruby's pantry is a hand up and not a hand out we are letting people know that we understand you need help and here is some food to help you, but we are not giving it to them ... Many of the people who come through our program are just above the threshold that is set by other distributions. They have got a job, but because they are just above that threshold, they are struggling to make the ends meet. Some of the other distribution programs that are out there, those people might be working too, but they are also on to some kind of subsidy program, maybe they have got EBT cards for food or maybe they have got their rents subsidized, *so they are a different type of people*, although we see some of them come to our program as well. (emphasis added)

In Nathan's analysis, hardworking middle-class folks are ignored by the system and have slipped through the cracks while public resources continue to be funneled toward poor people. Thus, since the government does not support these deserving citizens, RP has stepped in to fill that gap. Put differently, RP exists to help those people who work hard but do not meet the income-eligibility criteria for public assistance programs. In this discourse, policies and systems set in place to enable historically disenfranchised communities are viewed as harming folks in the mainstream. In the following excerpt, we see Nathan wrangle with the question of who is worthy of assistance:

> We do not have any income limitations, we don't have any frequency limitations, we do not have any quantity limitations, meaning if you wanted to come in and get more than one share we just ask that your contribution be equal to the shares that you get. This is where with other programs you get two weeks or three weeks of groceries, I don't know what those guys do but it goes back to *how does one make the determination that you are worthy?* You are not because you make just a little bit too much money. That young mother with young children just because she has a job that makes a little bit more money, she has daycare expenses, so really this mother here this week does not have daycare expenses, *what makes her more worthy than the other one that really could use that hand up and make use of nutritious food for the kids? I mean, so that is part of the problem, how do you make that determination and say you are the one.* I don't know how to answer that question. (emphasis added)

Although the more liberal steering committee members showed resentment for the explicit evangelism of the RP home office, they were easily recruited into the more conservative discourses of the marketplace, where dignity was attached to the ability to pay. They believed the assertion that paying twenty dollars offered clients an "opportunity for dignity," even as food justice concerns and concerns of equity were erased from the discursive space. When asked to describe the program, Kaitlin said: "Faith, respect, honesty, sharing, caring for others, and nondiscriminatory." Rev. Bard observed that from a spiritual perspective there was something moving about providing food for people: "Dignity. I think one of the things about this program is that it is a program that helps people stretch their food dollars, and I hope they are treated in a very dignified way. It is kind of a guest relationship." Notably, he was the only individual to point out that traditional food shelves do really important work because coming up with twenty dollars is a challenge for many people. Ellen, the most liberal member of the group, liked RP because it did not have eligibility criteria typical at traditional food shelves; however, she reverted to using language of accountability to talk about RP: "The other thing I like about Ruby's Pantry is that I truly believe, if people pay something they have more of a vested interest and they have retained some of their self-respect. They don't feel like they are getting charity. They feel like they are getting a deal; it's a whole different thought." Thus even Ellen, the most liberal member of the group, remained uncritical of the false distinction made between a hand up and a handout and reinforced the value of charitable capitalism.

Food Surplus and Cost Explained through Spirituality

RP is distinct from traditional food pantries because of the sheer quantity and type of food distributed. RP hands out massive, abundant, and spectacular quantities of food, anywhere from fifty to one hundred pounds of food per "share" (i.e., a preset amount of food distributed to each individual for twenty dollars). There are no restrictions on how many shares an individual can purchase so long as they pay twenty dollars for each share. Indeed, it is not unusual to see people picking up two or three shares for neighbors and friends. In the initial years, there was shock and awe on the part of clients regarding the quantity of food, including expletives of pleasant surprise: A whole twenty-pound sack of potatoes per share! Twenty cans of Coca-Cola sodas per share! A two-gallon container of boiled eggs! The quantity is so large that clients bring laundry baskets and suitcases to pick up their food and often need the help of volunteers, wagons, and shopping carts to carry food back to their cars. Because there is no government support, one does not see unfamiliar USDA commodities. Instead, the typical food distribution has many branded items, such as Coke, Yoplait, and Gold'n Plump chicken. Clients are expected to take everything because it makes the process more efficient; if they do not want an item, they are encouraged to redistribute.

The surplus food that ends up at RP is the result of an unjust system of food production; however, this injustice is never exposed and never part of the discourse. This is true of RP and food pantries in general. Consistent with an entrepreneurial can-do attitude, RP bypasses the Feeding America network and has its own system to procure surplus food. Sahr notes that corporations now call him up and say things like, "We have ten thousand pounds of potatoes, how soon can you pick it up?" Sahr spoke about a relationship RP has with Gold'n Plump chicken, a Minnesota-based company. He recounted a story about how Gold'n Plump uses a lot of Mexican immigrant labor, but because of language issues, mistakes are often made, and those "mistakes" come to RP. One time, a migrant Mexican worker injected the chicken with the wrong marinade, so a chain restaurant that Gold'n Plump supplies chicken to refused to accept it. This incorrectly marinated chicken ended up at RP.

In this brief example, we see how injustice is bursting at the seams of the hunger industrial complex. In an attempt to stave off hunger for people in the United States, the injustices that foreign migrant laborers face are swept under the table. Substandard pay, health hazards, poor working conditions, stolen wages, and debt all make migrant labor a modern-day slave trade (Gottlieb and Joshi 2010; Holt-Giménez, Patel, and Shattuck 2009). However, no one likes to talk about these issues because migrant labor subsidizes the US food system. For democrats and republicans, this is a win-win situation. Companies benefit from cheap labor, consumers benefit from cheap food prices, and the hunger industrial complex benefits from the surplus food that is created, which good whites get to dole out. In the feel-good spaces of charitable capitalism, these injustices are erased.

In official discourses, Sahr employs a spiritual framework to answer the question of surplus food. Sahr is extremely proud of the fact that RP is faith-based and self-sustaining without receiving any government funding: "Because we proclaimed to be faith based, many people privately told me that it was not possible to be faith based and receive any corporate donations. My response was always the same, 'We will not ever, ever be a secular organization! We will serve anyone and everyone but we will never hide what we believe'" (February 9, 2015). RP is only self-sustaining if we ignore political economic factors that allow FBOs to engage in spiritual entrepreneurialism—factors such as immigrant labor, government subsidies, tax breaks, and tax credits that incentivize food overproduction and corporate donations of surplus food (DeLorme, Kamerschen, and Redman 1992). Sahr sidesteps these factors in favor of spiritual arguments. RP has never run out of food because God provides, he says:

What about running out of food? Shortly after we purchased our distribution center in North Branch in 2005, we ran out of food. It was a Friday and there were two distributions the next day with no food in the warehouse. Not even a loaf of bread. It was 10:00 AM and I had already called every donating company I could think of. So I prayed and said, "God You have a problem. I didn't ask for this ministry. This was Your idea, not mine. So tomorrow I will have no choice but to go to the two distributions sites and tell the people the truth. You did not provide!" End of prayer. Within 10 minutes the phone started ringing and companies started calling us to donate food. ... We hauled food that night until 8 PM and we had more than enough for the distributions. We have never looked back. (March 1, 2015)

In focusing solely on God's blessing, Sahr ignores the global political economy that creates surplus food: neoliberal trade liberalization of agricultural commodities mandated by the World Bank and International Monetary Fund in exchange for loans to developing countries (Holt-Giménez, Patel, and Shattuck 2009), land grabs by multinational corporations, and the removal of tariffs that once protected farmers in the Global South, to name a few. Ignoring political and historical realities, Sahr praises the generosity of corporations: "Our food donors have been unbelievable with their generosity. We pray for our donors that God will bless their companies for their generosity" (April 10, 2015).

Poverty Governance at RP

By design, RP is meant to exclude those who cannot pay twenty dollars for food pantry food. The RP home office is full of critique for government income-eligibility criteria found at traditional food pantries but itself sets a fee of twenty dollars, which acts as a form of eligibility. The unspoken assumption is that charging twenty dollars makes it fair, just, and nondiscriminatory: a system open to all because the market is always fair and just. However, for highly food insecure folks, paying twenty dollars a share is a heavy price, so RP is not an option for them—at least, not a dignified one. What happens if a client cannot afford to pay twenty dollars at RP? In practice, this rarely happens, because most people call ahead to check prices and procedures. However, there was one "ugly incident" that Rev. Bard described as his worst experience with RP:

I think my worst experience was fairly early on. There was a woman who had come and was slightly belligerent to the person from our church who had worked to get this organized. She basically told her that if she did not have any money, it was her obligation to give her food. She kind of rubbed that woman the wrong way. The woman who started Ruby's Pantry was a determined sort of woman. She was not going to take that and she actually ended up calling the police who escorted the woman out. ... To be honest I would have managed the situation slightly differently, but I also did not feel that it was appropriate for me to over-step the woman who had gotten things going. She felt that this woman had really behaved badly and just needed to leave. I felt if that was her decision I was going to back her up. That was probably my worst.

Kaitlin also recalled the incident, but in her version of the story, layers of moral meaning centered on fraud and abuse were added on to the character of the woman: "It wasn't that she didn't have the money, but that she was asking for a free share. She was just asking for a free share because she was just trying to get loopholes, you know—like, oh, you said free, or a freewill donation or whatever or, so she took it out of context. I could understand if you don't have the money, but it wasn't like she didn't have the money, it was just like she was trying to fool the system or something." It is not clear how Kaitlin knew the woman had money to spare—they did not know each other from before—but what is clear is that there was no dignity afforded to this particular "guest," who was escorted out by the police.

In recent years, the RP home office has come up with a more formal pro-cess to handle such situations. The RP home office distributes gift certificates to each distribution site, which are awarded to people who cannot afford the twenty dollars. However, there are strict surveillance procedures for this, which are reflective of poverty governance procedures but at a smaller scale. A person who cannot afford to pay the twenty dollars is allowed to receive one free certificate per year for what is then no longer called a *share*, but a *blessing box*. The individual's name is recorded at the local site, and these names are sent to the RP home office. These names are also kept at the local site to verify that the same person does not receive more than one free box a year. Committee members say that it is quite tedious keeping strict accounts of it all and there is a lot of paperwork involved. Ironically, these procedures are similar to poverty governance procedures at traditional food pantries and that SNAP recipients undergo. In sum, for people who can pay twenty dollars, there is a "no questions asked" policy in place, but for those who cannot pay, moral and procedural accountability measures are set in place to ensure against fraud and abuse.

There were some behaviors that were deemed "fraud and abuse" as per the RP home office; these were behaviors that did not follow the rules of the marketplace. There were clients and volunteers who "abused the system" by going through the RP distribution line twice—in essence, getting a double share for the price of twenty dollars. There were also volunteers who tried to pick something they should not or get more of an item. Nathan rationalized this kind of abuse: "In any program there is always the possibility for abuse. We probably had some individuals that might take advantage of the program, but I think that is true of any program, and so what we have to do is just pray that that percentage of individuals that might take advantage of the program is negative. We do not have any way of tracking that. We do try to talk to the volunteers." Sahr noted cases of individuals returning food to the grocery store and encouraged people to report such behavior. He writes:

> In our effort to help people there is, and always will be, people who are critical of Ruby's Pantry and some that will actually cheat, break the rules and jeopardize the entire program. Over the past three months we had someone try to return some of our products to a grocery store for a cash refund. Recently we had someone try to return a product to a store to exchange it for one that was fresher. When this happens the manufacturers and suppliers are immediately notified by the store and they immediate call us. They have zero tolerance for this and we have to really seek forgiveness to pacify them. They get furious. In both recent cases we had to quit sending their product to those two particular distribution sites. What a shame. Like is so often the case, one person ruins it for everyone. ... Anyone caught selling food, returning food to stores for credit, exchanging for other items of the same or different product, or breaking any other rules pertaining to our program may be permanently banned from attending any Ruby's Pantry distribution. If you are aware of any of this behavior taking place please let your distribution site leader(s) know so they can address it. Doing the right thing will always be right and it will assure that the program will continue to bless many people in your area that need food. (August 10, 2015)

There is strong condemnation and reprisals for people who engage in this kind of behavior.

Ironically, RP's policy of charging twenty dollars but calling it a donation has raised some eyebrows and legal questions about whether this is fraud itself. Because of legal ramifications involved with tax write-offs, RP's position is that the twenty-dollar fee is not for the food itself, but a "donation" used to defray logistical costs. If RP charges people for the food, then food donors cannot receive tax write-offs for their donations—a key incentive for charitable giving. Thus, the website clarifies: "We give everyone the opportunity for dignity by giving a cash donation of $20 to help cover fuel costs and other associated expenses. **We do not sell food!**" In my interview with Celeste, a steering committee member, she often used the term *buy* or *purchase*, but would then stop short, saying, "Oh, 'buy,' wrong word! Nothing is purchased, it's *donated*." When I asked her why she didn't use the term *buy*, she said it was frowned upon by "corporate" because of IRS regulations. She then observed the contradiction: "A donation is an undefined amount. Again, this is not an undefined amount. This is a fixed-amount donation." There are several disclaimers that RP does not sell food, but as Executive Director Shaye Moris of Second Harvest Northern Lakes Food Bank pointed out, "Transit costs or not, they're still charging."

The Duluth steering committee meets once a month to make decisions about the operation and to figure out how to use the two-dollar fee per share that stays with them. The RP home office describes the two dollars as a "tithe back to the local sponsoring church" and encourages sponsors to be entrepreneurial with these funds. So far, the Duluth committee has used the money to purchase bags, wagons to help carry food out, and plastics to cover the tables. The money is also used to fund special requests in the community, such as a breakfast program at a local elementary school or the Red Cross. However, Cynthia noted that it was actually quite a burden to figure out what to do with the extra funds. She exclaimed: "There are so many people and so many issues in Duluth, how do we decide who or what to give it to?" She explained that now they just give the money to Chum or to one of the other organizations in Duluth because they are much more familiar with the needs of the city. The irony here is that Chum is a social organization that gives "handouts" to the poor and is part of the very same welfare state that the RP home office is critical of.

Conclusion

Deploying a combination of Christian conservative beliefs and business practices, RP carves out a unique space for itself in the charitable food assistance arena. The discursive practices of RP captured in the slogan "RP is a hand up, not a hand out" contribute to stigma against the food insecure by reinforcing divisions between the deserving and underserving poor. RP frames itself as a program for those who are hardworking and deserving, citizens who simply need a "hand up," whereas traditional food pantries are for the paradigmatic Other—a raced and classed group of people who receive undeserved handouts in the public imaginary. RP reinforces the idea that poverty is a problem that some people have that stems from moral, spiritual, and cultural factors, not from forces of structural violence. In this framework, spirituality, self-help, and market-based approaches are the solution. Amid the hustle and bustle of organizing surplus food for people, the roles of whiteness, capitalism, and Christianity in the production of negative difference are obscured. The lack of critical thinking around the discursive practices of RP means that it is just one more way by which stigma is reinforced against the poor.

Volunteers, even the more liberal ones, were easily recruited into neoliberal definitions of dignity. Stuart Hall (1988) once argued that the power of neoliberalism (or Thatcherism) was its ability to constitute subjectivities and discourses about the world that made sense to people in a range of different social positions. This was certainly the case with RP. Steering committee members rejected the religious evangelism of the RP home office on the one hand, but applauded the conservative link between dignity and economics on the other. Individuals and organizations were framed as potential entrepreneurs that, through a can-do attitude, could put aside their differences and come together to end hunger. In this fun and festive space of giving and getting, the language of equality, social justice, and rights was erased, while entrepreneurialism, abundance, industrial surplus food, big brands, and the generosity of corporate America was celebrated.

Implications for Policy and Practice

The resurgence of hunger and food insecurity can be linked to neoliberal policies at local and global scales, yet neoliberal solutions like RP continue to be offered as solutions to fix the hunger problem. At the national level, as long as there is underemployment, unemployment, low wages, structural racism, and gender inequity, there will always be people who need food assistance. At a global level, as long as food continues to be controlled by monopolistic food corporations, neoliberal multilateral organizations, and powerful nation-states, there will be increasing food gaps (Holt-Giménez, Patel, and Shattuck 2009). From a policy perspective, what is needed to end hunger is a radical transformation of the food system, increased entitlements, and increased opportunities for people to provide food for themselves. There is an urgent need to build a joined-up local and global movement that can resist corporate food regimes. There is a need to orchestrate a food system based on sustainable ecological production, community control, and social justice (Allen 1999; Poppendieck 1999; Riches and Silvasti 2014).

The point of this chapter is not to isolate RP as a singular organization engaged in this kind of charitable capitalism, but to draw attention to a growing trend in the food assistance arena: the turn from welfare to entrepreneurialism as a way to solve the structural problem of hunger. Indeed, this is happening not just in the emergency food assistance sector, but also in the broader food movement with its celebration of community gardens or what Pudup (2008, 1228) refers to as "organized garden projects," whose goal is to put "individuals in charge of their own adjustments(s) to economic restructuring and social dislocation through self-help technologies centered on personal contact with nature."

With regards to stigma, the shift to entrepreneurial models has at least two important considerations. First, organizers need to carefully consider the broader implications of their discursive practices. A neoliberal logic is often used to dismantle stigma, where money is equated with power and dignity, but this comes with consequences; it reinforces stigma against those who receive government assistance and against those who have limited means and resources to participate in such entrepreneurial projects.

A second point to consider is the question of how neoliberalism, justice, and faith are brought together in the food arena. In FBOs, there has been a semantic (and material) stretching of the market into the realm of social action and charity. Capitalist logics of mass production; supply and demand; and branding and marketing are used to sell charitable goods and services. By most accounts, including my own, neoliberal values are not in sync with justice-based approaches because of the reliance on individualistic conceptions of freedom and prosperity that involve the commoditization of goods and services. That said, neoliberal projects are complex and not always ideologically coherent, as seen at RP. Although neoliberalism always implies entrepreneurialism, entrepreneurialism does not always imply neoliberal values and goals; one can use the fruits of capitalism for the redistribution of wealth and toward the attainment of social goals as seen in the historic case of the Black Panther Party (Broad 2016).

In practical terms, for organizations engaged in entrepreneurial solutions, they must remain focused on the voices of the oppressed and constantly illuminate the intersectionality of oppression—to ask questions about who is missing from the picture. Whose voice is not heard here? Who is being left out? Perhaps entrepreneurialism can be in sync with justice when it is used for the self-determination and liberation of oppressed communities—when it is grounded in a deep critical understanding of the links among capitalism, race and class, and histories of oppression. There is some evidence to suggest that even neoliberal spaces of governmentality can be successful when they put their trust in people who appear the least deserving and allow participants to write their own scripts (Pudup, 2008). RP falls far short of this ideal; because even as it doles out massive quantities of industrial food, it reinforces age-old stigmatizing scripts centered on the politics of race, class, and gender.

6 A Culture of Suspicion: Making the Invisible Visible

Interviewer: Do you believe there are some people that use government assistance that don't need it?
Darlene: She doesn't need it. So, yes.
Interviewer: They abuse the system?
Darlene: Yes, right. That's why I don't like to use it. I told my girlfriends that I kind of feel about government services the way white women feel about being fat. It's like your worst fear. ... The thing is, I found out after the fact [that] if I had applied right after I got laid off even though I was getting unemployment ... that I probably would have qualified. But I didn't know and I was too proud.
Interviewer: So do you feel like there is a stigma attached?
Darlene: Definitely. I don't know if it's especially for women of color, but I feel like it is because I am a woman of color. I guess, I don't know.
—Darlene, African American female, RP client

The Queen Is Dead, Long Live the Queen!

Darlene is a thirtysomething Black woman with three young children; she is also one of the few people of color at RP–Duluth. Her first and only experience at RP was fairly pleasant; the staff and volunteers were friendly, and she recalls a volunteer apologizing because there was not much food that day. "I was like, oh great, my luck! The day I need it the most." Luckily for her, this was also the day they were giving out books, and she felt like she had won the lottery. A voracious reader, she was happier with the quality of the books than with the food. Darlene initially tried RP because she was laid off in 2009 and needed help making ends meet. She is well-educated and uses humor and metaphor in powerful ways, like when she says: "I kind of feel about government services the way white women feel about being fat" or when she says "Right now I'm working a full-time temporary job, which I can't wait to end, really. It's a lot like dating somebody you're never going to marry, you know? I'm done, emotionally." An eternal optimist, Darlene always felt that she would find a job again, but she has faced a lot of rejection. Her husband does freelance writing work, but there is not much money in it. For these reasons, when she heard of RP she thought it would be a good idea.

Darlene is extremely health conscious. In response to the question "Do you perceive yourself to be a healthy person?" she says: "I do ... Because I don't smoke, I don't drink. I make my own foods. I drink a lot of water. I don't always drink pop. I started drinking coffee at work. I never drank coffee before. I drink three cups of coffee a day now. It helps me focus, I'm not kidding." Darlene has started buying only whole grains and whole-wheat tortillas. She bakes all her own bread, and usually it is brown bread. In fact, some weeks ago her husband begged her to make white bread, which her seven-year old said "tasted funny." She adds, "He thought something was wrong. And all it had ... was a teaspoon of sugar, but he said it tasted sweet." Darlene makes massive meals on the weekends and freezes them for later. She also freezes single portions to bring in her lunch container to work. Because she is health conscious, she never went back to RP; the quality of the food was too poor. She says, "I only used it that one time. I didn't feel like the food that I got was food that I would buy if I had twenty dollars."

Just as Darlene is health conscious, so too is she keenly conscious of the negative racial stereotypes that circulate around her. Her thinking is informed by the flood of welfare discourses floating around in American society that violate her on a daily basis. These discourses, though emergent in welfare arenas, also find their way into charitable food assistance settings. Darlene remembered that once when she told her coworkers that she used RP, they said that they preferred to use coupons. She said: "I'm like, I use coupons. You can do both. There is no law." Darlene manages racial and neoliberal stigma by always policing her words and actions. During the interview, when asked whether she uses food pantries besides RP, Darlene responded, "We have, we've gone to other food shelves. I won't lie.

Probably once a month we go to a food shelf at the Vineyard or Salvation Army." The question was not intended to assess overutilization of services, but by using the phrase "I won't lie," Darlene revealed her awareness of the negative assumptions that follow her around. The phrase is typically used when people recognize that what they are about to say has negative meaning in the broader culture. It is a technique to "manage stigma," as Goffman (1963) pointed out, by directly addressing the stigmatized attribute- in this case preemptively taking ownership for something perceived to be contentious in the public eye—the overutilization (or abuse) of benefits. Age-old welfare discourses have also impacted Darlene's participation in legal entitlement programs. As seen in the excerpt that opens this chapter, she did not sign up for SNAP, to avoid stigma. In fact, rather than sign up for SNAP, Darlene sells her blood in downtown Duluth as a way to make ends meet. She has donated blood plasma four times now and has made $115—money that she is saving for the future.

Not only does Darlene evaluate, regulate, and police herself according to parameters set by racialized systems of poverty governance, Darlene also evaluates other people according to those parameters—including other Black women. In the opening excerpt, when Darlene says "she doesn't need it," she is referring to her husband's ex, who she claims is abusing the system. In her portrayal of the ex, Darlene taps into the trope of the quintessential "welfare queen," saying: "Because I know my husband's ex, they never got married. She got pregnant, decided she was done with him. I think she just wanted another baby, but anyway. It was her second one out of wedlock. So she doesn't work. She lives in public housing. I was complaining recently to John, my husband … and Jake heard me. My stepson. He went and told his mom. It made me seem like I was the bad guy. I'm like, how is that fair? First of all, honestly, I think she just uses the money for cigarettes." In Darlene's portrayal, the ex has become the paradigmatic cigarette-smoking Black welfare mother undeserving of public assistance—a trope that was widely circulated during the welfare debates in the 1990s (McCormack 2004; Seccombe 2011). More specifically, Darlene is drawing upon a nearly forty-year-old political discursive strategy used by President Reagan that framed welfare recipients as manipulative, dishonest, and not interested in working hard.

During his campaign rallies in 1976 and all through his presidency, Reagan regaled his audiences with stories of people, women in particular, who deceived the welfare system and were living the highlife—as in the story of the "Cadillac-driving Chicago welfare queen," who Reagan proclaimed had "eighty names, thirty addresses, twelve social security cards and is collecting veteran's benefits on four nonexisting deceased husbands. ... Her tax-free cash income alone is over $150,000" (McCormack 2004). The welfare queen was a con artist, lazy, and Black in the story, and unashamed of taking money from hardworking citizens. Using these stories, Reagan marked millions of poor citizens as scam artists and in doing so promoted a neoliberal agenda, which ultimately led to the passage of the Welfare Reform Act of 1996 and a more muscular and punitive era of poverty governance. The putative "welfare mother" served clear political interests; these stories had a strong moral component, linking hard work to citizenship and making the welfare queen a scapegoat for the economic and social changes threatening the middle and working classes (McCormack 2004; Seccombe 2011).

These discursive practices were powerful in that they established a commonsense understanding of welfare, such that people across social arenas—politicians, caseworkers, and welfare recipients—came to share these understandings. McCormack (2004, 358) writes: "Ronald Reagan was instrumental in constructing the image of the Welfare Queen, the penultimate abuser of a system designed to help the poor. The welfare queen lied and cheated to take money from the state while she lived well, drove expensive cars, and owned a nice home. While the welfare queen in Reagan's speech ... was shown to be a fabrication, the image of the welfare queen lived on, long past Reagan's presidency."

In her study with women a year after the passage of welfare reform, McCormack found that even while women on welfare understood the hardships of economic deprivation, they too echoed the sentiments of the lazy, manipulative welfare mother. McCormack (2004, 360) found some differences in how women responded to these discourses based on where they lived and their position in society, but for the most part, the women all "acknowledged the power of the welfare mother and employed various tactics to escape from the damaging effects of this putative Other."

Astonishingly, more than twenty years after the passage of welfare reform, these discourses still affect and influence the everyday lives of people who receive public assistance and live in spaces of poverty like food pantries. New language may be attached to these issues, but they are grounded in the same ideological assumptions about welfare users. This is seen in the case of Darlene, a woman who has experienced hardship herself, but who portrays her husband's ex as the quintessential Black welfare queen and welfare mother who is lazy, manipulative, and unhealthy. In this moment, Darlene becomes an agent of governmentality, surveilling and exerting discipline on others. In this moment, a collective history of oppression is replaced by racial and neoliberal ideals of citizenship perpetuated over the course of several centuries.

The persistence of these discourses through history can be attributed to the fact that neoliberalism is not just political doctrine but an ideology that creates a shift in identity and relationships—that is, how we engage with each other and in community. Neoliberalism influences identity through the creation of *neoliberal subjectivities*, a term denoting the ways in which market logic increasingly pervades the thoughts and practices of individuals (Del Casino and Jocoy 2008; Rose 1989). In this situation, the ideals of individualism, efficiency, profit, and self-help become internalized within individuals such that all other determinants of well-being are overlooked. Larner (2000, 19) writes: "Political power does not just act on political subjects, but constructs them in particular ways." Economic identities become the new basis for political life, displacing social citizenship and creating in-groups of hardworking individuals engaged in the market and out-groups of lazy people framed as a burden to the in-group. This neoliberal shaping of identity informs and influences the ways in which individuals conduct themselves in society—how they relate to each other and systems of poverty governance. This influence is discernible in the kind of self-regulatory behaviors individuals display. Larner argues that in a neoliberal era regulation occurs through practices designed to "facilitate the governing of individuals from a distance" (6). A key characteristic of neoliberal governmentality lies in the process of creating citizens capable of self-regulation (Rose and Miller 1992). For instance, Darlene, caught up in the trope of the Black welfare queen, will not sign up for SNAP. She disciplines her own behaviors and informs on the behaviors of her husband's ex. In so doing, Darlene has become an agent of governance: an autonomous agent surveilling and exerting discipline on others—discipline that she herself has been subjected to.

Drawing on this notion of neoliberal governmentality, I argue that neoliberalism, through its discursive practices (ideology and institutional frameworks), reformulates personal identity such that even exploited people can be recruited into conservative political projects. This is why people across social locations can be found to reinforce neoliberal ideologies, even when these positions are clearly against their own self-interests. The constant barrage of demonizing neoliberal discourses turns individuals into self-policing agents, who become increasingly conscious and self-conscious about how they talk and are constantly engaged in surveilling themselves and others. Some psychological aspects of self-policing involve self-surveillance, self-discipline, and self-censorship of behavior and opinions. As in the case of Darlene, citizens begin to compare themselves favorably to their fellow citizens who are not living up to the ideal of good economic citizens. Notably, in the stigma literature, Goffman (1963) referred to these sorts of self-policing behaviors as *stigma management* and documented various strategies individuals used to preserve impressions and manage their "spoiled identities" in the face of stigma (e.g., directly correcting the stigmatized attribute, seeing stigma as a blessing, reframing nonstigmatized individuals as actually needing help and sympathy, and using humor to break the tension).

In a neoliberal era, this kind of self-policing, monitoring, and managing of stigma does not occur everywhere and among all people, but is most alive in spaces in which the state has the strongest hold—typically spaces of poverty and disenfranchisement. These behaviors create and reinforce a culture of suspicion in these spaces, which destroys a sense of community and solidarity among people. These policing behaviors pit people against each other and replace what should be communal forms of living with suspicion, resentment, and paranoia. Importantly, the culture of suspicion exists not because poor citizens are uniquely different from the rich but because they are subject to more governance procedures that surveil and threaten action against them. Cultures of suspicion typically manifest at the point at which relations of power are exercised, such as between volunteers and clients, the state and claimants, and the researcher and participants; this is why even some portions of the interviews were rife with stigma management strategies. In these moments, ordinary citizens engaged in processes to defend against neoliberal stigma by highlighting their own self-worth, comparing themselves favorably to others, or pointing to and informing on others.

Goal of the Chapter

The goal of this chapter is to show how neoliberalism creates a culture of suspicion in spaces of poverty through its ideological formations and institutional frameworks. The chapter demonstrates ways in which hungry and food insecure citizens, living in conditions of fear and scarcity, become agents of discipline. Age-old welfare discourses inform the way in which food insecure people think about themselves and others who are like them such that they are constantly engaged in self-surveillance. In these spaces, people are always surveilling themselves and others for behaviors that are inconsistent with dominant values.

This is a story that remains invisible to a great many people who donate to, volunteer at, and work in food pantry spaces and the broader food system because these meanings only emerge in deep conversation and dialogue with citizens. By highlighting activities such as self-surveillance, self-discipline, and self-censorship, the chapter shows how stigma impacts not only people's access to food, but also their sense of identity and belonging to a community. It shows how individuals both reinforce and resist neoliberal narratives. As seen in the opening excerpt, Darlene demonstrates an oppositional consciousness with regard to neoliberal logic but simultaneously deploys neoliberal stigma to mark some people as unworthy.

Scarcity Model at the Food Pantry

The hunger industrial complex runs on surplus food created by capitalist modes of production; indeed, the food system is set up to produce excess food and then redistribute the surplus to the hungry. Yet many food pantries still operate within a food scarcity model, in which rationing food given to clients by setting time limits and eligibility criteria is normative. Instead of viewing people's access to food in terms of rights and legal entitlements, food is rationed, controlled, and subjected to governance procedures. This means that though fraud and abuse do not exist in a real sense at food pantries, these discourses find themselves here as well. Shaye Moris, director of Second Harvest Northern Lakes Food Bank, acknowledged that food pantries were rife with myths and misperceptions about fraud. She said: "I hear that people are selling product. I don't know, I don't know that to be true. It's not something that we've experienced or witnessed firsthand

... so to me that's a myth that you hear." In an earlier chapter, we saw Chum volunteers circulating these stories at the Chum food pantry. Volunteers invoked discourses of fraud and abuse while remaining silent on more deeply rooted issues of structural racism and their own whiteness. Typically, in this setting, fraud and abuse were constructed as selling food pantry food, lying about how many people were in the household, overutilization of the food pantry, and lack of genuine need. However, as Shaye pointed out during our interview, there is no such thing as fraud and abuse in food pantry spaces because industrial food is not scarce and their business is about giving away surplus food:

Interviewer: So in terms of Feeding America, then, and Second Harvest, there's no notion of fraud and abuse? This does not exist? Is that what you are saying?

Shaye: Correct. Yeah, there really isn't ... We're here to supply food that's otherwise going to end up in the landfill so we want it to be utilized ... If that means one household needs a lot more food than another household, we're happy just to make sure that they have food.

Interviewer: So there's this perception of scarcity—

Shaye: I was just going to say the scarcity model, yep. Yep, we see that definitely in our communities. Can't understand it, scratch our head about that because even we'll hear a news report where a food shelf says we don't have any food and whatever. And we think, "Oh my gosh! Call us if you're ever at that point because we have a warehouse full of food and we have relationships with these agencies." I think there is that scarcity model of there's never going to be enough food to provide needed food to people who need it.

Interviewer: Right, that's not something you believe, it's not scarce.

Shaye: No.

Interviewer: So you're saying there's an abundance of food?

Shaye: We feel that there's adequate resources. There might be volunteer scarcity, where it's hard to find people to help with the food shelf, certainly. But in terms of food, there are abundant resources.

Chum's food shelf director, Frank, also talked about the scarcity mindset among volunteers. His goal is to give food away—as much as he can— but this often conflicts with how volunteers understand their roles. For example, they currently have an abundance of bread, so they give it away for no points—this means giving as much bread as people want. They ended up moving the bread to the waiting area to prevent bottlenecks. "We just said, it's free if you want it, and when you walk by you can grab your bread. You want bread, take bread. You want just a loaf of bread and walk out the door? Do it." The volunteers were horrified and could not stand the lack of control. There was fear that people would take too much bread—even though that was the whole point- to get rid of surplus bread. Frank asserted: "In a grand scheme of things, it all has a perishable date. The cans will last five years. But if you're sitting on milk or eggs, they're just dying. Every day that they're not out and given away, is another day they're dying ... The goal is to literally get rid of it." Frank added: "It's this hard thing ... And it's taken a while. There's only a few volunteers left that are super, super sticklers. It's hard. You have to shift the entire dynamic of everything."

In talking to food shelf directors, I have learned that a much harder problem to solve is one of logistics: food is not scarce, but how to keep food flowing in and out at a steady pace is challenging. Although there is an abundance of food "out there," it is harder to bring the food to the food pantry for a variety of reasons: insufficient space to store the food, insufficient refrigeration, lack of staff to pick up available food, the wrong kind of food ending up at the food shelf, too much fresh food arriving at one time. It is easy to give food away, but harder to ensure a steady supply of the food that people want. Food pantries also have to be on the lookout for the best deals for food because food banks do not always get the best prices for products. For food pantry staff, if they take a few extra but tedious steps, they can do better and get more food for clients. This speaks to the tenuous relationships among actors in the hunger industrial complex—the food pantries, food banks, and Feeding America, which controls most of the operations. Each of these stakeholders has somewhat different priorities and agendas, which in the end makes the food pantry a complex and chaotic place to work.

Reluctant to Complain

Clients at Chum spoke warmly about the volunteers; they appreciated the food and the extra steps volunteers took to help them. They typically did not linger on the negative interactions at the food shelf but tended to put them down to a volunteer having a bad day. Ashley talked about her appreciation for the volunteers because they give her as much fresh fruit and vegetables as she wants. "I know they really make an effort to allow you to take as much of the fresh stuff, which is cool." Gabrielle said: "They have always been sweet and respectful to me." Clients attributed faith and ethical beliefs to volunteers' motivations. Violet referred to volunteers as "missionaries" doing God's work. Scott, a white elderly man, was full of praise for Chum volunteers, saying: "I'd say they're very giving and have empathy ... I'm not saying the trick word but they're definitely religious people, Christian, whatever you want to call them there. They're nice people. Nice people do and trying to do ... Love God and love people, so they treat people wonderfully." The volunteers were there by choice, which clients marveled at. Renee, a Native woman, stated: "They can be on vacation, spending money or whatever, but they're here helping the people that need help in this community."

Although clients showed gratitude to volunteers, the language of charity created a spiral of silence in which some were hesitant to complain and policed their language. Even the few participants who mentioned any dissatisfaction obfuscated it. Their articulations illuminate the complexity of being under the dual threat of poverty governance procedures and charity. Xavier, a fortysomething Black man, said that volunteers do the best that they can, but sometimes things go wrong. When asked if he has had any negative experiences with the volunteers, he said, hesitantly: "You have people that go off on you, say things to you because they maybe can't get an extra bag of beans or something, because being on that side, I've seen that and you can only do what you can. For myself, personally, if a person came and said they had twelve kids or a rough situation and asked if I could sneak them a bag of something, I would try to do it for them. I'm a firm believer of karma, you know. I believe that what you put in is what you get out. I tell my kids you don't put nothing in, no deposit. No return. Even if you put in, it doesn't always mean that you get back." Xavier was one of the few participants who inverted computational neoliberal logic, noting that we should give, *even when you may not get something in return*. Susan, a middle-aged white woman, was the most blunt about her experiences: "When you volunteer, you work ... You should not snap at people. I have no idea. Sorry to say, I know there are the people who have been there and that stay there, they are like helping out but then I can hardly tell why they are there."

Cadillacs and Lincolns: Making Favorable Comparisons

In the context of scarcity and poverty governance procedures, it is no wonder that Chum clients engaged in self-policing strategies to present themselves in a good light. In a typical pattern, clients justified their own food assistance patterns and compared themselves favorably to others, often telling or "informing" on these others to prove their point. Stereotypes of welfare recipients as lazy, greedy, bad health citizens, and selfish came up in client characterizations of each other. Food assistance was talked about as though it were a zero-sum game, a scarcity model, in which taking food for oneself meant that someone else was not going to get it. Indeed, a similar belief restricts potential SNAP recipients from signing up. Clients made moral judgements about why people should and shouldn't be at the food pantry based on perceptions of other people's "genuine needs"—a moral discourse of need. People were deserving of the food if they "genuinely needed" it, but what constituted genuine was never made clear.

For Ashley, a young white woman who worked as a janitor, accusations of fraud and abuse applied to other people, but not to her. She avoided public assistance programs as a way to manage stigma. She explained: "I feel like there's sort of that image of people that abuse the system or are lazy. I know that is the case in some situations, but I don't feel like that's my situation. I try to do my best not to use it." She added: "Some of them, people here that I know, I feel like they could figure out a way not to use it. To some extent I feel like they're a little lazy. I think it's a bit of both. I feel like more often there are people that are just sort of maybe not trying to intentionally take advantage of the system, but they are. They are being overly grabby about it. That's not everybody." Ashley is aware of the negative stereotypes surrounding her—a poor, white, working-class woman—and both defends herself and compares herself favorably to others as a way to manage stigma. Like Darlene, against her own self-interest, she does not use assistance until she crosses some personal threshold for pain and suffering.

Across the interviews, moral discourses of need were employed to compare oneself favorably to others. Victor, a thirtysomething Native man, detailed how some people sell their food stamps to pay rent and phone bills and buy alcohol and cigarettes. When asked if he sees a lot of it going on, he responded: "I don't see a lot of it going on at all. I know it's happening, though. It is, it's happening out there. I've been asked to buy some. That's how I know what the price is. No, I don't sell mine. I never will." He adds: "I get a little upset at some of them that I know have a lot of money and don't need to be here. Like I said, since I started working I have not been here yet. I'm still behind on bills and everything. There's other people out there that need it a lot more than I do ... This guy has a Lincoln for sale for $3,000.00. He does! A brand-new 1999 Lincoln." Here Victor invokes the scarcity model, making judgments about who needs it more. By invoking the "brand-new Lincoln," Victor draws upon the forty-year old conservative trope of welfare recipients owning expensive cars like Cadillacs. In her book *So You Think I Drive a Cadillac?*, Karen Seccombe (2011) addresses misperceptions about welfare recipients and how these racialized discourses influenced the passage of the Welfare Reform Act of 1996.

Jermain, an elderly Black man, similarly invoked the Cadillac trope, clarifying that he only used the food shelf sparingly. He said, "I get $2,700 a month, and I only use this when I need it. I don't abuse it. I don't." When asked what he meant by "abuse," he explained: "I've seen people that come here and go to one of the other food shelves the same day. I see cars pull up, nice cars. I'm saying if you can afford an eighty-thousand-dollar car, and you're in a line where somebody else is just pulling a cart, looking as though they do need it, you know. And that's what I mean. People abuse it." Despite the already oppressive system of governance, a few clients felt that there should be stricter controls at the food pantry. Paula, a middle-aged white woman, wished there were tighter regulations because of the "Cadillacs": "I see 90 percent of the people need it, but then I also see people pull out with Cadillacs using the food shelf, so that really kind of gets me a little bit. I've seen it few times here. Forty-thousand-dollar cars coming here to the food shelf, really."

Constructing "Us and Them" at RP

At Chum, clients tended to distance themselves from other clients, but at RP clients reinforced their similarities with each other. Contrary to the culture of suspicion forged at Chum, at RP a culture of unity was created.

Participants found it easy to relate to each other, and perceptions of social distance were minimal. "Everyone is in the same boat" and "RP is for everyone" were common refrains heard. *Everyone* in this context was *not* a nod to marginalized groups but a nod to more well-to-do folks. Julie, a white middle-aged woman, noted: "When I first started, before, I thought it was only for poor people but it is not. It is for anybody." Tony observed that there were a lot of different kinds of people at RP, but "we're pretty much all in the same boat." Participants met people they knew at RP, which contributed to feeling like this was a program for Us. Chris described the clientele as "just regular people just come in trying to get by and find a great deal. You have students in there from colleges. You have seniors in there. You have mentally disabled. Physically disabled." There was a well-instituted practice of helping friends, family, and neighbors at RP— an outcome of the connection they felt with each other. Families and friends came to RP together, and people picked up shares on behalf of neighbors.

At the center of this perceived unity was the ideological formation that RP was a place for "nice people," "working people," "the working poor," "people doing the best they can," and "people with pride." Bernadette saw herself as similar to the other people at RP "because they all need help with their budget and stretching things any way they can, and they're willing to pay for it, and they've got a little more pride in what they're doing. I just feel it that way … We're all in the same boat." Chris pointed out: "They all seem nice, working people. They all have families. They're all just trying to provide. It's a great deal … I didn't see anything wrong with some of the people there. They all seemed like nice people. They sat there all interacting with each other and talking with each other. There wasn't any negative energy in the air or anything. It was great. They're all open. It's just like, 'Oh, hey. How's it going?'" And Claire similarly said: "I think pretty much we're all the same, we're just trying to make ends meet and do the best with what we have … I just don't see the economic difference in anybody, anywhere, I try not to. I try not to see color or race or social and economic difference." In short, the people at RP were normal, Us, and there was nothing *wrong* with them.

Clients thought RP had a lot of diversity in terms of income levels, age, and ability. The fact that RP was a nearly all-white space was not mentioned;

in fact, race was rarely brought up among RP clients. Dennis, a young white man, observed that unlike the food shelf, which has a more homogenous population in terms of income, RP is much more diverse. From the looks of it, Jennifer thought that the people who came to RP were generally middle income. Darlene observed that RP clients seemed to be "the working poor" and people who were not on food stamps—different from the folks at Chum.

Interviewer: What are your impressions of the clients who use Ruby's Pantry?

Darlene: Ruby's Pantry, I think, is unique in that it's a different clientele that goes to a food shelf like Chum. They are a different group of folks that get assistance from food stamps ... The majority of people that are in Ruby's Pantry, I don't believe that they get any food stamps or anything that. They just don't appear to be in that same category of financial situations. I think that those who come to Ruby's Pantry tend to be, just a strange word or term, the working poor. They tend to be folks that have jobs, in fact, they might be juggling two or three jobs, but it's just not enough. And so they are accessing this program.

Because RP is open to "everyone" and there are no eligibility requirements, the primary ways in which fraud and abuse are thought of in traditional food pantry spaces were erased here. In this arena, there was no need to discuss how many household members one had or how often one used RP or even if one *really* needed food assistance. In a letter, Lyn Sahr, director of RP, urges people not to judge each other—ironically, given that conservative discourses over the last five decades have been geared precisely toward fueling such judgment toward others. His letter, however, demonstrates the power of discourse to interrupt age-old ideologies: "Some people are still stuck on looking around at who comes and judging whether they should be using the program or not. I still have people saying, 'They're just using you!' My answer is always the same, 'That's why we exist, to be used!' Please remember that Ruby's Pantry is for everyone that eats. It gives people an opportunity for dignity. Ruby's Pantry is a hand up, not a hand out program ... Therefore, be thankful for a program that no one has to pay for with their tax dollars and is totally funded by the donations of the guests who use the program" (August 19, 2015). According to Sahr, because no tax dollars are used to fund RP, it is a dignified form of assistance and one that actually "gives back" to the community. In these articulations, individuals are invited to think about themselves in a new way: they are not welfare recipients of a government program, but "guests" of a private entrepreneur.

RP creates frames of reference for clients that they now can use to construct their identities differently from traditional food pantry recipients. Clients brought up moral issues of overutilization and lack of genuine need, but then rejected those allegations in line with Sahr's exhortations. Pat was initially surprised by who came to RP, but does not judge anymore. She explained: "I mean of course you get to see many people who you think that you know they really need this. You can just tell. You can see it by the clothes they are wearing, what they look like, but then are these people that are surprising like. I have seen clients like my mailman and I think that person is supposed to be paid decent, *but it's for everybody, so you don't judge.* You think that maybe they are having or going through some problem or something." Chris has seen clients with expensive cars at RP—the Lincoln again—but he too does not think any less of them: "It's very mixed. I know a lady that goes there, she's not a close friend but I would consider her a friend, who gets a new Lincoln every year. She comes to Ruby's Pantry in her Lincoln … We are all there for the same thing. I don't think any less of them because they are there." In these articulations, we catch a glimpse of how age-old stigma *can* be interrupted through strategic communication that intervenes upon these negative perceptions.

Apart from Darlene and Trinity, the two Black women who talked about racial stigma, white clients did not experience stigma in their use of RP. Austin, a thirtysomething white man, said that in fact it was quite the opposite, with people always asking about RP. People want to know, "What did he get?" Does he like it? They are very inquisitive about RP. And when he tells them that he got a massive bag of potatoes, six boxes of ice cream, or six energy drinks, their jaws drop. In response to a question about why he feels there is no stigma, he says: "Probably because they know it's a good deal, especially with things today in the economy." According to Bernadette: "With Ruby's Pantry nobody says anything because you're paying for your food. You have a sense of pride about it, and, I mean, it's the American way. If you can get a good deal, you go for it, you know." The twenty-dollar fee was significant in shaping clients' sense of identity and dignity. Janet, an elderly white woman, clarified: "I mean, you pay for the food. Pretty much everybody in my life knows my situation. So it's not that they would say anything, but like the girl whom my roommates work for was afraid she would run into someone. If you did, they are here for the same thing you are ... I pay for what I get here, and that gives you a little bit of dignity as well."

Denouncing "Them"

We could argue that the creation of this space of unity at RP was positive, except for the fact that it reinforced social distance between "guests" at RP and clients of traditional food assistance programs. RP participants were comfortable using RP, but not so comfortable receiving food assistance through SNAP or from traditional food pantries like Chum. This was despite the fact that 80 percent of clients across both sites received some form of government assistance. Similar to Chum clients, RP clients were careful about their language and actions and engaged in self-policing when it came to government and charitable forms of food assistance. Claire observed that though she uses RP, she would never use the food shelf. She is trying to find work, and using the food shelf would hurt her chances: "I just don't want the people to think, 'Oh, you're going to the food shelf' because I'm not trying to diss people who go to the food shelf at all. They can use it. Go for it, but for my style, I'm very talkative and I just don't want to be looked at wrong." Her impression is that people who use food shelves are looked down upon and that only poor people use food shelves. Ashley has used food stamps in the past when her husband was unemployed, but she does not qualify now. However, even when her family did qualify for food stamps, there was always a feeling of guilt—a feeling that there were other people who needed it way more than they did. "I mean, there's people that are way worse off than we ever were ... Sometimes, I would feel kind of guilty for using it. You know, we always feel kind of guilty but it's like I tell my husband, you have to put pride aside, every once in a while, and just do it. You need to do it if it's just a couple of days, once in a while, it's not like we're making a nuisance out of ourselves."

Participants at RP directed suspicion toward people who use SNAP and traditional food shelves, like those at Chum. Katherine noted that though many people need support, there are some who abuse the system: "Naturally, there's going to be people that they don't really need it. Maybe a drug dealer is capable of working but he's out selling drugs instead and he might get food stamps, whatever the program is. I don't know if they still use food stamps or not." The reference to drugs is reminiscent of the stories of welfare recipients manufactured during the welfare debates of the 1990s. Some RP clients were much more explicit in their disdain for people who used traditional food pantries, as seen in a conversation with Bernadette, a white, middle-aged woman and a longtime volunteer at a local food shelf:

Interviewer: Do you feel people look down at other people for using food shelves?

Bernadette: I think sometimes it's the ones that are constantly abusing it, and there are people that will abuse it. Like I said, I helped manage a food shelf for about three years for the Salvation Army and I know of the different abuses because Northern Star would call us and say, "Did this person come over?" Then they got a network going that you'd have to put it on a computer every day and they'd have which ones came to this one and which ones went to the other ones, and knowing that one. They'd go to hit the same places sometimes at the same time so they could track them that well then.

Interviewer: You saw it firsthand.

Bernadette: Mm-hmm [affirmative sound]. We have one at our church right now—a food shelf too. Like I said, yesterday there were forty-one people or forty-one families that came through. They know that the food drive just went through too where you get a lot more, so they figured they're going to get a little more right now and they come out in droves then.

In this excerpt, Bernadette chastises people for taking advantage of the opportunities available to them to provide security for themselves and their families. In using phrases such as "hit the same places" and "come out in droves" and in her eagerness to police the abusers, we catch a glimpse of the deep-seated and negative ideas running through her head about people who use traditional food assistance programs.

Suspicious Skin

For people of color, racial stigma and the stigma of food assistance were inseparable. They had negative experiences riding the buses, conversing with neighbors and coworkers, and even just walking home from the food shelf. People of color who used Chum felt hypervisible at Chum and in the streets; their darker skin color marked them as suspicious in the eyes of others. They policed themselves more intensely and were also more subject to policing by others. Jermain, an African American man, clarified the racialized nature of stigma, saying that sometimes when he is riding the bus or sitting somewhere, he hears people say that "only Natives and Black folks use the food shelves, you know. I hear it, and I go, you know, if they feel like that, and if they don't use it, well ... [laughs] ... it would be more for us." Citizens talked about feeling hypervisible in the streets, like people were staring at them, when they used the food shelf. They also noted that perhaps it was simply paranoia that made them feel that way. For instance, Michele, a young Native woman, doubted her own perception of reality.

Interviewer: Do you think people might sometimes look down on you for using a food shelf or a food program?

Michele: No, no. I get that feeling, it might not even be true.

Interviewer: Where do you get that feeling?

Michele: When you take your little bags from here and get on the bus with them. Maybe it's just me thinking, "They're just looking at my food shelf food." But I don't care. I'm still going to get it. I don't care what people think.

Renee, another young Native woman, talked about people looking at her "funny" on the street and saying things like, "There, she's going to the food shelf," or, sarcastically, "Already at the food shelf today?" In these instances, the psychological impact of neoliberal stigma is clear; it oppresses people in terms of access to food but also shapes their identity and impacts how they live out their lives in community with others.

When asked if he felt people looked down on him for using the food shelf, Isaiah, an older Black man, responded: "I don't know if they look down on me. They were probably thinking that you know I might have sold my food stamps or made a mistake. They really don't know I only get sixteen dollars." Like Darlene, not only did clients use food assistance less because of neoliberal stigma, but they were also more vigilant about how they talked about receiving assistance. Gabrielle, in telling her story, started to describe how long she had been using the food shelf, but then, realizing that this made her look "irresponsible," stopped short:

Interviewer: So, when did you first use the food shelf?

Gabrielle: It has to be, my baby girl is twenty-two and we came here when she was two. So, I'd have to say, I'll give it eighteen years ago, maybe.

Interviewer: So, you've always used the food shelves for eighteen years?

Gabrielle: Always, always, always. *You know, I probably, just let me clarify this* (emphasis added), I've always used it but there was a time when I worked. I'm now looking for work again, and there's been a time I've worked so I might not have used it for a long time because, man, it was like, "We haven't seen you," you know, like that. So, it's not like consistently, just lately consistently because I've been out of work. August will be a year.

There was no need for Gabrielle to clarify this in the interview (or to anyone for that matter), but in doing so we see how the state and its multiple arms create powerful technologies that force individuals to position themselves as defendants in the system (e.g., Fraser 1987).

For Darlene, whom we met at the start of the chapter, stigma occurs at the intersection of her gender and color. She experiences it in government and charitable food assistance settings. Darlene has two boys, so she has used WIC—a government food assistance program for families with little children. Through WIC, she gets four gallons of milk and about twelve dollars' worth of vegetables, juice, eggs, and cereal for the month. "Some days I just go up to the store for WIC and it's wonderful. I come back, they love eggs. The kids will live on cereal if I let them. So that's nice. I appreciate that." But she has had multiple experiences of stigma at the WIC office, mostly revolving around her ability to be a good mother: "One lady, I don't know if it was just a bad day or what, but she asked me if my little one is drinking out of a bottle. I said, well yeah, he's eleven months old. She's just like, well, you know that they need to stop drinking at one year of age? And I was just like, all of my kids have stopped drinking at one year of age. At their birthday, they get no more bottles. And they're fine with it. I was just like, 'wow, you are so judgmental.'" Darlene, a Black mother on welfare, carries the burden of her demographic markers. Falling into the trope of the "Black welfare queen," neoliberal stigma is intensified for her because of the racial subtext. In the last decade, the new public health paradigm inscribed with neoliberal values of self-help, personal responsibility, and "choice" has also heightened stigma experiences for women like Darlene (Kirkland 2011). In this paradigm, good health is maintained through proper diet, exercise, adequate sleep, a healthy environment, and good child-rearing practices. In this responsibilization narrative, mothers must institute proper eating habits for children, such that they do not become an economic burden on society. Nearly twenty-five years after the passage of the Welfare Reform Act, a scapegoat is still found in women of color and mothers. Finding legitimacy in science, these mothers are accused of bad parenting and bad decision-making, as shown in the bottle-feeding discussion at the WIC office.

Trinity described the intense stigma she confronted while trying to sign up for SNAP. She explained that there was a four-year period in her life when her kids were little and her marriage had ended and she found herself in need of public assistance. For each month of those four years, Trinity found herself interacting with several county offices while seeking assistance. For Trinity, "the cruelty was extraordinary" when her son fell sick and she still had to beg to receive her assistance in a timely manner. Her thirteen-year-old son had a snowboarding accident and ruptured his spleen. She tried to apply for food stamps, but the caseworkers gave her the runaround. She finally had to threaten them with legal action, after which she received her food stamps pretty quickly, but it had taken a month to reach that point. Trinity was disrespected, stigmatized, and abused. Her gender, motherhood, and marital status played an unquantifiable role in the multiplicative forces of oppression she faced in the public assistance system. Indeed, as Seccombe (2011) points out women like Trinity, separated from their male partners with multiple children, "the welfare mothers" and "welfare queens," were at the heart of public discourse leading up to the Welfare Reform Act. These discourses helped secure public support for the removal of welfare entitlements, as well as the mobilization of a series of punitive workfare programs that continue to oppress women today.

Field Note: Racist Talk

There was a lull in clients today. I noticed Frank, the food shelf director, and Cindy, a longtime volunteer, shooting the breeze, so I went to join them. They talked about fish for a while. Cindy said she hated freshwater fish and could not understand how people in Duluth love walleye. After a while, I politely changed the subject by asking what they do with all the client data collected from the intake interviews. Cindy explained that it was all entered into a database and kept on file. Frank is not sure why they collect the data or what it is used for. Cindy mentioned that the data helps them to keep track of who is getting what. This reminded her of an article in the newspaper a few days ago about two people in Wisconsin committing food stamp fraud. She said with relief: "It wasn't at our level [meaning the level of the intake interviewer], but at a higher level." Frank remembered the story and said that the woman was in jail and had sold her EBT card for pennies on the dollar, to which Cindy replied, "Oh yes, for a cigarette here or some cocaine there."

At this point, a white female client came in, a thirtysomething, wearing a tank top and jeans, about forty pounds overweight, and wheeling a pushcart to carry out her food. She was flustered, out of breath, and consistently wiping her brow, and she gasped in a loud voice, "I haven't been in here in a while." Cindy replied in a friendly voice, "Go grab a form, fill it out, and I'll take care of you right here." Frank said, "Take a breath, we're in noooo hurry [giggling]." When I saw her come in, I moved to the other end of the room so that she could have privacy while being interviewed, but I was still hovering around. She stated in a loud voice, "I'm pregnant, that's why I'm so hot."

While she was filling out the form, Frank and Cindy continued their conversation about food stamp fraud. She overheard the conversation and, a moment later, scanning the room and finding me in the far corner, chimed in: "I don't mean to be like that or anything, I don't meant to offend anyone, I mean I don't mean any disrespect. Seriously, I have a ton of Black friends, but really it's the Blacks that do it. I mean, they're the ones that do this stuff and then turn to you and say, 'You are a racist.' You know, they do the same thing with cops, they do that stuff and then look at the cops and say, 'You're the racist.' I mean, I literally do not have any food at home, that's why I'm here. I'm pregnant and so I need food. I literally do not have any food at home, this [pointing] is all the food that I have." Frank had a thoughtful smile on his face as she said this, although it was hard to read what that smile meant. Cindy asked her for her ID so they could go through the procedures. I said nothing. Life just seemed to move on at the food shelf that evening without skipping a beat.

I went back into the pantry, my heart pounding as I waited to escort her around the food shelf. I welcomed her, but I was still shaky from the symbolic violence that had just occurred. I should note here that while I call it symbolic, the effects of racism are physical and embodied. Quite simply you feel its effects coursing through your body. Your heart rate increases, your body goes cold, your palms start to sweat, you can feel blood rushing to your brain—and, in my case clouding it over, your hair stands on end, your voice catches in your throat, and you feel as if someone just dug out your stomach with a blunt instrument. This is not something white people in their racial comfort zones ever experience in the presence of racist talk, but it is a commonly shared experience for people of color—and it shows up in the health disparities literature as increased cortisol levels, heightened stress, and lowered life expectancy.

The client was bubbly as we went around, polite, and continually apologetic because she kept forgetting how many points she had left. I had to repeat everything over and over again. She said it was her ADHD and said many times to me, "You're awesome, you're so awesome." When it was time to pick her grains, she said, "Nope, I don't want cereal, I'll take the pasta because I have WIC, so I am already stocked up on cereal." When we got to the milk, she said the same thing: "Nope, I don't need milk because I am already stocked up on that because I have WIC." It made me think back to her earlier statement, now seeming more and more disingenuous: "I literally do not have any food at home, this is all the food that I have." Usually, this would not have bothered me. In fact, having only milk, eggs, and cereal in a context of relative deprivation is indeed literally nothing; however, her racial accusations made me evaluate her statement more harshly.

By the time we got to the end of her "shopping," I had forgotten about her racial aggression and ended up giving her a lot of extra little hygiene items: conditioner, shampoo, and soaps. I even picked the best name brands from the lot to give to her because I knew clients appreciated brands they could recognize. As I write this entry, I am angry at myself. I wish I had the presence of mind not to have given her extra stuff. Maybe there is something about my own colonized mind that cannot hold on to hate. At the time, all I was thinking about was the fact that she was pregnant and how awful my own pregnancy was. Nice-smelling things like a new shampoo or soap felt so good in those months—a little respite. And I wanted desperately to be able to give her that. A clean body and a cup of tea. But even now I remain puzzled about why, even after she saw me, she continued to air her ugly racial aggression. Sure she made several disclaimers before she spewed her nasty comments, but the fact that she named out loud the "Blacks" as the "ones who do it" is disconcerting to me. If she had thought I was Black, surely she would not have singularly identified Black people as perpetrators. Perhaps I coded Native to her and she is privy to the tensions in Duluth between poor Native and Black populations. Or perhaps she correctly profiled me as being from India and knows that Indian culture carries within it colorism and severe anti-Black racism. So either she thought I would agree with her claims because I harbored anti-Blackness within me or she just did not care what I—a brown, female, immigrant-looking body—thought. Either way, I was just too insignificant in her eyes, except for some pitiful "I have a Black friend" type disclaimers. I am also grateful that I am usually not in the room when such racist talk occurs. This incident illuminated for me the racialized subtext for the discourses of suspicion that exist in food pantry spaces.

"White Folks Used to Whip Black People, and ... Now They're Living Together"

Consciousness as a form of agency and resistance is an important theme in Black feminist thought. Patricia Hill Collins (2004) writes about consciousness as a sphere of freedom and a sphere of activism for historically oppressed groups—in particular, Black women, who in their material realities are forced to conform to the prevailing social order:

> If Black women find themselves in settings where total conformity is expected, and where traditional forms of activism such as voting, participating in collective movements, and officeholding are impossible, then the individual women who in their consciousness choose to be self-defined and self-evaluating are, in fact, activists. They are retaining a grip over their definition as subjects, as full humans, and rejecting definitions of themselves as the objectified "other." ... People who view themselves as fully human, as subjects, become activists, no matter how limited the sphere of their activism may be. By returning subjectivity to Black women, Black feminists return activism as well. (114–115)

In her work on marginality, bell hooks (2004) argues that for oppressed groups, the margins can be spaces of creativity, radical openness, and possibility—the possibility to develop a radical perspective from which to see, create, and imagine an alternative world. She points out that there is a difference between marginality imposed by oppressive structures and marginality that one chooses as a site of resistance and radical openness. The margins as a site of radical openness is not a mythic space but one that comes from lived experience—a place that the oppressed come to through struggles, through suffering and pain. The margins provide those who are within them with an *oppositional world view*, a mode of seeing that is unknown to the oppressor, that sustains oppressed peoples and enables them to transcend poverty and despair and build solidarity. She writes: "For me this space of radical openness is a margin—a profound edge. Locating oneself there is difficult yet necessary. It is not a 'safe' place. One is always at risk" (156).

The voices of Black women and men in this study revealed complexities and contradictions that went far beyond Us and Them dichotomies and in so doing revealed sites of radical openness. Indeed, the small-minded naked racism that they encountered at government offices, in employment situations, in stores, in the neighborhoods where they lived, and on streets and buses stood in stark contrast to their own rational, progressive, and educated articulations. In their voices, the notions of consciousness and oppositional consciousness through the pain of lived experience rang clear. Jermain noted that the racism in Duluth really "gets under my skin." When asked to elaborate, he explained:

> Well, it's up here. You got your Scandinavians, Swedes, and, you have your Black folks, and Natives, and they look down upon them. They think that all Indians drink, you know, get drunk. And they think that Black folks are not supposed to own anything. That's how they were raised, that's how they were taught. All behavior is learned. Nobody's born a racist, that's learned. So, I just look at them and I just wonder, I know what their parents were like. Because, it's all learned. I mean, when I was growing up ... I remember my aunt and my grandparents saying, "You have to watch yourself with white folks," because of their past experiences; back before civil rights, they experienced the white and the Black bathrooms, and all of that stuff, so it's hard for people to change. It's hard. How could you experience how white folks used to whip Black people, and then believe that now they're living together. It's hard for them to comprehend that.

In this astute sociological analysis, which links racism that exists today with the violent brutality of racism of the past, Jermain articulates a deep understanding of the role of structural racism. Toward the end of the interview, Jermain disclosed that he had a biracial daughter and that explaining racism to her has been challenging. He said: "So, she's well-rounded. She's well-rounded. It tickles me, because a couple weeks ago, she came into the house, and she said, 'Dad, a red truck just went by, and called me a nigger.' And we were laughing, because that was the first time somebody had called her a nigger. And she was laughing. It stamps her Black side. She's like, 'I am Black.' We laughed about it." In this instance, we catch a glimpse of the margins as a site of resistance. Here father and daughter use humor to resist the brute force of racism hurtling toward them.

For many of the African American women and men in the study, the phrase "we all bleed the same" came up over and over again as way to make sense of, live with, and transcend everyday racism and structural racism. Consistent with hooks, this was not some clichéd vision imposed on them by the oppressive structures around them, but a vision that they chose as a site of radical openness through embodied experiences of discrimination. Clayton methodically described four of his most recent experiences of racism in Duluth, which included the "N-word," being followed around in a store, and having his possessions checked for stolen items. In a typical pattern of whiteness, someone reported him as being suspicious. He recounted: "'Well someone told us that you were probably doing some stealing.' I was like, you know what, let's go back in the store and I want you to look through each and every bag, I want to see what you see that's not on this receipt of purchase. Excuse me for getting melodramatic, but it burns me up when people are that ignorant, very ignorant." Despite being enraged, Clayton offered a vision of racial unity and interconnectedness, using the phrase "we bleed the same": "I don't see it being a Black and white situation. I don't see that because like I said we're all human, we bleed the same blood, we have dreams, we have nightmares, we cry, we laugh, we eat, we sleep, we live, we die, we fall, we buy dessert—I mean, what's the difference between our skin color? It's not where you come from, it's who you are right now and what you can do later on down the road of life." Gabrielle, who used to be a certified nurse assistant has experienced plenty of racism in her life and, like Clayton, boils it down to ignorance. She said: "I always say to myself they're ignorant, and they're ignorant because we all bleed the same."

Antoine, a fiftysomething African American man, noted that he has lived with racism for so long that it does not bother him anymore. He grew up in the Deep South with memories of Jim Crow fresh in his mind:

Interviewer: When did it stop bothering you? How do you get to that place?

Antoine: As a child. I was in a cotton field, so I've seen what my grandparents went through. You know what they had to go through with the color?

Interviewer: Yeah.

Antoine: Be it N-word or whatever. My grandmother said don't you never hate nothing because of the color. Because you don't even know nothing until you talk to that person. I can't hate nothing. I can hate what you hate, because you hate it, but I ain't never going to try to ... I don't have it in me. I'll just leave you alone. If you hate me it's all right, but you got to deal with that. I can go on with where I am because we're all connected. That's what people don't know. We're all connected. We're all different colors. We're all connected and a lot of people don't know that ... Once you learn that then you can accept whatever color, I love you either way.

He goes on to provide a spiritual solution to the problem of racism, while also noting that the markings of race can be a blessing:

Interviewer: What do you think would change minds? How would you, for instance, teach a white person everybody's connected? When is that going to happen?

Antoine: I don't know when that's going to happen. You have to get that for yourself. You have to really look, you have to really sit down and talk to somebody and everybody isn't the same. Everybody's different, but you're going to have to learn to be different yourself ... You just can't hate because of a color because you can't judge anything by the color. We hate because something looks different. It can be a blessing to you really. Somehow you have to get there for yourself. Number one, it's valuable to you. You have to start praying; nobody will give it to you. That's how I got it. I know that the Bible, I can say Lord helps that person. Then they'll know we all connected from the beginning. I hope you know that. I'm glad I know it.

Despite the crushing burden of racism that Antoine carries, the interconnectedness of human beings across racial lines and the power of prayer create a site of radical openness.

People of color typically expressed a sense of solidarity with others at the food pantry. They inverted neoliberal logic and discourses of fraud and abuse by demonstrating empathy and trust of people's motives. Antoine provided a thoughtful analysis of who was at the food shelf: "If you got kids you got to feed them first and they always will pull your coattail. I'm hungry, I'm hungry. That's not good to hear. I think some of them are worse off than me, especially when you have kids. They're pretty much doing the same thing I'm doing—trying to stay alive with food." Renee, a young Native woman, also described a similar understanding of why people were at the food shelf, without offering any caveats: "I really have no impression; if they need food, that's it. They need some help; I don't think they're just doing it because they're just doing it, they need food." Clayton expressed empathy with others at the food pantry: "I mean, they are here for the same purpose I'm here—to survive, to eat, to make sure they have enough food on the table for their family. They are the same as me." He adds: "People that stay in glass houses should dare not throw stones. If you are in the same situation as they are, then don't criticize and don't belittle because you're in the same boat." In using the phrases "in the same boat" and "they are the same as me," Clayton powerfully speaks to the possibility of unity and community even in spaces of scarcity.

Conclusion

This chapter shows how age-old welfare discourses can still be found in food pantry spaces today, with a few updates to the language. These discourses, when deployed, reinforce separations between Us and Them—the paradigmatic Other. In this chapter, neoliberal narratives were at the front and center of the ways in which clients processed their identities; economic identity became the primary parameter through which citizens evaluated themselves and others. Neoliberal stigma created a culture of suspicion at Chum, where people were hypervigilant and self-conscious about their language, opinions, and behaviors. Clients engaged in continuous self-surveillance, self-discipline, and self-censorship and, by the same token, cast suspicion on the motives, intentions, and behavior of others. For people of color, the stigma of race intersected with the stigma of welfare, multiplying the effects of stigma but also creating sites of radical resistance, by which Us and Them dichotomies and neoliberal logic were disrupted.

In this study, the suspicion that citizens levied against each other resonated with the phenomenon of horizontal violence described by Brazilian adult educator and organizer Paulo Freire (1970) in *Pedagogy of the Oppressed*. Freire's life's work involved organizing working-class people to achieve political freedoms—people who were primarily descendants of African slaves brought by Spanish colonizers to Brazil. Drawing on Marxist theory, Freire observed that *horizontal violence*, violence perpetrated by people in the same economic class against each other, emerged for two reasons: divide-and-rule strategies employed by the oppressor, and a lack of class-based consciousness among disenfranchised groups. He argued that because people do not have any consciousness of themselves as an oppressed class, each man retained his individualism and desire for property, conditioned by what he has seen before him. All in all, divide and rule strategies turned people within a socioeconomic class against each other and were necessary for colonizers to achieve their goals.

At Chum and RP, Reagan's "Cadillac-driving Chicago welfare queen" story was still the discursive and ideological linchpin that severed the community. This forty-year-old antipoor agenda was taken up by citizens who turned on each other and did not see themselves as being in the same boat. In this context, however, what made a difference to collective identity was whether or not organizational discourses directly addressed this linchpin. Organizational discourses played an important role in reformulating identities. For instance, RP engaged directly with welfare discourses by constructing clients as hardworking, responsible, and proud Americans. Through talk, text, and practices, RP situated itself as separate and different from traditional government assistance programs, stating boldly that there was no fraud or abuse to be had at RP. RP brought people together in ways that affirmed their identities, relationships, and class positions in society while otherizing citizens who used more traditional food assistance programs. On the other hand, Chum did not engage in any meaningful discursive work to reframe its food pantry or clients as such age-old welfare discourses ran full steam ahead. In the absence of counternarratives, citizens continued to perpetuate discourses of Black welfare queens, Cadillacs and Lincolns, and fraud and abuse. Whereas RP brought people together, creating a culture of unity and community, Chum reinforced a culture of suspicion, in which feelings of shame, guilt, and anxiety were ever present among clients. The problem with cultures of suspicion is that they work actively to prevent people from joining together.

Implications for Practice and Policy

The system of public assistance in the United States has inscribed within it a variety of oppressive ideologies. Food pantries cannot and will not end hunger, but what they do instead is manage hunger and control the poor through the perpetuation of neoliberal forms of stigma. The problem with entrepreneurial pantries like RP is that they reinforce neoliberal logic when it comes to food taking us further away from rights-based approaches and legal entitlements. Traditional food pantries would do well to tackle neoliberal stigma by shifting stigmatizing narratives surrounding legal entitlements in the United States, where the term *entitlement* has often been cast in a negative light, being associated with welfare discourses, government overspending, and national debt. However, the term itself is inherently positive, connoting security and collective solidarity (Jost 2003). These new narratives are important to interrupt the culture of suspicion, which prevents the creation of spaces in which people can gather, discuss, and organize resistance in solidarity with each other.

In comparing Chum and RP, we find that stigma is not natural or inevitable but created and disrupted through discursive practices that mark people. Instead of creating stigmatizing narratives like RP, pantries can create new stories and narratives that identify and debunk common tropes and stereotypes about welfare recipients (e.g., the Cadillac trope, moral discourses of need, etc.), and point toward prosocial positions of antiracism, antisexism, legal entitlements, and citizenship. Food pantries should replace stigmatizing narratives with narratives inspired by Clayton, who from his site of creativity, radical openness, and possibility was able to say, "We're all human, we bleed the same blood, we have dreams, we have nightmares, we cry, we laugh, we eat, we sleep, we live, we die, we fall, we buy dessert." Food pantries should replace narratives of fraud and abuse with those that emphasize the right to adequate food, food sovereignty, and community food security perspectives. Educating staff, volunteers, and clients about the meaning of legal entitlements would go a long way toward shifting how they perceive their roles. In time, these new stories using the language of justice, equity, and rights may eventually displace the neoliberal language of fraud and abuse, hard work, and personal responsibility.

7   Health Citizens: Choosing Good Food amid Scarcity

Interviewer: What do you typically pick up from the food pantry?

Victor: I pick up cereal, cheese, milk, bread, vegetables, yes, that's what I get from here. Peanut butter, of course. Peanut butter, and tuna ... What else is there? Ramen noodles, ramen noodles and macaroni and cheese.

Interviewer: You get canned vegetables?

Victor: Canned vegetables and fruit also. I try to get fresh vegetables also, green peppers, onions, tomatoes, and cucumbers.

Interviewer: When it comes to getting food from food shelves, what are you thinking about when you choose that food?

Victor: I'm thinking about how many different meals I can make with the certain foods I'm getting. I'm not used to cooking for one or two people. I'm used to cooking for the kids also and all of that. How many different meals can I make with these kinds of foods? I quickly glance over everything and see what's on the shelves and then I go from there. Basically, when I have the kids, it's basically all about them. What will they eat? I can eat anything and the kids won't. That's how I looked about everything when I first came in. You always get the milk, cheese, bread, and cereal, you always get that stuff no matter what. I do, at least.

Interviewer: What about food from the grocery store when you're using your own money or SNAP, what's important to you?

Victor: Same thing. Same thing, yes, same thing. You treat yourself a little better with your food stamps; you can buy anything, basically. Some things I do not, there's generic stuff that you can buy that's just as good as the regular stuff ...

Interviewer: So cost is important to you as well?

Victor: Oh yes, that's basically the biggest thing. If it's not on sale, I don't go shopping ... I try to get the best deals and the best coupons for everything.

—Victor, Native male, Chum client

Politics, Public Health, and Citizenship: America's Harvest Box

Victor is a thirty-seven-year-old Native man and a single dad who shares custody of his children with his former partner. Victor represents the group of single parents with children that suffers disproportionately from food insecurity. Although the average rate of food insecurity in the United States is about 15 percent, for households with children headed by a single man, food insecurity is 23.1 percent; for households with children headed by a single woman, it is 34.4 percent (United States Department of Health and Human Services 2014). As we see in Victor's interview, he is thoughtful, enterprising, and judicious in how he procures food for his family. The Chum food pantry does not distribute enough meat, so he buys meat from the store with his SNAP benefits. At Chum, he gets milk, bread, and any available proteins, like tuna and peanut butter. Victor uses his SNAP benefits carefully to get the best deals on food. He has a car, which allows him to compare deals at different stores almost daily. SNAP allows him a bit of dignity, because unlike the food pantry he gets to choose what he wants at the grocery store. As he notes, "You treat yourself a little better." His top priorities are "what is going to last longer" and "what do the kids want."

Discourses surrounding men, and Native men in particular, rarely if ever portray them as caregivers—dads involved in taking care of the kids. Welfare and SNAP recipients are further demonized, with suspicion cast on their character, choices, and morality. In this snapshot, we see Victor, the paradigmatic Other, at the heart of family, caregiving, and food. We see Victor making careful choices, balancing cost, nutrition, and the desires of his family as he picks up food at the grocery store and food pantry.

Even as Victor goes about making careful food choices every day, the political system continues to denigrate his character and decision-making skills. In February 2018, the Trump administration unveiled a proposal for America's Harvest Box as part of the 2019 budget. In one fell swoop, the proposal called into question Victor's agency and hard work and the care that he takes to procure food for his family. In one fell swoop, the modicum of dignity that Victor experiences at the grocery store has been placed in jeopardy. The proposal plans to replace half of the money households receive via SNAP with a box of government-picked, nonperishable foods every month (Thrush 2018). Instead of allowing people to choose their own food, the plan is to give them a box of prepackaged industrial surplus foods—USDA foods. The Agricultural Marketing Service (AMS) wing of the USDA purchases a variety of American-produced and American-processed commodity food products, which are delivered to schools, food banks, and households across the country to be used in federal assistance programs; these are called *government commodity foods* or *USDA foods*. USDA foods are typically subsidized through the Agricultural Farm Bill and thus are subject to government priorities and the availability of surplus; therefore, they serve government and corporate interests. The plan developed by the USDA was praised by Agriculture Secretary Sonny Perdue as "a bold, innovative approach" (as cited in Thrush 2018).

Significantly, in addition to "saving the government billions," America's Harvest Box is being touted for its capacity to provide more nutritious food to poor people than they typically have access to. How does the foremost agency responsible for addressing hunger and nutrition in the nation propose a plan that serves up cheap industrial food to forty million food insecure people and call it nutritious? Marion Nestle (2002), in her landmark research on the relationship between the government and the food industry, pointed out the conflict of interest created by the USDA's dual mandate to protect agricultural interests and advise the public about healthy diets. The government subsidizes food production via price supports for sugar, corn, and milk and facilitates lower tax rates and marketing programs for commodity foods. Agricultural corporations benefit from these subsidies and lobby Congress to continue this support, which becomes sedimented in the Farm Bill and other agricultural policies. Thus, as Nestle notes, "Dietary guidelines necessarily are political compromises between what science tells us about nutrition and health and what is good for the food industry" (30).

America's Harvest Box puts on display the double standards related to food in the United States. Similar to food pantries and soup kitchens, America's Harvest Box is just another receptacle to channel industrial surplus food to the poor. The good food movement has done much to show how whole foods, fresh fruits and vegetables, whole grains, lean meats, and minimally processed foods are the kinds of foods we should be eating—good food—yet access to these foods is consistently denied to the poor, who are then blamed for making bad choices—a key logic of neoliberal stigma. In a neoliberal era, the doctrine of *health citizenship* is deployed to control the bodies of the poor and food insecure. Health citizenship uses the language of "rights and duties" and encompasses the idea that people should take responsibility for their bodies by eating good food and limiting harm to others through lifestyle changes (Zoller 2005). Sidestepping issues of access, good health citizens contribute to the economy and do not burden the health system with excess sickness and disease. Conversely, when people are seen as irresponsible and not making good choices, they are blamed for it. These negative attributions serve to legitimize the less than adequate legal entitlements provided to the hungry.

In the case of America's Harvest Box, the bodies of Victor and his family are used as sites of control to serve the interests of political and business entities; as Dickinson (2013, 9) points out, the trap of cheap food is an "embodied form of discrimination." The distribution of bad food is normalized, even justified, because people like Victor are deemed irresponsible. The idea of America's Harvest Box continues down a well-worn path of removing access to good food for the poor and replacing it with cheap, high-fat, high-sugar, processed industrial foods. It also follows a well-worn path of casting aspersions on the choices, responsibility, and moral fiber of people on welfare. For Native people, this is not a new phenomenon. Native communities have identified America's Harvest Box as the same type of federal food assistance that tribes have historically received as part of the Food Distribution Program on Indian Reservations, with devastating implications for health and stigma (Thrush 2018). Indeed, the Food Research and Action Center noted that America's Harvest Box would be "costly, inefficient, stigmatizing, and prone to failure" (Evich 2018).

It is clear today that poor citizens do not get to choose or make genuine choices about what they eat; they have different economic means and therefore differ in their ability to purchase certain foods. Nestle (2002, 15) writes: "We select diets within the context of the social, economic, and cultural environment in which we live. When food or money is scarce, people do not have the luxury of choice; for much of the world's population, the first consideration is getting enough food to meet biological needs for energy and nutrients." There is a complete failure to acknowledge political and systemic factors that remove choice for people. In the absence of adequate entitlements, proposals that serve up boxes of industrial food to families are just another vestige of stigma against the poor—stigma that is antithetical to the goals of food justice. Although the proposal will likely never be enacted because it is so impractical, it has already had an effect. It communicates a stigmatizing message about people like Victor, which goes something like this: "We think you make bad food choices, so we'll continue to give you bad food, but food that is slightly better than if you had to choose for yourself."

Goal of the Chapter

Against a backdrop of top-down political proposals and stigmatizing discourses, the goal of this chapter is to show how hungry and food insecure citizens navigate food choices and perform health citizenship amid material constraint. The chapter sheds light on how citizens choose diets in the context of social, economic, and cultural environments, even in the absence of genuine choice. The chapter reports on what *good food* means to food insecure people and the strategies they use to stretch food. In the meanings attributed to good food, we find that food insecure individuals have a good understanding of what foods they should be eating and what foods are bad for them; however, in practice, their food choices are constrained by context and access to resources. The chapter shows how stigma is tied to the quality of food, which is implicated in visible markings on the food—either through rotting food or name brands. In the voices of the hungry, we hear about the importance of good food, the occasional treat, gardening, and nutrition; how they feel more energetic after eating good food; and the shame they feel when given bad food.

Quantity and Quality of Food at Chum and RP

The food distributed at Chum falls into the categories of grain (bread, pasta, rice, cereal), protein (frozen meat, peanut butter, and canned tuna/salmon), dairy (fresh milk, powdered milk, and yogurt), canned soup/meals (mac and cheese, condensed soups, hamburger helper), and fruits and veggies (canned and some fresh). Canned veggies include corn, peas, a variety of beans, spinach, and even sauerkraut. Much of the food is processed (boxed and canned) to allow for a longer shelf life and ease of transportation, but because of this it also has higher levels of sodium, sugar, and preservatives compared to fresh foods. In terms of fresh produce, there was a range of freshness depending on which "generation" the food was. At Chum, I saw fresh brussels sprouts, apples, pears, butternut squash, pallets of red tomatoes, potatoes, and multicolored peppers, but I also saw rotten produce and vegetables that were past their prime. Chum might receive fresh heirloom tomatoes directly from an urban garden, in which case the vegetables were in excellent condition. However, if the produce came from Second Harvest, which got it from another donor, which got it from a third donor, then this third generation of food was of much poorer quality. Other than produce, the range of food choices that clients encountered each month was the same: grain, protein, dairy, canned soup/meals, and fruits and veggies. There were typically no sugar-sweetened beverages distributed, but clients could get ground coffee (four ounces), tea (four to five tea bags), hot chocolate (a couple of small packets for the household), or bottled/canned water (one per individual in the household). Most chose the coffee because even a little was unaffordable to them at the grocery store. Depending on the size of the household, clients took away anywhere between twenty pounds of food (for a one-person household) and 150 pounds of food (for a seven-person household).

Although both food pantries relied on industrial food, there was a big difference between Chum and RP food in terms of quantity and nutritional value. At RP, clients paid twenty dollars for a share and received one hundred dollars' worth of food, which they carried away in laundry baskets, suitcases, and cartons. The quantity, even for a single person and regardless of family size, ranged from between seventy-five to one hundred pounds of food. RP typically distributed some protein, dairy, grain, and fruits and vegetables, but the exact form, quality, and nutritional content of these items was not certain. For instance, *vegetables* could refer to a twenty-pound sack of potatoes or a ten-gallon Ziploc bag of carrot puree—the kind that a restaurant would use. Consistent with RP's conservative agenda, there were far fewer regulations and restrictions on the kinds of food distributed. This meant that food quality was really hit or miss. You could get a twenty-pound sack of potatoes, but more than half of those potatoes could be rotten. Volunteers spent a lot of time sorting through bad food, but even so one could end up with a lot of rotten food at home. In addition, the nutritional quality of the food was also hit or miss. For instance, RP often distributed large tubs of ice cream, whipped cream, and packs of soda; ice cream counted as dairy and frozen cakes and bakery items counted as grains. RP did not have a nutritional breakdown of food and, unlike Chum, nutritionists were not involved in ascertaining food requirements.

Meanings of Good Food

The meaning of the term *nutritious* has undergone several shifts in the past century, from vitamin-enhanced processed foods being good for you to these very same foods being seen as responsible for atherosclerosis and other "diseases of civilization" (Dixon 2009). Client articulations reflected these shifts, uncertainties, and anxieties. Clients talked about nutrition as comprised of (a) the biochemical components of food and/or (b) whole, nonprocessed, and nonindustrial foods. With regard to biochemical understandings, the role of vitamins in nutrition was stressed. Michele, a middle-aged Native woman, noted: "The definition of nutritious to me would be something that's healthy, that gives you your vitamins and stuff that you need. Your vitamins. It feeds your body more than just making you full." Claire, a white woman, enjoys barbecued chicken, fish, baked potatoes, and fresh tomatoes. In her family, she says, "nothing is cooked too much, because it takes the vitamins out of it." There were several men who, concerned about getting enough nutrition, took vitamins to supplement their diets. Gary reached into his bag and pulled out a bottle, saying: "I take these vitamins every day. There is a regular multivitamin, and thiamin, and Vitamin B1 or something. If I really don't eat that well, I'm still getting some vitamins." Taking these supplements was more affordable for these men than buying good food.

Jane Dixon (2009) writes that nutritionism has given rise to the "nutricentric citizen," whose life is ruled by abstract biomarkers such as "good" and "bad" cholesterol, daily calorie and protein requirements, and the body mass index (BMI). Tyrone, a young Black man, around twenty-two years of age, is an apt example of the nutricentric citizen. He is careful, even anxious, about his food choices, making sure to eat fruits and vegetables with as many meals as he could. Tyrone used to be a "big guy" but was determined to lose weight; he lost over eighty pounds by walking and biking one whole summer when he was out of school. These days, Tyrone "gets his nutrition" in whatever way he can, including vegetable juices, which he finds is a more cost-effective way to consume fruits and vegetables. He explained: "Yeah, because sometimes I don't eat it as much so, like I say, I try to buy the juices that has all of it in there so I can get the intake more instead of me eating just the apple or an orange and eating broccoli, spinach. I can buy two different kinds that either have one of the same things or both of them together."

Different from nutricentric clients, other participants talked about good food as food that was "fresh" and "nonprocessed." Ashley, a young white mother, explained that good food was "not overly processed" and a "balanced diet." She makes sure to have at least three food groups with every meal and food with a lot of nutrients. "I try to get fresh veggies, low-fat meats, and stuff like that." Ashely is health conscious and started a "cleanse" a few months ago, in which she cut out all meats, sugars, and processed foods. Paula, a middle-aged white woman, noted that she had become more conscious of consuming processed foods after her husband passed away from cancer: "Yeah. I try not to eat processed foods if I can. Pizza or something, every once in a while is alright. Yeah. Processed foods are going to be bad for you. I've been eating more vegetables and leanest cuts of meats."

Across race and gender, participants articulated a mind-body connection when it came to food. Rick, a thirtysomething white man and a client of RP, noted "feeling the difference" after eating a balanced meal compared to fast food. Unfortunately, as a teacher, he rarely got time to prepare his own food, and even buying lunch at the cafeteria was too expensive, so he eats fast food a few times week. Bill also noted feeling the difference when he had not eaten right:

> If you're not feeling the best because you haven't been eating right, or you haven't had a meal, you're a little stressed about that, or you're tired, and a little bit worn out, because you've lost energy from not eating. And of course, that not only saps your physical strength, but it saps your mental strength as well, and you're much more susceptible to mood swings and other people's mood swings and, you know where you'd just turn around and walk away from somebody if you were feeling good, because they're being such a pain in the butt and you want to grab them by the neck and squeeze them till their head pops, you know. But, which is totally socially unacceptable

Trinity discussed the positive effect good food had on her body and mind: "Instead of buying for $3.33, a McDouble, a small fry, and a large pop, for that same three dollars, you could buy a banana, half a pint of milk, and a package of peanuts and you would feel so much better. Your body would actually have energy and your brain would be crisp and refreshed. Where with the soda and the fat is going to bog down and slow down your brain, bog down, slow down your body." Trinity was also quick to acknowledge the difficulty of maintaining a healthy diet. While she tried to be health conscious, there were times she did not have the resources to do so.

People of Color and the Long Arc of Food Injustice

People of color articulated anxieties linked to eating industrial food—concerns that were linked to their histories and biographies. Jermain showed a distrust of scientific experts and encouraged a return to traditional and cultural foods:

> Well, I don't listen, I remember they used to say, "an apple a day keeps the doctor away," then I heard them say apples wasn't as good for you as they said. And, it seemed like everything that they used to say was good for me, well now it's bad for you. So, I don't know. I know, they say fried foods are not good for you. I don't know, but my grandparents, they lived on fried foods. They lived to be ninety and eighty-seven years old. You know, if I live that long, I'm good, you know. So, I think you can over, over-analyze stuff, you know. It is what it is. You know, God gave us this for nutrition, for us to eat. So, why should I find fault?

For Jermain, nutrition should not be overcomplicated but should involve following traditional food ways. His views resonate with Dixon's recommendation to follow a "preindustrial ecological nutrition approach," which moves beyond the biochemical orientation to include social, cultural, and environmental dimensions.

Antoine grew up in the South, where he learned how to grow food as a son of a sharecropper. He does not trust the industrial capitalist food system; for him, growing your own food is the only real solution. In his words, we catch a glimpse of the intersection between hunger and history as Antoine evokes Jim Crow segregation and white supremacist policies of the USDA:

Interviewer: Have you ever done gardening?

Antoine: I've done that. I come from the South. That's how we ate. We had to get out there and dig in the dirt. It isn't easy, but it sure pays off. Food really is good when you get it when it comes up. That's a blessing.

Interviewer: If somebody gave you a little piece of land over here you would be ...

Antoine: Willing to get out there and do it? I like to watch it grow. I like to see stuff grow, especially food. I could get out there and do that. I did it when I was a child. When I was a little boy, I used to get out with my grand-mamma. In the South you had land; it wasn't our land, but we worked it. We ate from it. Corn, okra, watermelon, cantaloupe, all that stuff. I'd love that. That's the best food you can get, straight from the ground, the earth.

Interviewer: Yeah.

Antoine: I don't know what the government is feeding us now, but I know it sure as hell [ain't good] ... I think that's why most of the people have diabetes. Half the world has got diabetes, I believe.

In this brief narrative, we glimpse the long arc of injustice that people of color confront when it comes to food. Hinson and Robinson demonstrate how the Jim Crow era brought years of intense oppression for Black farmers, who, unlike white farmers, were unable to get assistance from the government and therefore could not purchase or own land (Hinson and Robinson 2008). Thus, many were forced into a system of servitude called *sharecropping*, in which Black farmers would rent land from white landowners in return for a share of the crops but often remained in debt and indentured to their landlords. Indeed, US agriculture and labor relations are predicated on structural racism: land was given to white people and taken away from African Americans, Natives, the Chinese, the Japanese, and Latinos (Guthman 2011). This was Antoine's story—and the story of many others as well. Antoine is hungry today, even though he spent his youth doing backbreaking work in the fields, producing wealth for rich white capitalists. However he still sees gardening and "getting it straight from the earth" as a way to protect against an untrustworthy food system. When asked where he had garnered this knowledge of food, he explained: "I think I got it from the South. When we were growing up, we had to grow our food and that's the best. You know what you putting in there and you know what you got. You know what comes up out of the ground, but once somebody else got it and you got your factories you don't know what's in it. I've worked in factories and I've seen people put all kinds of stuff in food and it's not right, but what can we say? I don't have a job any more. I eat nothing but a little bit here and there."

This racialized history is invoked in James's interview as well. James also grew up in Jim Crow South. The grandson of sharecroppers, he grew up growing and eating what today is commodified and sold as *organic*, which, ironically, he cannot afford:

Interviewer: What does the term *nutrition* mean to you?

James: Nutritious food. If I just go back in time, it's your freshly grown and freshly prepared foods. Everything now comes through a processing plant and whatever, so you can only trust that people are making things healthy for us since we've got to go in the store and just pay cash for what we need off the shelf or out of the bins. It's just that trust factor. Nutritious, that's just what I think, fresh foods, like growing your own vegetables, having your own chickens, getting your own eggs fresh out of your own barn. Nutritious, to me, is just country living. It's not city living because what I heard was everything has become instant ... That nutrition thing, it's iffy in the world today. Again, if you were not farm raised or whatever, you've got to deal with what our food processors put out here for us to eat.

Interviewer: What do you suggest us city people do who don't grow all our own stuff?

James: Woo-ee, city people. All I can tell us city folks is, "Hey, when you go to the grocery store, just shop for the best." Organic is so high, and they need not be taxing us for wanting to take care of ourselves. I think everything is just overpriced. They're making it so hard for people to take care of themselves. It's just really hard. When they came out with organic, that just said all the other food is crap. Then they charge you an arm and a limb for organic, so I don't even bother. I've been growing up eating this food all this time. Y'all don't need to be making me spend this extra money that I don't even have to go organic. I can't afford to go organic.

James knows the value of eating good food and wants to eat fresh, whole, and organic foods but cannot afford it. Equally importantly, history and biography make paying such high prices for what should be everyday food—the norm—an added travesty.

In Context: Good Food Is Safe Food

While participants at Chum and RP showed ample knowledge regarding what counts as good or bad food and what is healthy or unhealthy, they adjusted how they thought about healthfulness when confronted with material and physical realties. For instance, Chum clients were health conscious, food conscious, and concerned about industrial food, but when they were at the food shelf, *food safety* was their number-one concern. Industry experts note that expiration dates are rarely used anymore; instead, "best by" dates are used, which tell us that food is still safe to eat past the date, even if it may not look or taste perfect—yet another practice that works in the interests of corporations rather than poor citizens. After all, which one of us, if our child asks for food, would offer them a can of tuna that has lost its flavor, texture, and color? At Chum, clients were aware that they could eat food beyond the best by date, and many did so; however, personal experiences with food poisoning had made them anxious about doing this.

Lived experience had taught clients that food safety should be their top concern at the food pantry. For Isaiah, the quality of food at Chum was fair, so long as he spent time checking the food before bringing it home. He has suffered from food poisoning in the past, so he is careful about what he eats. Victor noted that the food at Chum was okay with some adaptations: "Yes. It's edible, yes, especially if you cook it right." Charlotte pointed out that Chum food was not very good: "It's been sitting too long or it's bruised, and then it starts to ... especially some of the vegetables or fruit, it's rotten." Renee has gotten bad food several times: "Just fresh vegetables and stuff like that that go bad, the milk is sour sometimes." Ashley has even come up with her own strategy for choosing safe food: "I've had issues with noodles, where you get mac and cheese in the box and there's been bugs in them. That kind of stinks. I tend to shy away from the ones that are in boxes because I've had that experience. I look for things that are sealed and a date, or shrink-wrapped or something, so I don't have to worry about that." Xavier was concerned about falling sick from unsafe food: "So, you know, I worry about that kind of stuff because I guess you can get sick. You know what I mean? You see some things like, you might see a spot on a bell pepper or an onion and you cut around it and work with what you can, but that kind of stuff makes me feel like, well, why is this?"

Clients were troubled by the quality of food given to them and where the food came from. These factors made clients anxious about their health. Receiving food that looked bad and was unsafe to eat was not something they took lightly. It communicated to clients that they were not worthy or deserving of decent food. It made them feel otherized, like third-class citizens, and negatively valued. Gabrielle is appreciative of the food from Chum, but feels mistreated when confronted by unsafe food: "I do want to say one thing, that maybe ... Just to say that, maybe the people that volunteer here and that do that food stuff, that they look ... That they don't put stuff out here that's expired. I mean, I could see one or two days, maybe you could work it, but I don't know where it was from, but one time, I was giving him these noodles, and it had bugs in it ... Don't put something out that you wouldn't eat. You know what I mean? You know what I'm saying?"

Clayton is appreciative of Chum, but his food choices are constrained by safety: "Program, thumbs up. In some cases, forgive me, you know, some items are a little out of date, like if it's expired by let's say a few days, a month or so, but I don't relish on it, because if you see something that's outdated, you have a choice, avoid it, improvise, go onto something else, no hard feelings, but I believe whoever is giving them the food should look over the items and say, 'I don't think they should have this one.'" Clayton has concerns about E. coli and salmonella and fears that he or his children will fall sick: "That is very important, because not only am I going to consume it, my children will consume the food as well, so it's very important to ensure the safety of your food." In a statement telling of the experience of stigma, Clayton said: "Just because people need food it doesn't mean that they need any old food. Just don't get them anything. That's just like tossing a bone to the dog with no meat on it. You don't know how long that bone sat on the kitchen table."

In Context: Good Food Is "Fancy Food"

Clients at RP evaluated the food there in the context of their overall foodways; as such, even highly processed industrial food was seen as good food because it was part of a "balanced diet" and because it was food they would usually not have access to. A few clients talked about the poor quality of food from RP. For instance, Katherine worried about the healthfulness of RP food, saying: "Sometimes I feel that ... Sometimes I think the programs set up to help people aren't really giving them the right kind of food. At Ruby's Pantry there's a lot of fattening food that they give, and I just think it would be good if they could give people more fresh produce. There's very little fresh stuff that's ever given out." Notwithstanding critiques, many clients, including those who valued whole foods and fresh foods, thought RP food was of high quality despite how industrial it was. Claire exclaimed that the food was "awesome" in taste: "Everything is really incredible." She added, "I think it's very good quality. Some of the things like tater tots have calories, but those are healthy calories rather than eating a bunch of French fries from McDonald's. I think it's very good quality." When asked about the quality of fruits and vegetables, she said: "I think it's really cool, I'm very thankful for anything we get there because then I don't have to put my pennies for it in the big store, which is expensive." Bernadette also enjoyed the food from RP: "It is good. I don't think they hand out much that is not nutritious except for the cookies one time were really good, another time they handed out so many poppy-seed muffins. Those were so good ... I think they do their best to hand out a well-balanced option, staples, like I said, potatoes and onions and egg, some sort of meat, usually chicken and then other things." The quantity was so vast that people felt they had struck a good deal even on one item. A prime example of this was chicken. The cost of a large pack of chicken thighs or breasts ranges from eight to twelve dollars at the grocery store. RP often distributed two packs of frozen name-brand chicken, a retail value of at least twenty dollars, so clients no doubt saved a lot on just this one item.

The phrases *balanced* and *a good mix* came up frequently. Tony made accommodations for the quality of the food, stating: "All things considered, when you see what's in each delivery, you know, it's pretty much well-balanced. There's usually meat, dairy, some kind of bread product, quite often a pasta, potatoes, vegetables. It's pretty much all around well-balanced." By using the phrase "all things considered," Tony implies that there are other factors to consider beyond quality when assessing the value of food. For Penelope, getting treats from RP was justifiable, given that there was a "good mix of everything": "They try to do a good job of making sure it's a good mix of everything. They try to give you basic staples and they'll like throw in something fun, like the last time we went in, there was ice cream. That's something we normally don't put on our grocery list. You have a lot of good stuff but then you have that treat thing. You know that, everybody needs a little treat once in a while. Or another time, it was cookies, we'd have a ton of cookies." Bernadette admitted there was not much produce at RP, but added, "I mean, it's nothing you can help, but then I can make that up by going to the grocery store with my food stamps and I don't have to worry about that." Here too we see Bernadette making adjustments to her way of thinking about healthy food because of the context in which food was received.

Participants appreciated RP because it gave them access to big-name brands and "fancy food" items that were otherwise unaffordable to them. Although the food was not in the best condition or past its best by dates, the fact that these were name brands made recipients feel valued, special, and like they were getting a good deal. People's eyes would light up on seeing brands like Coke, Malt-o-Meal cereal, Gold'n Plump chicken, and Dole strawberries. These were brands they couldn't afford usually; they usually bought store brand and off-brand foods instead. I heard a little boy exclaim, on seeing the Coke, "Sodas! Oh, that's the best part!" His mum was also excited that they got to take a twelve-pack can of sodas home with them—and they could choose from a variety of products: regular Coke; Coke Zero; Sprite; Dr. Pepper in regular, diet, vanilla, or cherry variants; Mello Yellow in diet or regular variants; and Fanta in diet or regular variants. Another mum shrieked in delight on seeing the sugary kid's cereals, saying, "Well, I don't know who wouldn't like those Choco dynos." Getting name-brand items—even if they were snacks, sodas, and treats—was exciting for families because they were novelties; it made them feel normal and mainstream. Penelope gushed: "It's nice to have sweets in the house once in a while too. That's kind of a good thing for us. Wow … Oh, I can't even … Gosh, I can't even … I know there was yogurt and there was granola and oh, my God, we just died and gone to pig heaven." Claire enjoyed coming to RP because of the "fancier" foods—including juices—that she otherwise would not have access to:

Claire: I always have a meal for myself but this is fancier food that I would have never been able to buy at the store because I live in the dollar store … Tater tots seemed fancy.

Interviewer: If you didn't have this food from Ruby's Pantry, would you substitute it from somewhere else?

Claire: Definitely, I would be buying cheaper things but having those hamburger patties they had one time, that was a big treat. Nothing like that at my house usually. It's usually a sandwich for dinner and I put the veggies on that. Never fills you up enough compared to a hamburger, to be honest … I think it's helped me just to have some nicer quality things that my family doesn't have to buy for me. I don't have to spend fifteen dollars on some hamburger patties at work, that's expensive! I can have fifteen dollars of fancy things for myself.

Claire made her food budget work by cobbling together a variety of resources, but she still could not afford name-brand items—or anything special, for that matter. She said: "Yeah. The Coke was awesome. The fancy juices were nice, not typical that I go to a gas station every day to buy a fancy bottle of juice. Wow, that was really fancy for me. Just have a nice sit-down juice."

Field Note: Two Purple Eggplants
Two eggplants per share! These were the fresh vegetables that RP gave out today. It caused quite a riot! I got a variety of responses from people to these eggplants. Some people had no idea what they were—not even a guess. They looked at me and said, "What's that?" This surprised me because they are always available in the grocery stores in Duluth. With many people, their eyes opened in amazement at how big and beautiful the purple eggplants looked—big smiles for the most part. Some had seen an eggplant before but never eaten one, many did not know how to cook eggplant, and some said, "Ah, there's fancy stuff here today." For people at RP, it was not just the industrial foods that they found fancy, but also vegetables like eggplants that were culturally unfamiliar and that would have been too expensive for them to buy at the store. Most people accepted the two eggplants; there were only three people who refused the eggplants from me point-blank. One person asked me if I had a recipe sheet for how to cook the eggplant. Today, I am reminded about the joy of trying out new and culturally unfamiliar foods.

Stretching Food and Health Concerns

Similar to Victor, who we met at the beginning of the chapter, other clients at RP and Chum were also strategic in how they spent their food stamps at the grocery store and how they used their points at the food pantry. Michelle uses sales and coupons and buys family packs to save money. She is preoccupied with keeping count of how much she has left on her EBT card and in coupons. She explained: "They are on my mind a lot because you can break them down and you've got to count. I am counting because every

thirty days to get meat is a long time so I want to stretch it as far as I can."
Clients hated to go grocery shopping because of the stress and anxiety of
not being able to afford food, let alone good food. A deciding factor in what
to pick up was how long the food could be "stretched." Foods that could be
extended across multiple meals and made people feel full were best. Isaiah
explained:

> Well, I look at the fact of what I need to take to be full. So I allow myself to have
> a decent meal. You know, sometimes I take chicken, which would last me if I cut
> it in half, it would last two different meals, so I freeze half and cook half … They
> give you one pack of meat, according to how many people you have in your
> household, so that is kind of hard. They say it is a week's worth of food but that's
> one pack of meat a week, you know. So then you have to get other things like
> macaroni, things that stretch your food.

For Isaiah, making right choices at the store is important, so he does not go
to the store when he is hungry. "So a lot of times I drink water before I go.
You know, so it fills me up and I make better choices."

There were several health concerns and dietary restrictions running
through clients minds at the grocery store and the food pantry. Morgan is
diabetic and has Crohn's disease and cardiac stents, so she is on three different diets. Gabrielle has type 2 diabetes, so she stays away from sugary foods,
pastas, breads, and potatoes and tends to eat a lot of greens and meats.
Gabrielle gets twenty-three dollars in food stamps, which she uses to get
milk and bread at the grocery store. "Sometimes I'll buy salad stuff because
I love salad. So, lettuce, tomatoes, cucumbers. In Super One, I bought two
tomatoes and crackers for almost two bucks." Renee uses her SNAP benefits
to buy meat at the grocery store and uses the food shelf to get sides. She
has high blood pressure, so she tries to cut down on salty and fatty foods.
Instead of salt, she uses seasonings and steams or bakes her food. She is also
conscious about the meat she buys: "I try to stay off the pork, but that really
is the cheapest stuff; the beef stuff is really high, so it's a struggle there." She
usually ends up buying chicken and ground beef. James understands that
as an African American he is more susceptible to heart disease and diabetes,
so he watches his sugar and salt intake. He likes to eat a well-balanced diet
of fresh and whole foods, something he has been doing since his younger
days as an athlete. Michelle's entire family suffers from diabetes, so "she
knows the drill," although it is a challenge: "I know what to eat. I've been
diabetic for years, so I know the whole carbohydrates, and the sugar … to

be honest. I do to a certain extent. I'm not going to have pops, pops I don't do. The Kool-Aid they'll do, I won't do it because of the sugar. I'll do the regular juices. I already know that you're not supposed to eat a lot of pasta and whatever, so I don't eat a lot of it."

Food insecurity for households with children headed by a single woman is a whopping 34.4 percent (Coleman-Jensen, Gregory, and Singh 2014). Ashley, a working-class, single, white mum, belongs to this group. She is exemplary when it comes to being a good health citizen. She is extremely health conscious and picks up a lot of fresh and whole foods at the food shelf. "I got a lot of whole grain stuff because I've been trying to do that as well. There were beans and stuff like that to get protein from a nonmeat source because, I guess, it's better for you." She added: "I try to make sure that half our plate, like they say in the picture, half a plate of veggies, then a grain and a protein. I'll do lots of veggies and then just use the grain." Here she is referring to MyPlate, the USDA fruits and vegetables campaign. Ashley buys at lot of oatmeal at the store because it is nutritious and filling. For someone who is both food insecure and health conscious, oatmeal is a staple for her:

Ashley: Oatmeal, I'll always buy oatmeal; because oatmeal I can even use water. It fills you up and it keeps you full for a while. Outside of that there's never any leftover fruits or veggies. There's never that. It's usually always at the end of the month we're not eating fresh fruit, until we get the money to buy more groceries.

Interviewer: You might even eat oatmeal for a meal?

Ashley: Yes, oh yes. Often that's probably like the last two weeks that's probably what I eat for breakfast and sometimes lunch.

Disordered eating is typical in Ashley's household. Typical of food insecure families, Ashley encourages her daughter to eat sparingly and eat a little good food along with fillers so that they can stretch out their food. So she explains to her daughter: "Don't eat the whole bag of grapes in one sitting; you won't have any left for tomorrow. Eat some grapes and eat some crackers and something else; you know, it's stuff like that." Ashley rations out the food, but by the end of the month, there is no food left, so they spend the last week eating mostly industrial food. She explained: "I know that what we eat changes as to what we have in the fridge. At first we're eating all fresh stuff. The minute we get our food we're usually eating the fruits and stuff like that right away. Towards the end it's sort of like a lot of the cheap processed foods towards the end of the month."

Clients varied widely in how many fruits and vegetables they picked up. Some clients did not take any fresh produce, while others took a lot. Many clients opted for the fresh fruits, such as bags of grapes, apples, and pears from the grocery store. They enjoyed fresh leafy greens, as well as the convenience of bags of salad. Salad bags, when in good condition, tended to move quickly. One evening we ended up giving away six gigantic butternut and spaghetti squashes to one client. Clients who did not opt for the fresh produce at the food pantry did so for a variety of reasons: their families would not eat the vegetables and they did not want to see them go to waste; or they carefully picked through the vegetables and, not finding any that looked good, moved on to the cans; or they felt like they would not be able to cook and eat the produce in a timely manner. For others, the issue was one of storage. John and Morgan live at the Chum homeless shelter across the street, so the only food they picked up was canned and microwaveable food that could be easily stored.

Making Adjustments: One Bad Potato and Tomato Bisque Soup

There was joy and delight when clients talked about what they liked to cook and what their favorite meals to eat were. They were adept at figuring out ingredient substitutions and how to stretch meals. Clients from Chum and RP had knowledge and cooking skills consistent with most Americans, but unique to this group was a keen knowledge and ability to stretch food and to make food choices based on nutrition and what was going to last longer. With a big smile on his face, Clayton said: "I don't think I'm a good cook, I *know* I'm a good cook." He has taught his kids to cook, and they even cook for him on special occasions. Participants talked about cooking "American classics" such as mac and cheese, hamburger, and stews and soups; when resources were available, they also cooked gourmet, slow-food, and foodie-type meals. Soups, stews, and roasts were favorites because they could be made in a healthy manner with a medley of ingredients from the food pantry. They were also relatively inexpensive per meal per head. These dishes were not tied to particular ingredients and allowed for easy substitutions: swapping one vegetable for another, one meat for another, and even fresh food for canned foods and vice versa. Renee loves to cook pot roast: "You get some roast and you just simmer that down and then there's a bunch of vegetables; it's really simple, really. Put your fresh vegetables, sometimes it's hard, I just use the canned vegetables." Jermain loves red beans and rice because it is filling, and when he has a little extra to spend he flavors it with catfish, ham hocks, or smoked neck bones. "And then you can season ... you have it hot this time and spicy maybe next time, something different, you know. But, I like that, because everything is right there, and you are full."

Participants had learned to make do—to adjust their cooking based on what was available to them with their meager food assistance. Jermain has a special signature dish called *messed-up eggs*, made with eggs, onions, and other vegetables, which he loves to make and eat. Janet enjoys cooking "slow food" but is still learning how to adjust ingredients: "I just like to cook. I love soups, anything that kind of takes a while, I like to chop things and I like to simmer and you know unfortunately again the things that have fresh vegetables for making soups, I used to make it all the time and I am a little limited now, although I am learning to adapt, but yeah I like to make food for people." Rick likes to make a good soup, but this can be problematic with food pantry food: "Sometimes it's hit or miss and sometimes you know if you are working through Ruby's Pantry, specifically you get one of those large things of mashed potatoes or if you got one bad potato in that bunch, it's going to taste like that one bad potato. So I mean you know sometimes it turns out as fantastic, other times its wow, what happened? So I really enjoy playing with soups and spices to be able to make it more exciting or interesting yeah."

Pasta was a staple as it was filling and could be used to stretch more expensive foods. Tyrone's favorite meal is spaghetti and meatballs, but he is health conscious, so he uses a mix of ground beef and turkey sausage for the meatballs. Like many, Violet uses hamburger and potatoes as a way to make food last longer: "If I get a small thing of hamburger, I might use a sandwich bag or something to divide that up and take it, thaw it out, and then use a little potato that I got. I just make a portion just for one person. I'm sort of good at stretching until I can actually go to the grocery store or whatever." Portioning and freezing were common techniques used to stretch food. Morgan used to be a chef at the country club, so she has tremendous cooking skills and knowledge. She made what she called "natural soups"—soups with a lot of fresh vegetables and whole grains. She is also adept at making and freezing pasties—typically a batch of twenty-four.

The language of fresh, whole, and simple food, with allusions to Mediterranean and low-carb diets, showed that participants were influenced by foodie discourses. Rick explained that his favorite food to cook varied by season: "If its summer time, I like making simple bruschetta that has tomato and cucumber topping. It's real simple. Its butter, olive oil, garlic, let's see here, mustard. Anyhow, you slice up your bread, you put a little dollop on each slice of bread and a little bit of parmesan cheese, bake that in the oven, you chop up your vegetables fresh and for me it just tastes like summertime. So that will be my favorite summer time meal." Darlene talked about her favorite dish to make, Alton Brown's Baked Brown Rice: "It's so good. I don't know. And it's so easy. You just boil the water with olive oil and whatever seasonings you want. You pour it over your rice, throw in the oven for an hour, and it's done. They like it too. They were so anti brown rice when I first started this, but now they're coming around. Probably because I don't serve white rice anymore unless John makes it." Her husband, John, also likes a tomato bisque soup she makes, but since they are health conscious, she does not use heavy cream and does not strain the soup; this retains all the nutrition. There are nights they have tomato bisque soup for dinner; on other nights, when Darlene is ferrying her kids around to their evening activities, they have peanut butter and jelly sandwiches. This is also a way they save on food.

Urban-Rural Gardening

There were many folks who had interest, skill, and experience in growing food—and there was much joy in these conversations. In the city of Duluth, which is in close proximity to more rural regions of the state, clients spanning age and racial categories were experienced with growing food, although white clients had more access to land to do so. This disparity, even in a relatively small sample, spoke volumes about the lasting legacy of the discriminatory practices of the USDA—one of the biggest contributors to the decline in Black farming and Black wealth in contemporary US history (Hinson and Robinson 2008). Overall, across groups, clients knew the health and monetary values of growing their own food, having either grown up with vegetable gardens and farms or tried their hands at gardening themselves.

Penelope, a white female client of RP, maintains a lush organic garden that does not use any fertilizer. "It's all organic," she says. She grows potatoes, onions, squash, and tomatoes, as well as herbs like oregano, basil, lemongrass, and chives. She still runs out of vegetables, so she has to buy the rest from the store. Bernadette, also white and a client of RP, has a raised-bed garden, which she calls a "garden in a box." In this box, she grows peppers, lettuce, carrots, beets, onions, kale, zucchini, and radishes; she also has fresh herbs growing indoors. Gary's dad grows all kinds of different vegetables and fruits in his garden and also has a raspberry patch and apple tree. Gary receives some of this bounty in exchange for helping his dad around the house, which he says "helps quite a bit" with his food security. John, when he lived in Minneapolis, had access to a 20 × 40 square foot plot of land from the city, surrounded by deer fencing. He grew everything on this land: potatoes, corn, broccoli, cauliflower, carrots, and cucumbers. He said if somebody gave him a plot of land, he would be delighted to grow a garden again.

Many clients of color said they would love to grow a vegetable garden, but the lack of land and resources were obstacles. Renee, a Native woman, loves plants and the outdoors and thinks a garden would be therapeutic for her anxiety issues—but she does not own her own house, so having a garden is impossible right now. Victor's dad, also Native, was a potato farmer, so Victor is very comfortable gardening and farming. In the past, he has grown tomatoes, cucumbers, and other vegetables. "That was a lot of fun ... it would save you money too." He is confident about his gardening skills, saying, "Oh yes, I've been gardening my whole life straight through." Violet would like to grow a garden, but lives in an apartment building and so cannot. She recognizes the value of having a garden, both in terms of nutrition and cost benefits. Some clients attempted to garden, but without success. Darlene explained that when they first bought their house, they were excited about growing a garden. "But then the soil wasn't really prepared for that, and we didn't have the money to do so, so it's just something we will revisit when we have more money, I guess."

Commodity Foods

Similar to RP clients, Chum clients also enjoyed getting name-brand foods. Once there were Tyson frozen chicken nuggets available for families to take, but because the exterior branded box had been removed, clients did not know it was Tyson chicken. I recall showing multiple clients the large, empty cardboard box as evidence that it was really Tyson-brand chicken. Their faces lit up. Receiving familiar name brands took them from politely appreciating the food to delighting in it—as was the case at RP. Conversely, on several occasions clients at Chum would stop short when they saw the huge blocks of cream cheese at the food shelf. The reactions were almost the same each time: first excitement that they were getting cream cheese, then puzzlement, and then disappointment when realizing that these were the dreaded government commodity foods.

In the 1960s, government commodities suffered a poor reputation and were highly stigmatized. In fact, until the 1990s, USDA foods were branded with distinctive white-and-black labels that simply said "CHICKEN" or "BEEF" with a sketch of a chicken or cow. Today USDA food items retain their private labels, so it is much harder to tell which foods are commodity foods and which are regular foods for retail. This was done to remove the stigma, but also because it ended up being more economical for the USDA. Most commodity foods do not say USDA on them today and look like regular retail products, but since the labels were not familiar, clients guessed that they were USDA foods. On some days, with some convincing, I could get clients to take this food, but not always. These reactions serve as an important reminder that food is not just about chemical components but is inscribed with memory, histories, and political meaning, all of which influence food choice.

In her poem "Why I Hate Raisins," Natalie Diaz, a Native Should poet and writer, Mojave and an enrolled member of the Gila River Indian community, captures the profound simplicity and complexity of what it means to be hungry and food insecure in the United States. Her poem also captures the stigma of having to eat government commodity foods, most likely commodity foods that arrived in a box as part of the Food Distribution Program on Indian Reservations—a program similar in form to the proposal for America's Harvest Box.

Why I Hate Raisins

And is it only the mouth and belly which are injured by hunger and thirst?

Mencius

Love is a pound of sticky raisins
packed tight in black and white
government boxes the day we had no
groceries. I told my mom I was hungry.
She gave me the whole bright box.
USDA stamped like a fist on the side.
I ate them all in ten minutes. Ate
too many too fast. It wasn't long
before those old grapes set like black
clay at the bottom of my belly
making it ache and swell.

I complained, *I hate raisins.*
I just wanted a sandwich like other kids.
Well that's all we've got, my mom sighed.
And what other kids?
Everyone but me, I told her.
She said, *You mean the white kids.*
You want to be a white kid?
Well too bad 'cause you're my kid.
I cried, *At least the white kids get a sandwich.*
At least the white kids don't get the shits.

That's when she slapped me. Left me
holding my mouth and stomach—
devoured by shame.
I still hate raisins,
but not for the crooked commodity lines
we stood in to get them—winding
around and in the tribal gymnasium.
Not for the awkward cardboard boxes
we carried them home in. Not for the shits
or how they distended my belly.
I hate raisins because now I know
my mom was hungry that day, too,
and I ate all the raisins.

In this childhood reflection, the family does not receive cash benefits
that are sufficient to meet their food needs. They cannot manage their food
insecurity by simply going to the store and using legal entitlements to purchase food of their choice. Instead, Natalie and her family must eat government food predetermined for them. In this poem, the invasive, paternalistic,
and marked role of the government in the lives of poor communities is evident when she discusses the bright box of raisins with "USDA stamped like

a fist on the side." These are USDA commodity food boxes, which restrict food choices for poor citizens. Instead of being able to eat a sandwich, the young girl is forced to eat a box of sticky black raisins. The most likely scenario here was that there was a glut of raisins in the market and the price of raisins fell; to avoid farmers losing money, the USDA bought the raisins and distributed them as commodity foods to food insecure households. But the little girl wants a sandwich—a staple of the American diet, but as I learned through this study, for most poor citizens bread, ham, and cheese were some of the most unaffordable items at the grocery store—and these items because of their restricted shelf lives were also not easily accessible at food pantries. Diaz's poem reminded me of Ashley's story—Ashley, the extremely health conscious mum who eats oatmeal several times a day to save money and is forced to say to her child, "Don't eat the whole bag of grapes in one sitting; you won't have any left for tomorrow. Eat some grapes and eat some crackers." Eat raisins.

Diaz's poem bears witness to the multiple effects of hunger. Hunger means facing the very real physical sensation of pain, a kind of gnawing in the belly that won't go away and will not let you do much else, but it also means experiencing complex feelings linked to what it means to be oneself, what it means to be the paradigmatic racial Other in a world of white privilege, what it means to be poor and isolated in a world of commodified middle-class lifestyles, and what it means to look at yourself through the eyes of those higher up in the social hierarchy. The young girl cries: "At least the white kids get a sandwich. At least the white kids don't get the shits." The poem illuminates the physical pain of hunger, as well as the meanings that hunger carries in the social and political world. Being hungry means suffering not alone, but in the context of family and community—at times sharing the pain and shame with loved ones, but often hiding these feelings from them or arguing with them. Being hungry is about living in an unjust system grounded in white supremacist and neoliberal "capitalism with the gloves off" policies such as America's Harvest Box, which affects people of color and poor white folk in devastating ways.

Conclusion

Dominant political and cultural discourses demonize SNAP recipients, portraying them as lacking in discipline, enacting poor food choices, and unconcerned about their health and well-being. This chapter shows food insecure individuals like Victor, Violet, and Ashley—parents, who perform health citizenship in extraordinary ways. Participants showed tremendous skill in navigating limited food choices. Individuals were preoccupied, anxious, and concerned about eating well and were particularly concerned about eating unsafe and industrially processed foods. Citizens like young Tyrone took great pains to try to get the most nutrition that they could out of the food available to them. Many recognized the value of growing their own food, in terms of both nutritional quality and financial savings. People of color talked about their food choices in the context of history and biography; there was a lack of trust in the dominant industrial food system—not only because it delivered bad food to people, but also because it was steeped in a long history of racism. These themes also were reflected in how clients responded to seeing commodity foods at the food shelf. Foods that were fresh—and looked fresh—as well as name-brand foods took away some of the stigma associated with hunger and poverty. Name-brand foods, whether Tyson or Coke, made recipients feel special because they were foods they would not typically buy for themselves. Unique to food insecure families, participants cooked stews, natural soups, "messed-up eggs," and tomato bisque soup, using recipes that allowed them to use food pantry food in creative ways. They ate filler foods like bread, pasta, and crackers to help stretch out more nutrient-dense foods over a longer period of time. Food choice *should* depend on a family's preferences, culture, dietary restrictions, health consciousness, and contradictory desires; however, for food insecure families, "choice" is determined by what is available through charitable capitalism and meagre SNAP benefits.

Policy Implications

Food policy, enacted through government and charitable food assistance programs, forces people to rely on cheap industrial food as a way out of hunger. SNAP benefits are inadequate for purchasing good food—fruits and vegetables, whole grains, nutrient-dense foods, culturally acceptable foods, foods for the body and the mind, foods for a balanced diet, and foods that allow you to live, work, and play better. Indeed, cheap food is an "embodied form of discrimination" that should result in new kinds of policy actions, as Dickinson (2013, 9) points out. The USDA currently uses the Thrifty Food Plan to make recommendations about what SNAP entitlements should look like. The plan is a race to the bottom for the cheapest food possible and holds stigmatizing assumptions about who the poor are. The Thrifty Food Plan, like America's Harvest Box, is in effect a sedimentation of the double standards and contradictions of food assistance policies: we want people to eat nutritious food, but not too much, for fear of incentivizing "welfare." In a typical pattern of neoliberal stigma, the poor are consistently denied healthy options and are then blamed for making bad choices. So the first step to rectifying an unjust food system is to increase SNAP entitlements for households, such that people can eat good food and an adequate amount of food every week of the month.

In this chapter, people's forays into urban gardening resonate with food sovereignty discourses, which argue that communities' rights to grow and produce food are critical to the long-term food security of communities (Alkon and Mares 2012). There is a growing body of literature on urban gardens, which on the one hand argues that this is a vital strategy for enhancing food security, but on the other cautions that as a strategy, it is only possible when resources of land, money, and time are available (Alkon and Agyeman 2011; Ghose and Pettygrove 2014; Levkoe 2006). In the case of urban gardens, care must be taken to ensure that programs are not subject to the same paternalistic forces of poverty governance found in the rest of the food system. Furthermore, from a policy perspective, it is important not just to create new urban farming and gardening programs, but also to work on redressing historical travesties. For instance, farming in Black communities today garners contradictory responses because of its problematic associations with slavery and sharecropping. With regard to racial equity, the fight must be for reparations for communities that have lost their farms, their lands, and their livelihoods to white supremacy. In an ethnographic study of the voices of Black farmers, Carter (2017) found that though the USDA has a well-known history of racism, farmers were able to point to instances of incremental progress, such as the *Pigford Settlement*, one of the largest civil rights settlements for Black farmers in the history of the United States. More settlements like these for African American, Native, and Hmong communities, are required to shift the compass on racial equity. In short, even as we continue to think about and enact food justice programs and policies, it must be done carefully and with a view toward racial equity. This means not quickly jumping onto new strategies, but methodically and passionately working for reparations, rights, and representation for exploited communities—remembering that the unjust food system has a long arc that reaches deep into history and that the way people eat is just the tip of the iceberg.

8   Conclusion: Imagining a Future for Food Pantries

But ... it is also easy to see the shortcomings in the conduct of the Samaritan. There is no suggestion that the Samaritan ~~organized~~ sought to investigate the lack of police protection on the Jericho Road nor did he appeal to any public officials to set out after the robbers and clean up the Jericho road. Here was the weakness of the Good Samaritan. He was concerned [*merely?*] with temporary relief, not with thorough reconstruction. He sought to sooth the effects of evil, without going back to uproot the causes. Now, without a doubt Christian social responsibility includes the sort of thing the Good Samaritan did. So we give to the United Appeals, the Red Cross, to all types of unfortunate conditions ... But there is another aspect of Christian social responsibility which is just as compelling. It seeks to tear down unjust conditions and build anew instead of patching things up. It seeks to clear the Jericho road of its robbers as well as caring for the victims of robbery.[1]

—Martin Luther King Jr., "The One-Sided Approach of the Good Samaritan," Montgomery, Alabama, 1955

Neoliberal Stigma and the Problems of Hunger and Food Insecurity

The problems of hunger and food insecurity are problems of food justice. If food justice means "ensuring that the benefits and risks of where, what, and how food is grown and produced, transported and distributed, and accessed and eaten are shared fairly" (Gottlieb and Joshi 2010, 6), then clearly, for approximately 15 percent of the population food justice is not a reality. The lack of access to adequate and affordable food means that households are disenfranchised not only in terms of food, but also in their physical, emotional, and social well-being. The lack of food means that families are forced to enter the restrictive and punitive world of government and charitable food assistance, in which shame, humiliation, gratitude, servitude, and "embodied forms of discrimination" take a toll on their social identity formations: how individuals see themselves, how others perceive them, and their capabilities for political action.

As pointed out in the introduction to this book, the problem of hunger in the United States is not natural or inevitable. Nationally, there is no shortage of resources; we have sufficient food, technology, expertise, and information (Carolan 2011; Sen 1983). Hunger is the outcome of neoliberal "capitalism with the gloves off" policies that commodify food but fail to provide decent living wages or entitlements for people to access those foods. The government has a legal obligation to ensure "access by all people at all times to enough food for an active and healthy life," but this obligation has not been met. Hunger is a problem of entitlement failure and a democratic system that does not represent the people it serves. In a neoliberal era, charitable food assistance programs are central to the government's solution to end hunger. When food banks emerged in the 1980s, they were meant to be stopgap measures, but charitable assistance today is necessary for supplementing meager SNAP entitlements (Fisher 2017; Poppendieck 1999). Indeed, unlike Deuteronomy 15:7–10, which proclaims that "you shall open your hand to him [the poor man], and lend him sufficient for his need, *whatever it may be*" (emphasis added), these programs deliver just enough food to prevent bloated bellies, but not enough for people to achieve their aspirations, to live "a good life," and to be *citizens* in the fullest sense of the word.

Specifically, this book has argued that the phenomenon of *neoliberal stigma*, by which people are marked by negative meanings centered on work, personal responsibility, citizenship, economic productivity, and wealth, is the ideological fulcrum that legitimates entitlement failure and food injustice. Neoliberalism offers a set of neutral rhetorical resources necessary for the justification of the social order, in which hard work and personal responsibility are foregrounded while history and structural forces are dismissed as irrelevant. In an era of health citizenship, the food choices people make are subject to intense scrutiny and discipline; individuals are chastised for their alleged lack of motivation and desire for self-improvement. They are the so-called bad citizens, who harm themselves, their children, and the national debt by not taking care of their bodies. Individuals are held responsible for eating industrial foods and for their purported lack of food-related information, knowledge, and skills. All these stigmatizing discourses come together to justify neoliberal and racial projects while masking the real issue: exploitation that takes place at the hands of a global capitalist food system. Stigmatizing ideologies are inscribed and reproduced in policies and procedures at global, national, and local levels—even the level of food pantries.

The effects of neoliberal stigma on people who are hungry and food insecure are devastating. Neoliberal stigma is pivotal to the Us and Them mindset so rampant in food assistance spaces today. For people in positions of vulnerability, this means managing stigma by distancing themselves from people and places. It involves processes of blaming, shaming, and silencing that take a toll on identity and social well-being. For people in positions of power, this means constantly trying to discern who is deserving and underserving, what counts as fraud and abuse, and identifying scammers. Neoliberal stigma pervades food assistance spaces, unleashing a culture of suspicion in which volunteers are suspicious of clients and clients are suspicious of each other. Neoliberal stigma results in less access to food and good food, reductions in SNAP benefits, and the excessive monitoring and policing of clients through poverty governance procedures. Stigma has the ultimate effect of enhancing perceptions of social distance and actual distance among groups of people—keeping people away from each other. Stigma is divisive and silencing: it builds a solid wall of separation between those on the giving and receiving ends, as well as within class groups, and in so doing it reinforces the status quo. Stigma in any form is dangerous because what starts out as symbolic eventually leads to the building of real walls: border walls, sanatoriums, mental asylums, and prison-industrial complexes, to name a few.

Because my research is focused on food pantries, my recommendations are geared toward change at this level, although there is work to be done at every level of the food system. As I noted in the introduction, food pantries are small actors in a much larger food system, but because there are so many of them, they have the potential to become formidable allies in dismantling the food system. This means redefining their function. In addition to collecting and distributing food, I argue that food pantries should become centers for the production and distribution of new narratives. Specifically, in this chapter, I argue that a genuine food justice approach to hunger requires developing new versions of food pantries, ones designed not just to dole out food, but to develop the *critical consciousness* of people who enter them as donors, staff, volunteers, and clients.

Critical pedagogue Paulo Freire (1970) referred to this process of consciousness raising as *conscientization*, or the process of developing a critical awareness of social realities through reflection and action. We might also think of these as processes geared toward developing an *oppositional consciousness*—a consciousness trained to invert dominant paradigms of thought, whether they be religiopolitical, white supremacist, sexist, or capitalist. It is "an empowering mental state that prepares members of an oppressed group to act to undermine, reform, or overthrow a system of human domination" (Mansbridge and Morris 2001, 5). It is a consciousness that counters dominant ideologies, directs attention away from personal explanations to structural and institutional forms of oppression, and provides "symbolic blueprints for collective action and social change" (Morris and Braine 2001, 26). Dr. Martin Luther King's sermon, excerpted at the beginning of this chapter, is a powerful example of what an oppositional consciousness looks like. Aptly titled "The One-Sided Approach of the Good Samaritan," King ([1955] 2007) applauds the Samaritan for caring for the victim but chastises him for not taking steps to "uproot the cause" and to "clear the Jericho road of its robbers." The Samaritan did not talk to public officials or the police; there was no advocacy, no protest, no demands made of public officials. Indeed, King's theological orientation is not the theology of Sahr, which brings him to categorize people into three types, but the cumulative voices of people of color and people of faith speaking from below, inverting dominant paradigms of thought, oppositional and nonviolent at the same time.

Goal of the Chapter

The goal of this chapter is to first summarize key findings from the study and then provide a framework for how food pantries can start moving toward new versions of themselves that exert influence in the wider community and upward through the food system. Grounded in theories of social change, in which a key requirement is dialogical processes geared toward recovering, centering, and foregrounding the voices of the hungry, I present particular steps pantries can take to move toward the future, which involves consciousness-building and the creation of communicative or participatory spaces in which bodies and voices flow easily. To be sure, this is not a transformational approach—I am not recommending that food pantries be dismantled, at least not yet—but it is a pragmatic approach to move us one step closer to achieving that vision. To do so, food pantries and organizations must first build their capacity for antiracism and advocacy grounded in reflection and action. This chapter presents examples of the kinds of allies that food pantries can seek out as they move toward more justice-based versions of themselves. The chapter ends with an analysis of Appetite for Change, a community-led organization centered on food justice issues, as a vision of what food pantries can become.

Key Findings

Voices of hunger are powerful, complex, and full of desire.

Amid oppressive systems, this book bears witness to the complex, contradictory, and nuanced lives of the hungry and food insecure. In these recovered voices, we see personal responsibility, rational decision-making, critical consciousness, and agency. College degrees, work, volunteerism, giving back to the community, physical pain, mindfulness, prayer, and spirituality all constitute the "lived lives" of participants. We hear lives full of meaning: remembering and forgetting, reflection and action, regret and anticipation. Participants talked about the important role of God in their lives—a God of the oppressed who saved them from death and despair even as they moved through dark and lonely places of poverty, disability, unemployment, violence, anxiety, and depression. Participants described sticker shock at the grocery store, unemployment, homelessness, migration, physical and mental health issues, jumping through hoops, and histories of racism going all the way back to the Jim Crow era. Participants used complex, rational, and creative processes to juggle government and charitable food assistance. They showed skill navigating the complexities of food and nutrition even as they struggled to protect their families. They showed immense gratitude for public assistance but recognized how oppressive these forces were in their lives. They cared for each other—for children, sick relatives, family, and friends—but also battled with each other and with oppressive forces in their lives, like systems of poverty governance. Individuals inverted neoliberal logic on a daily basis but also reinforced it when it worked in their self-interest.

Overall, participants disrupted the binaries of knowledgeable/ignorant, moral/immoral, healthy/unhealthy, and good/bad citizens, often used in political discourses, and showed lives lived outside of discursive boxes and categories. In a letter written by Sahr (discussed in chapter 2), he placed people into three categories: those who are not able to work, those who are not able to find jobs, and *those who do not want to work*, with his wrath reserved for the last category. However, in the voices of the hungry, I found that people cycled through the first two categories many times in the course of their lives. *I never found people who did not want to work*; in fact, work was always talked about with great joy, as a source of positive identity formation and a source of privilege. Interview after interview, not one of these citizens could be placed in the third category. I soon began to realize that just like the "welfare queen" and "angry Black woman" stereotypes, this category of people does not exist. It is a socially constructed category with no basis in reality, but rather is constructed in the service of a powerful political project.

Stigma is intensified at the intersection of race and gender.
At Chum, Native and African American clients articulated far more experiences of neoliberal stigma than white participants. They felt it more and internalized it more. Racism, sometimes color-blind, was an important subtext for their experiences related to food assistance, which occurred in their own neighborhoods, in food pantries, and in government assistance systems. In their articulations, clients linked experiences of depression and anxiety directly to being negatively marked by their color. They used an intergenerational lens to make sense of racism and used a variety of ways to cope with racial oppression. Most often, they turned inward and looked to themselves for answers and solutions: long walks, prayer, hanging out with friends, using humor to diffuse the situation, and counting their blessings. Importantly, these stories were completely concealed and made invisible at the food pantry. They did not show up in the interactions between clients and volunteers. Citizens came in, waited, got their food, and left. Volunteers did the same. Time, procedural constraints, and racial distance played a role in concealing these narratives. So, shockingly yet inevitably, volunteers often had no idea who was standing in front of them—the vast history and biographies of the people who came there. They did not realize that some of the people they were serving grew up as indentured sharecroppers,

had grown organic food, made tomato bisque soup, and had lived several lifetimes before they got to the pantry.

The study also showed that women faced a heavy burden of oppression. Because of the gendered division of labor, women were often the primary caregivers for children and grandchildren, and because of these caregiving roles they were more visible at the food shelf and at the welfare office, making them easy targets of stigma. In households with single female parents and even in two-parent households, women typically were accountable for food preparation; the onus was on them to prepare healthy meals that maintained the family budget. Women of color, Native and African American in this study, experienced racism at government offices, at the workplace, and in their communities. Their stories were amplified by the violence of relational abuse, loneliness, addiction, and depression, thereby illuminating the broader context of structural violence within which hunger occurs. Even as women aged and became grandparents, they continued to shoulder the burden of providing food for food insecure children and grandchildren; this was true of both white women and women of color.

Food pantries function as whitened neoliberal enclosures.
Pantries like Chum and RP are a kind of "neoliberal enclosure" in which time and space are orchestrated to achieve particular mentalities, behaviors, and disciplines. In a Foucauldian vein, enclosures as a technique of governance act like machines, transforming and exerting control over people not by direct coercion but by creating self-regulating bodies through procedures of supervision, assessment, and evaluation (Foucault 1995). Within the enclosure of the Chum food pantry, with its rules and spatial barriers, both clients and volunteers were obedient to the arrangements of space and time, each following their roles precisely. There was a stark division in this space; clients queued up outside the food shelf waiting for it to open, while volunteers set up food and other formalities inside. Volunteers entered through a separate door and had their own space to take breaks, eat snacks, and chat, but clients were not allowed access to this space. This kind of disciplinary enclosure reaffirmed the separation between racial and class-based groups at Chum. Within these neoliberal enclosures, volunteers and clients were easily recruited into neoliberal modes of being and action, where ideals of individualism, personal responsibility, efficiency, and self-help were embraced.

In these enclosures, stigmatizing assumptions penetrated the subjectivity of people across a variety of backgrounds: people in positions of privilege and at the bottom of the social order. At Chum, age-old stigmatizing beliefs about poverty, race, and gender alongside neoliberal discourses of accountability, responsibility, and hard work were prevalent themes. These themes remained somewhat masked in this enclosed space. In other words, simply walking into the food pantry you would not know that forty-year-old stigmatizing beliefs about "welfare mothers" and "Cadillacs" were floating around in people's minds, but these themes came up consistently in interviews with volunteers and clients. It is no wonder then that people sat around subdued and in silence as they waited for their food—with no sense of community and not much cross talk or conversation. RP, on the other hand, was a very different kind of neoliberal enclosure; here paying twenty dollars offered clients a way to *buy* themselves out of the indignity of oppressive neoliberal narratives and construct themselves as hardworking folks. These unifying discourses created an open and welcoming space for clients but reinforced stereotypes about people who used traditional food assistance programs like Chum.

Religion produces charity but not advocacy.
At both sites, the power of religion to bring a great number of Good Samaritans together to do the most unsavory of jobs, like pitchforking their way through raw frozen fish and rotten potatoes, was notable. The question remained, however, how to refocus the energies of these Samaritans toward systemic change. A number of volunteers and clients at both sites had strong faith beliefs, which influenced their worldviews and actions. At Chum, religious beliefs often were described as the key motivation for volunteering. Volunteers talked about the role of Jesus in the lives of the poor and saw themselves as fulfilling a God-given mandate. At RP–Duluth, volunteers also saw themselves as doing God's work by reaching out to the hungry and opening their church space to the poor. These faith beliefs were not made explicit in the everyday bustle of collecting and distributing food; instead, the physical food distribution occurred in a secular and even postsecular way, in which humanistic values were applauded and only loosely tied to Christian doctrine. At Chum and RP, discourses of helping others and charity were prominent and seen as central to Christian social responsibility, but unlike King's sermon, rebuilding and creating new equitable structures

were not part of volunteers' faith beliefs. Many volunteers talked about the importance of advocacy but did not tie it to their responsibilities as Christians, and their identities had not changed because of it. In this space, their work was framed as "doing good" and there was mutual admiration and appreciation among them. Although volunteers did not make their faith explicitly known, clients assumed that volunteers were there because of faith commitments, although at RP this was complicated by the fact that volunteers were getting something in return.

Communication builds and fractures communities.
The study shows that stigma is neither natural nor inevitable, but created and disrupted through communicative or discursive practices that mark people in explicit and implicit ways. This is the work of discourse or, in the case of RP, *strategic* communication. The phrases "RP is for everyone" and "we're all in the same boat" created solidarity among people. Sahr put a lot of effort into addressing beliefs and assumptions clients had. Through strategic communication, he created a sense of community and destigmatized the RP food assistance program. At Chum, in the absence of strategic communication about who the hungry were and the causes of hunger, age-old ideologies hitched their carriages to new languages and events to create a culture of suspicion. Chum failed to articulate a coherent ideological project in which religion, economics, and politics could be brought in line with the value of social justice. Indeed, many voices could be heard at Chum—some reinforcing stigmatizing ideologies, others countering them. The lack of coherent narratives dealt a deathblow to community building and solidarity. Thus, Chum, even with its social justice position, was far less effective at creating a sense of collective identity and solidarity among its various internal stakeholders.

At both sites, "collective forgetting" and discursive erasures reinforced social and racial distance between Us and Them. These spaces were racialized not because of what was present, but because of what was absent. At Chum, the failure to remember the bloody and brutal enslavements of racial minorities in the past reinforced a neutral reading of Black and brown bodies in those spaces. There, the fact that all the volunteers were white reinforced the idea of white superiority; these were "good white women" reaching out to poor brown folks. At RP, focusing on the role of miracles in receiving surplus food but overlooking the role of the industrial food system reinforced the idea of hunger as a personal issue. There, the mostly white bodies in that space reinforced the social imaginary of whites as hard-working, proud, and responsible Americans, proud because they were paying for what they were getting, not simply taking so-called handouts. This occurred even though most people at RP also received government benefits in some shape or form—food assistance, unemployment, disability, or social security. This reinforces Fraser's (1987) argument that the US welfare system is a two-tiered system biased by gender, race, and class, in which participants in the "masculine" subsystem are positioned as rights-bearing beneficiaries and purchasing consumers of services, whereas participants in the "feminine" subsystem are positioned as dependent clients, welfare recipients, freeloaders, and morally defective.

Neoliberal ideology is flexible.

As scholars have previously noted, the values associated with neoliberalism are fluid and flexible and able to fit in with a variety of political orientations (Hall 1988; Larner 2000; Springer 2016). Simply put, there is something for everyone in neoliberal ideology—and it can be used by anyone for any purpose. This fluidity also has something to do with the opacity of ideology in general—the fact that individuals are typically unaware of the ideological dimensions of the positions they occupy and therefore not committed to them (van Dijk 1993, 2001). Holborow (2015) underscores the fractured and contradictory nature of social consciousness as it manifests in practice. She writes: "A dominant ideology may say one thing about people's lives which their immediate life experience contradicts and leads them to say something different" (6). The fluidity of neoliberal doctrine was seen in this study, in which values of hard work, economic productivity, and personal responsibility were able to slide around easily amid social justice discourses at Chum and conservative discourses at RP. At Chum, the mainly white volunteers easily articulated neoliberal rationalities of hard work, self-help, and accountability alongside ideals of justice and equity. At RP, the fluidity of neoliberal ideology was seen in the convergence and divergence of beliefs between actors at the home office and the local site. Actors varied widely in terms of their political and religious leanings but agreed that charging for food contributed to dignity and a destigmatizing environment.

Subversion is necessary but insufficient for transformation. The literature suggests that frontline staff in public services, as well as people who use those services, act to modify, disrupt, or negate the intended processes and outcomes of public policy. Barnes and Prior (2009) identify three ways in which this counteragency can occur: *Revision* occurs when objectives are modified to lead to different outcomes than those the policy initially demanded. With *resistance*, actions are taken to develop alternative strategies to achieve outcomes other than those prescribed in official policies. *Refusal* is a more passive mode of response to problematic situations and occurs when individuals decline to become engaged or involved in official strategies. Examples of each of these modes of counteragency are shown by volunteers at Chum and RP. Chum volunteers showed resistance when they adopted the choice model and engaged in breaking the rules by handing clients more food than they were allotted. At RP, steering committee members engaged in refusal when they refused to have religious content on site because they believed that people would not feel respected. In using the site for purposes other than food distribution, such as signing up people for health benefits, RP–Duluth also engaged in a form of revision. These acts of counteragency subverted official policies to the extent that they made accommodations for clients and attempted to better their experiences at the food pantries; however, they did not go far enough to be transformative or to activate against dominant structures.

Telling an Alternative Story

Drawing from the findings, I contend that at the individual, organizational, and community levels, dismantling neoliberal stigma can only come about by *listening to the voices of the oppressed*, allowing these voices to *change identities, our very being in the world*, and then using these reformulated identities *to shift dominant narratives about Us and Them* that hold the food system in place. These three processes are cyclical and unending, always feeding back into each other. If discursive formations operate to hold the system in place, then changing these narratives is important for the end goal of systemic change. Specifically with regards to identity, there are two important shifts that need to happen: consciousness raising with regards to racial oppression and racial equity, and shifting dominant modes of thinking from charitable to rights-based perspectives, in particular for faith-based communities. I make these recommendations while drawing on social movement theory and the work of three scholar-activists in particular: Paulo Freire (1970) and his method for conscientization, Nancy Fraser (1992) and her theorization of subaltern counterpublics, and, more recently, communication scholar Mohan Dutta's (2008) explication of the culture-centered approach (CCA). These theories of social change taken together provide a sense of what the pathway to more equitable decision-making and policy might look like.[2]

Unique to these approaches is the utmost importance of creating participatory spaces and anchoring our actions to the voices of the oppressed. In a world where we are always much more likely to listen to and believe those in positions of power, these approaches amplify the voices of those on the bottom rungs. Taken together, these theories demand the development of a critical or oppositional consciousness that recenters, refocuses, and reframes thinking and actions around the oppressed. The formation of collective identities leads to the telling of new stories, new frames for thinking about problems and solutions, and new demands, like the ones made by Dr. King "to tear down unjust conditions and build anew instead of patching things up." In sum, social change begins through dialogue and listening that foregrounds community voices as sites of knowledge production and implementation (Dutta-Bergman 2004). Through this process of *listening to the voices of the exploited and oppressed* we are changed; identities are reformulated to provide an unshakeable base from which to shift, resist, and invert stigmatizing discourses and structures, creating new stories and obliterating old ones.

What does this mean from a practical perspective? First, I should point out that this is not just the work of food pantries, but also the work of organizations and the broader communities that they are embedded within. We should not shift the labor of solving this problem to one entity. As a first step, organizations and communities should create participatory forums in which silenced voices can be recovered and brought back into focus. In most food pantries I visited, people often sat alone or with kids waiting for their numbers to be called. There was not a whole lot of interaction going on; people simply waited for their food. Following the CCA or Freire's method for conscientization, this time could be used to bring people into dialogue or discussion with each other and with staff and volunteers as equals. A starting point might be to ask people for feedback on the quality or quantity of food provided. This conversation could be used as an entry point to talk about stigma, welfare, the oppressive state apparatus, and dynamics of race and whiteness. Food pantries could even use available food justice documentaries to unpack these themes. This dialogical activity would provide insights into not only a client's caloric needs but also the kinds of meals they aspire to cook and how they think of themselves and their identity in the world. As these voices emerge, they will work to change and revise the identities of people in and around those spaces. Volunteers will no longer see themselves as Samaritans and saints, but as advocates—people of privilege who can use their privilege to tell new stories and advocate for the needs of people. Clients will no longer see each other as unworthy and undeserving scammers, but as citizens with legal rights. Through this participatory process, a collective Us can be brought into being, and political action becomes a possibility.

A second role food pantries can play is to produce discourse for internal and external audiences geared toward shifting cultural and political narratives. Social justice organizations must do the communicative work necessary to produce a coherent organizational identity, in which faith beliefs, economics, and politics are brought in line with the work they do and the broader vision of social justice. The goal of this discursive work is to create a counternarrative to the problem of hunger and food insecurity that moves away from individual-level causes to structural and systemic issues. Organizations must codify their ideologies—identifying core values and "values in action." Similar to Lyn Sahr, who produced discourse to serve a powerful political project, social justice organizations should produce careful discourse to serve the interests of poor citizens. Developing an organization's theory of change is important to ensure that everyone in the organization, from staff to volunteers, recognize and build self-awareness and system-level awareness. Producing discourse for public consumption is equally important; this means creating newsletters, antistigma campaigns, community forums, media stories, speaker bureaus, and memes, if necessary. Although social movements are punctuated with embodied and highly visible events such as marches and protests, much work also occurs in mundane but thoughtful communicative acts, like letter writing. Quite distinct from fundraising, the goal of all this discursive work is to invert dominant logics, frameworks, and narratives through a process of reflection and action centered on the voices and meanings created by the oppressed. This goes beyond organizational mission and vision statements to articulate a theory of change—and to show how this theory is different from dominant ones in use. Ivan Illich, a philosopher and Roman Catholic priest, once asserted: "Neither revolution nor reformation can ultimately change a society, rather you must tell a new powerful tale, one so persuasive that it sweeps away the old myths and becomes the preferred story, one so inclusive that it gathers all the bits of our past and our present into a coherent whole, one that even shines some light into the future so that we can take the next step. ... If you want to change a society, then you have to tell an alternative story" (as cited in Springer 2016, 2). Food pantries need to develop new, powerful stories grounded in the lived experiences and aspirations of the hungry. Food pantries need to capture the ellipses, the gaps, the silences in dominant narratives surrounding hunger. These counternarratives will play an important role in shifting the identities of people within food pantry spaces, such that even as volunteers dole out food, they can employ counternarratives to disrupt stigma.

Third, organizations and communities must find ways to channel citizen voices into the realm of policy grounded in rights-based thinking. This requires an explicit shift from thinking about individuals as clients, recipients, and guests to thinking about them as citizens. This could mean starting with small steps like setting up phone stations with ready-made scripts that people can read or having postcards that people can write and sign. Advocates note that small political acts such as these, though they do not take much time, can be extremely important for policy change. These are activities that can be done as people wait for their food, but they can also be made open to the wider community, so that in the same physical space people can learn how to come together to become citizens. These acts will serve to create a culture of advocacy and rights-based thinking among food pantries and stimulate discussions on the right to food, food sovereignty, and community food security perspectives. These stories can also be collected and curated for political purposes. Stories or oral histories from clients can be recorded and edited in traditional and digital media formats. Students from local colleges and universities can work on these projects, giving something of value back to organizations through their volunteering. Similar to photovoice methodologies, these stories can be directed at policy organizations such as Hunger Solutions or Feeding America. I have been at far too many meetings in which advocates have asked for stories;

we should always know and carry these stories with us. The purpose of these stories is to allow the wider public and policymakers an opportunity to bear witness and act upon what they hear.

The Challenge to Participation

In engaging with any of these activities, there are multiple challenges that organizations might face, a primary one being resource constraints. The question here is how organizations might garner resources to do the work of citizenship. This is something for organizational boards and committees to think about seriously. There is a need to think creatively about how to leverage resources not just to distribute food but for sociopolitical outcomes—for citizenship goals. How can organizations use neoliberal logic in their interests to apply for grants to achieve broader goals of social citizenship? Is there a way to use neoliberal parameters such as "accountability" and "assessment" in the interests of clients? Is there a way to use strategies of resistance, refusal, and revision to modify official policies such that the work of citizenship can occur in these spaces? How can the wider community be involved in this work of citizenship?

Another important debate that arises with participatory forums is whether they can actually lead to policy change given the complexity of power structures, issues of representation, and the dynamics of participation in these spaces. For instance, a common issue pointed out is that disenfranchised communities do not show up to participate. This is often framed in a negative way that perpetuates neoliberal stigma. Some may not be able to participate because of physical or mental disability, and some do not have the time or resources to expend on these kinds of activities. The onus is on organizations to make ways for people to engage that do not burden their lives even further. This means meeting clients where they are at in the course of their lives. This could mean paying participants for their work of citizenship, facilitating safe and quality childcare, and paying for meals and gas. It also means respecting people's rights to sit on the sidelines, just as well-to-do folks do, either because they are complacent or because they are afraid of retaliation—although I saw fear, fatigue, concern, interest, vigilance, and passion much more often than I ever saw complacency among the poor citizens that I spoke to. Finally, with regard to participation, it should be remembered that listening to the voices of citizens and implementing the changes they ask for will go a long way toward building trust in a group typically not used to being listened to.

Partnerships and Allies

To build the capacity of organizations and communities to facilitate successful and ethical participatory forums, it is essential to partner with institutions that have expertise navigating issues of race, class, and gender. Food pantries should *not* assume that they know how to do this work; indeed, no one should. In the emergency food assistance arena, there is a great need to build capacity with regard to antiracism and advocacy—in particular, with respect to Christian social engagement. Evoking consciousness and an oppositional consciousness with regard to these areas is a necessary condition to imagining future possibilities.

Racial Equity

With regard to racial equity, it is vital that food pantries seek out partnerships with institutions that are invested and committed to racial justice. These are organizations that use deep information and precise pedagogical techniques to teach adults how to "re-read" the world through the lens of racial equity. All racial equity workshops are not equal, so great care must be taken to partner with the right organizations—organizations that are committed to racial equity and not beholden to institutional power structures. For instance, even universities today offer several opportunities for "diversity training," but these trainings are geared toward creating "respectful" work environments rather than truly dismantling the underlying logic and structures of racism (Chun and Evans 2018). Although diversity officers have the ability to conduct more incisive workshops, they are constrained by dominant forces within the university that prefer the status quo, as well as by very real material threats posed by legislators, boards of regents, alumni, and donors. Especially when it comes to antiracism trainings, I believe it makes sense for organizations that exist in these troubled waters to outsource their work to racial equity institutes that have been vetted by communities of color to ensure that they are getting the right kind of consciousness raising. Some such institutes include the Racial Equity Institute (North Carolina) and the People's Institute (New Orleans), which are acclaimed for "going there" and doing the deep and hard work of building critical consciousness around issues of whiteness. Other organizations that have always done this kind of work are the National Association for the Advancement of Colored People (NAACP) and the YWCA. In the future, I hope that universities will play a much larger role leading the diversity shift not just within their compounds, but in their communities. For instance, in my vision all land-grant universities will fund chapters of these organizations in their states, the role of which will be to build the capacities of local people for antiracist work—these may even become part of university extension programs, which are currently geared toward providing practical education and training to people in areas related to agriculture, food, and natural resources to name a few.

In the absence of racial equity institutes in Duluth, an example of a relatively new coalition that could fill this role is Showing Up for Racial Justice (SURJ). SURJ's goal is to mobilize an expanding base of white people into racial justice action. At the national level, SURJ was founded in 2009 in response to the anti-Black sentiment resulting from President Obama's elections, as well as state-sanctioned brutalities against Black and brown bodies. SURJ has a chapter in Duluth called *SURJ–Northland*, which has been active over the last three years. SURJ's ideological position is that white supremacy is integral to economic injustice, patriarchy, and other forms of oppression, so destabilizing white supremacy is critical to ensuring all forms of justice. A central part of SURJ's theory of change is to maintain strong accountability relationships with communities of color, leaders, and organizers; however, SURJ does not believe that it is the role of people of color to teach or educate others about racism. Its goal is not to displace or silence the voices of people of color, but to be allies in antiracist efforts and to share the burden.

The methodology of this group is unique in that much of the work takes place through conversation and dialogue, often in small-group settings or even in one-on-ones, in which people can process collectively racialized events or incidents and uncover barriers to change. Unique to SURJ is that they have seen firsthand the workings of racism in their white bodies, homes, neighborhoods, and institutions, so they are able to reach people where they are. According to the SURJ Northland website, their work involves building "skills and capacity necessary for interrupting racist moments and conversation, and for engaging in multi-racial organizing without doing more harm than good."[3] Nathan Holst, a SURJ leader, observes that showing up for racial justice is a long process, which involves honesty, humility, and reconciliation. Individual realization and reflection are necessary to move forward to action and activism. Integrating the work of entities like SURJ into the work of food pantries can play an important role in raising racial consciousness and decentering whiteness. At Chum and RP, volunteers wanted to make a difference but did not realize how problematic their good (white) intentions were in a space of racialized poverty. Joining a group like SURJ (or participating in antiracist trainings) has the potential to reformulate identities—to change how volunteers perceive themselves and their own positionalities, as well as how they reach out to other clients.

From Samaritans to Citizens

A big challenge for food pantries is to shift organizational culture from one of charity to one of rights-based thinking. The goal is to push donors, volunteers, and community members from thinking of themselves as good people engaged in good works to political actors enacting policy—from saints and Samaritans to citizens and advocates. Here too shifting direction requires the help of professionals—people who know how policy and advocacy work and can provide assistance in an ongoing manner. Examples of organizations that do this kind of work include the Joint Religious Legislative Coalition (JRLC) in Minnesota and the Religious Action Center of Reform Judaism (RAC) in Washington, DC. JRLC is the largest nonpartisan interfaith public-interest group in Minnesota, and it brings people of diverse faiths together to lobby for the poor, whereas RAC identifies itself as the "hub of Jewish social justice work"—a nonpartisan group that mobilizes around federal, state, and local legislation. Some priorities for these organizations include increasing minimum wage, extending child care assistance to more families, and expanding tax credits for working families.

In the course of their legislative work, both organizations produce discourses that highlight linkages between faith and advocacy. For instance, JRLC stresses that serving the poor and human dignity are foundational beliefs among Christian, Jewish, and Islamic traditions; thus, poverty is a violation of God-given dignity. It uses dictates from Scripture and religious leaders to underscore these connections, such as "O believers, stand up firmly for justice, as witnesses to Allah, even against yourselves or your parents or kin" (Quran, 4:135) and "Politics is one of the highest forms of

charity, because it serves the common good" (Pope Francis). JRLC acknowl-
edges the role of charity but reinforces the fact that policy is necessary to
shift root causes. In a paper titled "No Poor among You," JRLC (2010) lays
out how change is possible, thereby intervening in the sense of hopelessness that middle-class folks typically experience. RAC also uses scripture to
validate the need for advocacy work around issues of hunger, such as Isaiah
58:7, which says, "God commands us to "share [our] bread with the hungry
and bring the homeless into [our] house." It too reinforces the fact that policy can make a difference to hunger: "The United States could cut domestic
hunger in half within 2 years, and lead a global effort to cut world hunger
in half by 2015, by spending approximately $7 billion more annually, or
7 cents per American per day. Many people believe that ending hunger in
America is entirely possible." These are examples of the kinds of discourses
required to build oppositional consciousness. Integrating these discourses
into food pantries can create the much-needed culture of advocacy and
activism in these spaces. Chum and its member congregations already work
with JRLC; indeed, it was because of Chum that I was first introduced to
JRLC. However, for conservative food pantries like RP, which are socially
engaged, such nonpartisan faith-based discourses could play an important
role in reformulating identities and practices.

Appetite for Change and Free Spaces

Poppendieck (1999, 317), in the final section of *Sweet Charity* wrote: "In my
most optimistic scenarios, I envision turning our kitchen and pantries into
free spaces, places where people can meet and interact across the gulf of
social class and the divisions of race and ethnicity, not as givers and receivers in ways that widen the gulf, but as neighbors and fellow citizens in ways
that strengthen social bonds."

Appetite for Change (AFC) and its restaurant, Breaking Bread Café, spoke
to that vision for me while also raising critical questions. In this section, I
provide an analysis of AFC, a community-led organization that "envisions
sustainable, local food systems, created and led by thriving, socially connected families and communities."[4] Founded in 2011, AFC uses a complex
blend of neoliberal ideology and social justice to nudge the food system
in a more equitable direction. AFC is not a food pantry, but rather one of
the many organizations spurred by the good food movement in the last

decade to address issues of food access and equity. In this analysis, I highlight some themes and tensions running through AFC that are relevant to
key arguments in the book. Some might see this blend of business and justice as negating the transformative capacity of activism. However, I point
to ways in which justice, for the moment, retains the upper hand at AFC
despite neoliberal constraints. I believe that AFC remains mission focused
by being deeply conscious of the dominant forces that surround the organization and by staying grounded in the voices of marginalized communities.
Quite different from Ruby's Pantry, which is set up to reinforce the Us and
Them dichotomy, AFC is set up is to reinvigorate the identities of people
with long histories of oppression. Also unlike RP, which uses wealth as a
proxy for personal responsibility, AFC assumes that people are responsible
and designs programs to create economic opportunities and wealth. AFC
operates very differently from traditional food pantries, so, indeed, I am
comparing apples to oranges; however, my point here is to precisely raise
the question of whether oranges can become more like apples and apples
more like oranges.

Founded by a small, multiracial group of women, Princess Titus, Michelle
Horovitz, and LaTasha Powell, AFC uses a social entrepreneurship model
that focuses on building community, economic development, and jobs. It is
located in a neighborhood in North Minneapolis comprised mostly of African American and ethnic communities. A site of disinvestment, North Minneapolis has been historically redlined and kept segregated from the rest of
Minneapolis through housing and urban policies. In 2015, North Minneapolis made national headlines for the police shooting of an unarmed Black
man—Jamar Clark. The area is a food swamp saturated with fast food, fried
food shops, liquor stores, and corner stores. In addition, 40 percent of the
residents do not have access to a vehicle, thereby exacerbating the problem
of food access.

Operating in this context of exploitation and oppression, AFC states
boldly on its website: "We grow food, families, leaders and community.
Planting seeds to build social change and justice." AFC has several social
enterprise initiatives, including Fresh Corners, which builds the capacities
of urban farmers from the community to channel their produce into local
restaurants, corner stores, and farmer's markets; Community Cooks, which
gives families—in particular, moms and youth—an opportunity to come
together to grow food, cook, eat, and learn; and leadership training on food
systems and policies through the Youth Training and Employment Program

(YTOP). In addition, the Breaking Bread Café serves food inspired by the cultural cuisines of North Minneapolis and is used to train and employ adults from the community. Kindred Kitchen is a shared commercial kitchen open to small food operations looking to launch or grow their business. And finally, Northside Fresh Coalition is a partnership working on food justice policy and advocacy efforts in the area.

Voice and Political Representation

Foregrounding the voices, interests, and cultural commitments of community members is an ongoing priority for AFC, which makes it different not only from food pantries but also from other hunger groups and coalitions. The founders, longtime residents of the North Minneapolis neighborhood, held cooking workshops in the process of forming AFC during which over 250 residents cooked, ate, and discussed what changes they wanted to see in their community. Through these conversations, AFC learned that people wanted more access points to food. There was a complete lack of diversity in food options and no capacity for people to make healthy choices. Michelle Horovitz, a white woman and the executive director of AFC, pointed out that this had nothing to with people not knowing how to eat healthy or not wanting a home cooked meal but with the lack of any good food options in the neighborhood. Lara, food justice advocate and staff person at AFC and an African American woman, pointed to the intersection between food and other stressors, saying: "If you're a mother and you have to choose between gassing your car, paying your rent, or buying kale, what are you going to do?" Michelle noted that since they began their work, people have become more open to accessing food in different ways; farmers markets used to be thought of as a "white thing," but this perception is shifting. She believes that since they started, there has been a notable difference in how people feel about their own power to change the system.

Consistent with theories of social change described earlier in the chapter, the process of reaching into the community and then out into the wider public for advocacy is important to AFC. However, even as community voices are foregrounded within AFC, there are concerns about how these voices are taken up in advocacy—something not usually described in the literature. Lara points out that most people in the community do not know how policy works and don't have the tools to navigate the political system. Furthermore, a lot of policy work happens beneath the surface and is structured by racism. She says, astutely: "And, you're entering a game where you did not draw the board and you did not make the rules. If you're coming to that game, with a set of rules that don't fit into the game, you might have a great set of rules, and you might have a great amendment to the way the game is played. But there are a number of players right now that like the way the game is played, so it's not going to work." She continued that even with grassroots advocates, there are entities with more political power because they have larger budgets, more privilege, and political capital. Many large hunger-relief organizations today engage in advocacy but have their own histories of perpetuating institutional racism, antiblackness, or antiqueerness. So though they might advocate for helpful changes, their work often does not produce equitable outcomes (alleviating hunger/poverty) specifically for those most marginalized in the country. In the end, indigenous people and people of color are called to the table and asked for their ideas, but there are no outcomes. This is extremely consequential, as Lara notes: "But, if they don't incorporate the things that we're actually saying, then it's useless. And, it's just perpetuating white liberalism. And that in itself is destructive to the communities that need changes for their livelihood and for the sustainability of their own generations."

White Liberalism: "Getting More Than It Gives"

Across this book, the capacity of white liberalism to bring about emancipatory change in the interests of people of color has been called into question. Lara explained the concept of white liberalism so powerfully and eloquently that I will provide the excerpt in its entirety:

Interviewer: What do you mean by "white liberalism"?

Lara: Oh, the concept of white liberalism. It's like a person who wants to march at the Women's March, and purchase their pink pussy hat, and has a Black Lives Matter sign in their front yard. But they're so quick when they hear the bass running down their street, and they see that Black man get out of the car. They're the person that calls the cops and gets scared. Or they're the person that crosses the street because they feel uncomfortable. They want to get defensive and say that they voted for Hilary. Or that they voted for Obama twice.

And that's the kind of thing where, instead of embracing and understanding that, just like we have to suffer from the destruction of our history, we're all suffering because of decisions that your ancestors made. And it's a disappointment, and nobody wants to be sitting here blaming white people, but that's just how it is. Because those are the decisions that were made. And you perpetuate the negativity. We can see it in the news, and we can see it with our people that have been killed, and shot, and aren't present with us anymore because of things that were out of their control.

And, so, that's why I call it white liberalism. Because, in all honesty, it's not like it's those that have the MAGA hats and the confederate flags that I'm scared of. Because I already know to stay the hell away from them. It's the people that are in my everyday work life that greet me and smile at me at Breaking Bread Café, that sit next to me at the legislature ... Because they're the ones in the [Twin] Cities that are influencing policy. And they're the ones that are here trying to say they're building relationships with communities of color, but they're not. And they're not for Black liberation. If they were, the way that they structure their program, the way that they handle PR, the way that they have the person design the flyer, and the representation on there, it would be different.

Lara's articulations are a very precise articulation of how color-blind racism operates today and is very similar to the tensions faced by food pantries described in a previous chapter—the problem of "good white women." Because of their own racial blind spots, many food pantries (and people who work there) do not recognize this tension. Furthermore, given that they run entirely on volunteers, they often have little control over this situation. This dilemma is top of mind for AFC. The AFC staff talked about the struggles they have with white volunteers. When they started programs, many folks assumed they were "teaching poor brown folks how to cook" and showed up. Michelle explained: "You know what I mean, they were like the stay-at-home mom coming because she loves to cook and thinks that she's gonna come and share a bunch of knowledge with folks from North Minneapolis, and it just sets up this Us and Them. It ... perpetuated white supremacy throughout ... They didn't see themselves as participating in the workshop, they saw themselves as leading it." They also got dietitians coming in to volunteer, who were critical of the ingredients they were using because they were not as healthy as they could be. This reinforced stigmas like, "Oh, you poor brown folks don't know what healthy eating is. You don't want healthy eating. You can't cook." The staff has also been concerned about experts coming in to do surveys and community health assessments, as well as college students doing projects; these are exploitative processes that occur especially when outsiders do not involve the communities or bring information back to the communities.

In all of this, there is a clear recognition that volunteers pose a threat to the communities they serve and typically get more than they give from the experience. To manage this problem, AFC has been protective of its communities by intentionally not having many volunteers in their programs and, when they do, ensuring that volunteers have had some consciousness raising occur. They hold orientations, trainings, and one-on-one conversations with individuals to learn more about why they are there and what they hope to get out of it. In fact, another staff member noted that their youth are too precious, so they do not let anybody near them unless they have had that orientation. For Lara, the dilemma is "not wanting it to be a closed club, but also wanting to make sure that you are holding your heart close and not leaving it open to being wounded." However, there are institutional—neoliberalizing—pressures that come with this. Volunteers lead to donors, and funders like volunteer programs: a bottom-line issue. So they are currently in discussions about how best to have a volunteer program but also protect communities. Michelle observed: "We want to find ways that they can actually add value to the organization, or remove things from people's plates that we don't have the capacity or time to do. But at the same time provide an education and training for them on how to be better volunteers."

Entrepreneurship and Justice

In terms of revenue, at AFC 35 to 40 percent is earned revenue that comes from five different sources (catering, café sales, renting the kitchen, produce sales, and selling cooking workshops), while 60 percent comes from grants (private foundation grants, government contracts, corporate foundation grants, and individual donations). An interesting detail here is that two of AFC's private funders are Cargill and General Mills (GM). Cargill and GM are, of course, big players in the hunger industrial complex and heavily implicated in industrial agriculture, commodity foods, and welfare politics. These multinationals are part and parcel of the very forces that AFC is fighting against. Michelle notes that this was initially a source of concern among the founders; however, in light of AFC's goals and place in the food system, it made sense to take their money. She explained:

And when we first took funding from Cargill it was like should we even be doing this? And we were so small back then that we couldn't say no. We were like, you know what, they helped create this system, and they should pay for fixing it, and if we were part of the solution then, you know … "Yeah they caused this they should pay for it." It's easy for a white female liberal to stand and say, "No we shouldn't take money from Cargill." You know what I mean, it's like, okay, well, can we really afford not to?

In nonprofit settings, there is a burgeoning literature on how actors resist neoliberal imperatives amid scarce resource (Barnes and Prior 2009; Cloke, May, and Williams 2017). Individuals interpret and reinterpret policy in light of their own values, identities, and commitments, as well as questions of what they consider to be right. In these settings, the ethical agency of staff and clients modify, disrupt, or negate public policy processes in the interests of their communities. This certainly seemed to be the case here. The argument reminded me of the fact that even the Black Panther Party, which was ideologically opposed to capitalism, in practice relied on redistributing the fruits of capitalism; its ultimate goal was to reduce dependencies and allow for self-determination in Black communities (Broad 2016). This also follows along with the idea of "microreparations"—the idea that the very least these corporations can do in light of historical and ongoing exploitation is redistribute some of its profits among communities it has violated. When I asked about whether AFC experienced pressures from these companies about keeping to their mission, Michelle pointed out that both corporations knew that AFC was involved in advocacy and, in fact, some of the funds to build local food systems in North Minneapolis came from them. She said: "I think they are glad they can say that they're supporting organizations that do this work, even if they are perpetuating the system." The intertwining of Big Hunger and grassroots resistance programs is an ongoing tension, and one that will need to be constantly reexamined.

In sum, the work of AFC provides an entry point to think about how entrepreneurship, accountability, and "vocabularies of the economy" can be used in conjunction with goals of equity and justice. AFC's work resonates with J. K. Gibson-Graham's (1996) claim that community economies are expressions of "diverse economies," which cannot be pegged as capitalism because they contest and resist particular features of neoliberalism. These economies can be spaces of ethical action, not just places where we submit to the bottom line. This point is reinforced by the fact that besides

Cargill and GM, Colin Kaepernick, the controversial African American quarterback, also donated $25,000 to Appetite for Change.

Blackened Shrimp and Grits, a Kale Salad, and a Latte

One of the first things I did at AFC was eat lunch with a staff member. She recommended the blackened shrimp and grits with a side salad of kale. It was incredible! It was tasty and made me feel good: a chef-prepared meal and authentic at the same time. I gave thanks (internally) that I was not eating another cold ham sandwich or a tasteless wrap—staples of the whitened diet I have come to suffer in Duluth. It was a perfect lunch and I did not waste a bite. Although the most expensive item on the menu was $13, this café would not be an option for some of the extremely food insecure folks at Chum, like John, the environmental chemist who could only afford the occasional dollar for a plate of fries. But, as Michelle noted, this restaurant provided an important access point for good food in a food desert and changed the look and feel of the neighborhood.

The day I visited, there were people sitting at most tables in the restaurant—people of color and a few tables with white folks. There was a group of African American men and women engaged in a serious business discussion, a white couple with their two young kids, and a couple of young women—perhaps Hmong—who after lunch took out their computers to work. I learned from my host that folks from the neighborhood often use the café for business and community meetings. The servers were African American, as was the chef and other people who operated the kitchen. The place was a typical restaurant, professional to a tee, but you just got the sense that there was a different set of rules being followed here. The air was set at the perfect temperature—not too cold, as restaurants sometimes are. There was an openness, a sense of fluidity to the space, people coming in and going out. There was some cross talk among tables. Most people appeared to be professionals, perhaps in the low- to middle-class income bracket. And for the first time in a long time, I was not the only person of color at a restaurant.

Breaking Bread reminded me of a space reconfigured to look not like it existed outside of capitalism and neoliberalism, but like it existed *despite* neoliberalism. It seemed to bend the rules of racist structures, white liberalism, and capitalism. The decentering of whiteness was palpable in the bodies present and how they moved in that space. Saldanha (2006, 22) argues that "race shows the openness of the body, the way organisms connect to their environment and establish uneven relationships amongst each other." Whiteness is about the "the sticky connections between property, privilege, and a paler skin" (18). Saldanha uses the term "viscosity" to capture the material ontology and performativity of race: "Viscosity means that the physical characteristics of a substance explain its unique movements. There are local and temporary thickenings of interacting bodies, which then collectively become sticky, capable of capturing more bodies like them: an emergent slime mold. Under certain circumstances, the collectivity dissolves, the constituent bodies flowing freely again. The world is an immense mass of viscosities, becoming thicker here, and thinner there" (18). In using terms such as *sticky* and *viscosity* , Saldanha is referring to how (white) bodies under particular conditions coalesce or disaggregate—like "emergent slime mold" (I love that imagery!). At Breaking Bread, I got the sense that white bodies became unstuck, looser, and "bodies were flowing freely again" (18) because whiteness was decentered.

Astonishingly, Breaking Bread reminded me of a restaurant I once used to hang out in fourteen thousand miles away in Bangalore, the city I grew up in. It was a place that decentered class and culture in similar ways. Although the food was not cheap, the small cups of coffee were, so it was a place where people would sip coffee for hours, talking, working, reading, and writing. There were folks from a range of social locations, rich and poor, different cultures, and you could always hear different Indian languages being spoken—not typical of the elite spaces I usually inhabited. You could sit there alone. You could joke around with friends. And while there may not have been cross talk, eavesdropping in this noisy space was the norm. Some people thought it was a bit pretentious because it was a hub for Bangalore intelligentsia, artists, and playwrights. But it was perfect because it seemed like everyone was trying to work out life in that space through and with others. And the thing is, you felt completely comfortable, even if you bought one cup of coffee and left six hours later. Breaking Bread reminded me of that place: not quite there yet, but perhaps in the process of becoming.

The different set of rules became clear to me when I ordered a latte after lunch. Michelle picked me up from the café, but because it was noisy and I was recording, we went back to the conference room. Perhaps nervous, I quickly packed up my stuff and followed her—without paying for my latte. I forgot to pay! Halfway through the interview, I remembered. I was embarrassed for having broken a pretty simple and key rule of capitalism. Two hours later, I went back sheepishly to the café to apologize, to explain, and to pay for my drink, when the woman behind the counter, who I did not know, said with the most generous and casual smile: "Oh no, you're good, you're good!" and waved me away. For me, the most important point of this story is that I forgot to pay—and, next, that they did not take my money. Because I wonder what would have happened if this was Starbucks? No doubt I would have been chased down and, as we know today, cops might have been called. But frankly, I would *never* forget to pay at Starbucks or any other restaurant. It just doesn't happen. Somehow, being in that space, what felt like a community (a "community economy") changed my identity. It moved me from a state of hypervigilance to *normal*; for a brief moment, I was not ruled by a capitalist or racial calculus. I wondered if that happened often, and the accountant in me hopes that it does not, but it was a powerful reminder that the way things work is not the only way they *can* work. There is always something deeper, more fun, and much more interesting below the bottom line—and we should always be interested in exploring that.

A Final Word

It has been nearly twenty years since Janet Poppendieck (1999) observed that fighting hunger had become a "national pastime." We are at an impasse. The prevalence of hunger continues at the same rate and is worsening. Indeed, in a nation of abundance, it is quite extraordinary that people are forced to eat a plate of fries for a meal, even as they are incredibly knowledgeable about the roles of vitamins, minerals, and fresh foods in their health. Food pantries manage the immediate problem of hunger but do little to solve the long-term problem of food insecurity and its intersecting needs and oppressions. They are just not set up to do that; they are set up solve logistical problems related to collecting and distributing surplus foods.

For me, the Chum food pantry represents the past, RP a problematic and tenuous present, and AFC a hopeful future for food access and assistance: ironic, of course, because they all exist at the same moment in time to remedy the same problem of hunger caused by economic deprivation. They are all also beholden in some way to the systemic pressures of industrial agriculture. On the one hand, AFC provides a good example of what food pantries might look like in the future, but is there a way for AFC to distribute *good food* to people right now, people who need it, like Trinity and John? Can AFC do the work that food pantries do, but with the same deep critical consciousness and connection to the histories and biographies of citizens? On the other hand, can food pantries like Chum and RP develop a deep critical consciousness like that I found at AFC? Can food pantries get away from the language of charity and good works? A language that silences the voices of those who are on the receiving end and leaves in its wake a culture of suspicion, dread, and disillusionment?

I began this book with an excerpt by Trinity, an African American woman who captured the essence of neoliberal stigma. Here she is again, capturing the essence of why we're at an impasse with charitable food assistance:

It's not charitable to give it to poor people because it's crap. It's processed, it's full of fat, it's full of salt, it's full of chemicals, and that aren't really going to help a person ... And so there's a part of me that's quite jaded and grumpy and that part of me says, "It's just a way for people to feel good. Look at us, we've salvaged this food and we're making sure people will get this food ..." But the fact is that it's going to go somewhere. And if it fills people's tummies, then I have to put on my other lens that says it is a tremendous thing to do. I mean, it's a huge undertaking to repurpose or salvage, whatever that is. It's a huge undertaking, obviously, they come with those huge trucks, they have to load those trucks and go to the sites and unload those huge trucks. And it's a great service. At the risk of sounding bipolar, on one hand, I think it's awful, and on the other hand, it is really a good thing.

It is precisely this "bipolarity" that we are trapped within. Trinity is not bipolar; the system is bipolar. On the top, you have the Goliaths—the corporations, governments, and transnational neoliberal institutions that make the rules. At the bottom, you have smaller players that dole out food in the service of faith and personal fulfilment. Concealed within charitable discourses, the many injustices of the food system remain hidden from view. The language of saints and Samaritans hides the injustice of legislation, corporations, structural racism, and the benefits received by millions of donors who participate in the hunger industrial complex. Food pantries are small players at the bottom of the food system, but they are not innocent bystanders—not anymore, not thirty years later. How can food pantries change their roles to work toward a vision of food justice? How can these individually insignificant players come together to bend, modify, and break the rules so as to chip away at the systemic forces they are entangled with? How can they create more liberating spaces where people can feel at ease, where there is a sense of joyfulness and moving forward, not suspicion, dead-ends, and standing still?

I believe that food pantries can become spaces of empowerment if they think of themselves more broadly as centers and sites for activism and the production and reformulation of new narratives. Food pantries are at the very frontlines of the hunger epidemic, closest to the people who experience the violence of hunger, and therefore are in prime position to generate new stories. For this to happen, the language of possibility, social action, and activism needs to enter spaces of food assistance and create identity shifts. Fortified by the stories of their clients—clients like Trinity—food pantries can take small steps to act as points of resistance and to eventually bring about the vision of food justice. We can only imagine if the thousands of food pantries were to actually become cognizant of and participate in building the critical consciousness of their staff, volunteers, clients, and broader communities; then the margins would truly become spaces of liberation and dissent, able to stand up to the crushing burden of neoliberal stigma.

Notes

1 Introduction

1. Terms used to identify people of color are textured by complex social and political histories, and are subject to change as we move through history. I use the terms "Black" and "African American" interchangeably throughout this book since both terms are used today in intra-group settings as well as across racial groups—although the term African American carries with it a particular history involving the African slave trade, Jim Crow, and the Civil Rights Movement, as different from the histories of recent African immigrants and refugees to the United States. Black, as per conventional editorial standards, is not capitalized because it is used as an adjective to describe skin color, rather than a racial or national designation. However, following the work of MacKinnon (1982) and Crenshaw (1991, 1988), I capitalize Black because I see it not merely as a descriptor of color, but as "a heritage, an experience, a cultural and personal identity, the meaning of which becomes specifically stigmatic and/or glorious and/or ordinary under specific social conditions. It is as much socially created as, and at least in the American context no less specifically meaningful or definitive than, any linguistic, tribal, or religious ethnicity, all of which are conventionally recognized by capitalization" (MacKinnon 1982, 516). Put differently, Black is capitalized, because "Blacks, like Asians, Latinos, and other 'minorities,' constitute a specific cultural group and, as such, require denotation as a proper noun" (Crenshaw 1988, 1332n2).

2. The data in this book draw from the research project titled "The Food-Based Community Economy: Understanding How Community Enterprises Provide for Those Experiencing Food Scarcity," a four-year, mixed methods project examining the various ways in which individuals who experience food insecurity provision themselves. All research protocols were approved by the Institutional Review Board of the University of Minnesota as well as Chum's Director and Executive Board and Ruby's Pantry Steering Committee in Duluth. Consent was obtained at the individual level for each client, staff member, and volunteer interviewed. Entrance to Chum and RP–Duluth was initially made by contacting the manager and program

heads at each organization. A formal presentation was made to the board of RP–Duluth, which voted to allow the study to be conducted. At Chum, entrance was gained through more informal personal relationships with board members and program directors. Semistructured interviews were conducted with twenty-two clients, eight volunteers, and three staff members from Chum and with twenty-one clients, ten volunteers, and two staff members from RP over the course of two years. Each interview lasted between thirty and ninety minutes, and participants received fifteen dollars in gift cards to use at the local supermarket. Interviewees were between the ages of eighteen and sixty-five. An additional twelve formal interviews were conducted with food experts, advocates, and leaders in the food movement. Three interview protocols were developed in an iterative manner—one for clients, one for volunteers, and one for staff/managers/directors. For the first two, the protocols contained several sets of questions, including questions about initial contact with the food pantry, relationship with volunteers, quantity and quality of food, methods for coping, faith beliefs, positive and negative experiences, impressions of clients, stigma, and relationships with other clients. For organizational leaders, questions focused on vision, institutional pressures, and program sustainability. The interviews were recorded, professionally transcribed, and analyzed for themes using NVivo. Except for the executive directors of the organizations, all other names of staff, volunteers, and clients were anonymized using pseudonyms. In addition, certain identifying details were removed to maintain confidentiality. I wrote field notes after each time I volunteered; the notes described the people present, the events that played out during the session, the roles and functions of individuals and groups, and the types of interactions. These memos and field notes were entered into NVivo, which was used to inform the analysis. The study also included an analysis of organizational documents (websites, promotional materials, press releases, and newsletters), which were key to understanding the ideological underpinnings. Finally, I attended numerous food conferences, including the Food Access Summits held in Duluth. Through these conferences, I engaged with actors in the food movement, including activists, legal aid representatives, staff from local food pantries and food banks, and legal, health, and government officials. On several occasions, I brought food home from RP to get a better sense of the quantity and quality of food distributed and with the goal of recentering the body in this research project about hunger. Approximately four hundred surveys were conducted at Chum and RP; however, given my interest in discursive practices related to stigma, the analysis in this book relies primarily on interviews and observations.

3. In this study, I used Charmaz's (2001) constructivist approach to grounded theory to analyze the data. This is a process-oriented methodology that organizes qualitative data and allows for new relationships and theoretical propositions to emerge. I used NVivo to code and organize the data. The first step in the analysis is *open coding*, which involves a line-by-line reading of all text (including transcripts and field observations) to code for "what is happening" in the data—a mostly descriptive

process. At this time, approximately 950 descriptive codes were identified, which were labeled variously (e.g., "talking about nutrition and whole grains"). The second step—*selective* or *focused coding*—involved moving the analysis from description to conceptualization; this was a way to reduce the data meaningfully. Here I brought together 950 descriptive codes into sixty more analytically incisive codes, representing the major recursive themes in the data. For instance, forty-one codes in the data were eventually brought together to constitute the theme and meanings of "food consciousness"—one of them being whole grains and nutrition. These codes came from twenty-seven unique interviews. Although I did not count how many times something was talked about, if the meaning was frequently occurring, repetitive, or displayed a pattern, then it was codified as a major theme and something to be presented in the final write-up. The last step of the analytical process involved *synthesizing* and *interpreting the data*. This was the most grueling part of the process because it happened in a fluid, ground-up, and organic manner. It had been my intent to study hunger and food insecurity as they related to health, healthy choices, and strategies for coping—and these were indeed the themes that I coded. Stigma was one piece of the study, along with all the rest. However, as I listened to participants and heard their stories, what bubbled to the surface were the multiple ways in which people experienced, expressed, and managed stigma around these more particular food- and health-related themes. The attributions of shame, blame, identity, and difference rooted in race, gender, religion, and politics formed connective tissue across the data. In terms of method, this now meant that instead of simply listing volunteer perceptions of clients, I was compelled to interpret these perceptions through the lens of stigma. This is where I began the work of theorizing neoliberal stigma, which involved a sequence of reading, reflection, interpretation, and continually checking ideas and assumptions to ensure rigor and richness. After this, I used several techniques to validate my findings. I kept memos to establish preliminary relationships between themes and clarify ideas, and I also ran the themes by folks who worked in such spaces paying attention to the standpoints and positionalities of these individuals. I had no idea when this study began that I would find myself so deeply in political and racial terrain; this emerged in a grounded sense from the voices of my participants and my own social justice sensibilities.

8   Conclusion

1. I would like to recognize Pastor Kathy Nelson of Peace United Church of Christ, Duluth, Minnesota, for her sermon on "The One-Sided Approach of the Good Samaritan" in July 2016, which called my attention to this lesser-known interpretation of the parable.

2. Freire's (1970) *conscientization* refers to a dialogic process through which people become aware of their own oppressed status and then take action to overcome oppression. Building a critical consciousness necessarily involves the incorporation

of a critical understanding of the sociopolitical context, as well as the cultivation of skills for social action. Through the development of a critical consciousness, the oppressed come to "read the world" and name and evaluate the problem. This process involves a problem-posing method consisting of a cycle of listening-dialogue-action, which enables participants to engage in continuous reflection and action. For Fraser (1992, 123), the *subaltern counterpublic* refers to a space in which "members of subordinated social groups invent and circulate counter discourses to formulate oppositional interpretations of their identities, interests, and needs." Subaltern counterpublics have a dual function: to function as spaces of withdrawal and regroupment for oppressed groups and to serve as training grounds for agitational activities directed toward wider publics. "It is precisely in the dialectic between these two functions that their emancipatory potential resides" (124). Importantly, subaltern publics are arenas not only for understanding beliefs and opinion, but for the formation and enactment of social identities, spaces where people can speak in their own voices, idioms, and styles. Simply put, there are no "masculinist bourgeois" rules that individuals are beholden to in these spaces; instead, the subaltern can freely express her personal and cultural identity here. Last, but not least, Dutta's (2007) conceptualization of the *culture-centered approach* (CCA) is founded on the principle of bringing the voices of people in the margins into focus. The CCA highlights the roles of culture, structure, and agency in this process. *Culture* is conceptualized as "a complex and dynamic web of meanings that is continuously in flux, as it interacts with the structural processes that surround the culture" (310–311). Culture is not static but is found in the continuous interweaving of the past, present, and future through meanings co-constructed by cultural participants. The CCA reinforces the importance of identifying structures and systems that perpetuate disparities because inequity ultimately resides in the social organization of societies and institutions. Finally, the CCA asserts that social change occurs through the agency of cultural participants expressed in communication at multiple levels—communication among community members, policymakers, program planners, and other communities in a manner that expands the network of influence (Dutta 2008).

3. See http://www.surjnorthland.org/calendar/.

4. See https://breakingbreadfoods.com/.

References

Adkins, Julie, Laurie Occhipinti, and Tara Hefferan. 2012. "Social Services, Social Justice, and Faith-Based Organizations in the United States: An Introduction." In *Not by Faith Alone: Social Services, Social Justice and Faith-Based Organizations in the United States*, edited by J. Adkins, L. Occhipinti, and T. Hefferan, 1–32. Lanham, MD: Lexington Books.

Alkon, Alison Hope, and Julian Agyeman. 2011. *Cultivating Food Justice: Race, Class, and Sustainability*. Cambridge, MA: MIT Press.

Alkon, Alison Hope, and Teresa Marie Mares. 2012. "Food Sovereignty in US Food Movements: Radical Visions and Neoliberal Constraints." *Agriculture and Human Values* 29 (3): 347–359. https://doi.org/10.1007/s10460-012-9356-z.

Allen, Patricia. 1999. "Reweaving the Food Security Safety Net: Mediating Entitlement and Entrepreneurship." *Agriculture and Human Values* 16 (2): 117–129. https://doi.org/10.1023/A:1007593210496.

Ambedkar, Bhimrao Ramji. 2014. *Annihilation of Caste: The Annotated Critical Edition*. Edited by S. Anand. London: Verso.

Arnold, Joan Hagan, and Penelope Buschman Gemma. 1983. *A Child Dies: A Portrait of Family Grief*. Rockville, MD: Aspen.

Atia, Mona. 2012. "'A Way to Paradise': Pious Neoliberalism, Islam, and Faith-Based Development." *Annals of the Association of American Geographers* 102 (4): 808–827. https://doi.org/10.1080/00045608.2011.627046.

Barnes, Marian, and David Prior, eds. 2009. *Subversive Citizens: Power, Agency and Resistance in Public Services*. Bristol, UK: Policy Press.

Beaumont, Justin, and Paul Cloke, eds. 2012. *Faith-Based Organisations and Exclusion in European Cities*. Bristol, UK: Policy Press.

Bielefeld, Wolfgang, and William Suhs Cleveland. 2013. "Faith-Based Organizations as Service Providers and Their Relationship to Government." *Nonprofit and Voluntary Sector Quarterly* 42 (3): 468–494. https://doi.org/10.1177/0899764013485160.

Biewen, John. 2017. "Episode 45: Transformation (Seeing White, Part 14)." Scene on Radio podcast. Center for Documentary Studies at Duke University. http://www .sceneonradio.org/wp-content/uploads/2018/01/SeeingWhite_Part14Transcript .pdf.

Black Lives Matter. n.d. "What We Believe." Accessed September 7, 2018. https:// blacklivesmatter.com/about/what-we-believe/.

Blue Bird Jernigan, Valarie, Eva Garroutte, Elizabeth M. Krantz, and Dedra Buchwald. 2013. "Food Insecurity and Obesity among American Indians and Alaska Natives and Whites in California." *Journal of Hunger & Environmental Nutrition* 8 (4): 458–471. https://doi.org/10.1080/19320248.2013.816987.

Boero, Natalie. 2010. "Fat Kids, Working Moms, and the Epidemic of Obesity Race, Class, and Mother-Blame." In *The Fat Studies Reader*, edited by E. Rothblum and S. Solovay, 113–119. New York: New York University Press.

Bondi, Liz. 2005. "Working the Spaces of Neoliberal Subjectivity: Psychotherapeutic Technologies, Professionalisation and Counselling." *Antipode* 37 (3): 497–514. https://doi.org/10.1111/j.0066-4812.2005.00508.x.

Bonilla-Silva, Eduardo. 2010. *Racism without Racists: Color-Blind Racism and the Persistence of Racial Inequality in the United States.* 3rd ed. New York: Rowman and Littlefield.

Bornstein, E. 2005. *The Spirit of Development: Protestant NGOs, Morality, and Economics in Zimbabwe.* Stanford, CA: Stanford University Press.

Bourdieu, Pierre. 1990. *The Logic of Practice.* Cambridge: Polity.

Broad, Garett. 2016. *More than Just Food: Food Justice and Community Change.* Berkeley: University of California Press.

Carolan, Michael. 2011. *The Real Cost of Cheap Food.* New York: Earthscan.

Carter, Andrew. 2017. "Soul Food: Examining the Narratives of African-American Farmers in the U.S. South." Paper presented at the National Communication Association annual convention, Dallas, TX, November 16–19.

Casey, Patrick, Susan Goolsby, Carol Berkowitz, Deborah Frank, John Cook, Diana Cutts, Maureen Black, Nieves Zaldivar, Suzette Levenson, Tim Heeren, and Alan Meyers. 2004. "Maternal Depression, Changing Public Assistance, Food Security, and Child Health Status." *Pediatrics* 113 (2): 298–304.

Centers for Disease Control and Prevention (CDC). 2013. CDC Health Disparities and Inequalities Report- United States 2013; Morbidity and Mortality Weekly Report, 62 (Suppl 3). URL https://www.cdc.gov/mmwr/pdf/other/su6203.pdf.

Charmaz, Kathy. 2001. "Qualitative Interviewing and Grounded Theory Analysis." In *Handbook of Interview Research: Context and Method*, edited by J. Gubrium and J. Holstein, 675–694. Thousand Oaks, CA: Sage.

Chilton, Mariana, and Sue Booth. 2007. "Hunger of the Body and Hunger of the Mind: African American Women's Perceptions of Food Insecurity, Health and Violence." *Journal of Nutrition Education & Behavior* 39 (3): 116–125.

Chilton, Mariana, and Donald Rose. 2009. "A Rights-Based Approach to Food Insecurity in the United States." *American Journal of Public Health* 99 (7): 1203–1211.

Chun, Edna, and Alvin Evans. 2018. *Leading a Diversity Culture Shift in Higher Education: Comprehensive Organizational Learning Strategies.* New York: Routledge.

Clair, Robin, and Lindsey Anderson. 2013. "Portrayals of the Poor on the Cusp of Capitalism: Promotional Materials in the Case of Heifer International." *Management Communication Quarterly* 27 (4): 537–567.

Cloke, Paul, Jon May, and Andrew Williams. 2017. "The Geographies of Food Banks in the Meantime." *Progress in Human Geography* 41 (6): 703–726. https://doi.org/10.1177/0309132516655881.

Coleman-Jensen, Alisha, Christian Gregory, and Anita Singh. 2014. "Household Food Security in the United States in 2013." ERR-173, US Department of Agriculture, Economic Research Service. https://www.ers.usda.gov/webdocs/publications/45265/48787_err173.pdf?v=42265.

Collins, Patricia Hill. 2004. "Learning from the Outsider Within: The Sociological Significance of Black Feminist Thought." In *The Feminist Standpoint Theory Reader: Intellectual and Political Controversies*, edited by Sandra Harding, 103–126. New York: Routledge.

Comstock, Betsy, and Carolyn Pesheck. 2013. *Facing Hunger in America*. Study project sponsored by the United Methodist Church West Michigan Conference Board of Global Ministries. http://www.ministrywith.org/files/96/Facing%20Hunger%20in%20America%20Report%202013.pdf.

Cone, James. 1997. *God of the Oppressed*. Maryknoll, NY: Orbis Books.

Connell, Carol, Kristi Lofton, Kathy Yadrick, and Timothy Rehner. 2005. "Children's Experiences of Food Insecurity Can Assist in Understanding Its Effect on Their Well-Being." *Journal of Nutrition* 135 (7): 1683–1690.

Corrigan, Patrick W., Jonathon E. Larson, and Nicolas Rusch. 2009. "Self-Stigma and the 'Why Try' Effect: Impact on Life Goals and Evidence-Based Practices." *World Psychiatry* 8 (2): 75–81.

Corrigan, Patrick W., F. E. Markowitz, and A. C. Watson. 2004. "Structural Levels of Mental Illness Stigma and Discrimination." *Schizophrenia Bulletin* 30 (3): 481–491.

Crenshaw, Kimberlé. 1988. "Race, Reform, and Retrenchment: Transformation and Legitimation in Antidiscrimination Law." Harvard Law Review 101 (7):1331–1387. https://doi.org/10.2307/1341398.

Crenshaw, Kimberlé. 1991. "Mapping the Margins: Intersectionality, Identity Politics, and Violence against Women of Color." Stanford Law Review 43 (6):1241–1299. https://doi.org/10.2307/1229039.

Cutts, Diana Becker, Alan F. Meyers, Maureen M. Black, P. Casey, Mariana Chilton, John T. Cook, Joni Geppert, Stephanie Ettinger de Cuba, Timothy Heeren, Sharon Coleman, Ruth Rose-Jacobs, and Deborah A. Frank. 2011. "US Housing Insecurity and the Health of Very Young Children." American Journal of Public Health 101 (8): 1508–1514. https://doi.org/10.2105/AJPH.2011.300139.

Dean, Stacy. 2016. "SNAP: Combating Fraud and Improving Program Integrity without Weakening Success: Testimony of Stacy Dean, Vice President for Food Assistance Policy, Center on Budget and Policy Priorities, before the Subcommittees on Government Operations and the Interior of the Committee on Oversight and Government Reform US House of Representatives." Center on Budget and Policy Priorities, June 9, 2018. http://www.cbpp.org/food-assistance/snap-combating-fraud-and-improving -program-integrity-without-weakening-success.

Dees, Gregory. 1998. "The Meaning of 'Social Entrepreneurship.'" Duke University, Duke Innovation and Entrepreneurship Initiative. Last modified May 30, 2001. https:// entrepreneurship.duke.edu/news-item/the-meaning-of-social-entrepreneurship/.

Del Casino, Vincent J., and Christine L. Jocoy. 2008. "Neoliberal Subjectivities, the 'New' Homelessness, and Struggles over Spaces of/in the City." Antipode 40 (2): 192– 199. https://doi.org/10.1111/j.1467-8330.2008.00583.x.

DeLind, Laura. 1994. "Celebrating Hunger in Michigan: A Critique of an Emergency Food Program and an Alternative for the Future." Agriculture and Human Values 11 (4): 58–68. https://doi.org/10.1007/BF01530417.

DeLorme, Charles D., David R. Kamerschen, and David C. Redman. 1992. "The First U.S. Food Stamp Program: An Example of Rent Seeking and Avoiding." American Journal of Economics and Sociology 51 (4): 421–433. https://doi.org/10.1111/ j.1536-7150.1992.tb02726.x.

De Marco, Molly, Sheryl Thorburn, and Jennifer Kue. 2009. "'In a Country as Affluent as America, People Should be Eating': Experiences with and Perceptions of Food Insecurity among Rural and Urban Oregonians." Qualitative Health Research 19 (7): 1010–1024.

de Souza, Rebecca, Ambar Basu, Induk Kim, Iccha Basnyat, and Mohan Dutta. 2008. "The Paradox of 'Fair Trade': The Influence of Neoliberal Trade Agreements on Food Security and Health." In Emerging Perspectives in Health Communication:

Meaning, Culture, and Power, edited by Heather Zoller and Mohan Dutta, 411–430. Mahwah, NJ: Lawrence Erlbaum.

DiAngelo, Robin. 2011. "White Fragility." *International Journal of Critical Pedagogy* 3 (3): 54–70.

Diaz, Natalie. 2012. "Why I Hate Raisins." In *When My Brother Was an Aztec*, 9–10. Port Townsend, WA: Copper Canyon Press.

Dickinson, Maggie. 2013. "Beyond the Minimally Adequate Diet: Food Stamps and Food Sovereignty in the U.S." Paper presented at Food Sovereignty: A Critical Dialogue International Conference, Yale University, New Haven, CT, September 14–15, https://www.tni.org/files/download/23_dickinson_2013.pdf.

DiFazio, William. 2006. *Ordinary Poverty: A Little Food and Cold Storage*. Philadelphia: Temple University Press.

Dinour, Lauren M., Dara Bergen, and Ming-Chin Yeh. 2007. "The Food Insecurity–Obesity Paradox: A Review of the Literature and the Role Food Stamps May Play." *Journal of the American Dietetic Association* 107 (11): 1952–1961. https://doi.org/10.1016/j.jada.2007.08.006.

Dixon, Jane. 2009. "From the Imperial to the Empty Calorie: How Nutrition Relations Underpin Food Regime Transitions." *Agriculture and Human Values* 26 (4): 321–333. https://doi.org/10.1007/s10460-009-9217-6.

Doane, Ashley, and Eduardo Bonilla-Silva, eds. 2003. *White Out: The Continuing Significance of Racism*. London: Routledge.

Dougherty, Debbie, Megan Koch-Schraedley, J. Wickert, and Angela Gist. 2016. "Revealing/Concealing among the Unemployed: Body Class/Text Class Discourses of Food Insecurity." Paper presented at the National Communication Association annual convention, Philadelphia, PA, November 10–13.

Drewnowski, Adam, and Nicole Darmon. 2005. "The Economics of Obesity: Dietary Energy Density and Energy Cost." *American Journal of Clinical Nutrition* 82 (S1): 265S–273S. https://doi.org/10.1093/ajcn/82.1.265S.

Dutta-Bergman, Mohan. 2004. "The Unheard Voices of Santalis: Communicating about Health from the Margins of India." *Communication Theory* 14 (3): 237–263.

Dutta, Mohan. 2007. "Communicating about Culture and Health: Theorizing Culture-Centered and Cultural Sensitivity Approaches." *Communication Theory* 17 (3): 304–328. https://doi.org/10.1111/j.1468-2885.2007.00297.x.

Dutta, Mohan. 2008. *Communicating Health: A Culture-Centered Approach*. Cambridge: Polity Press.

Dutta, Mohan, Agaptus Anaele, and Christina Jones. 2013. "Voices of Hunger: Addressing Health Disparities through the Culture-Centered Approach." *Journal of Communication* 63 (1): 159–180. https://doi.org/10.1111/jcom.12009.

Elisha, Omri. 2011. *Moral Ambition: Mobilization and Social Outreach in Evangelical Megachurches.* Berkeley, CA: University of California Press.

Ellingson, Laura. 2017. *Embodiment in Qualitative Research.* New York: Routledge.

Evich, Helena Bottemiller. 2018. "Trump Pitches Plan to Replace Food Stamps with Food Boxes." *Politico*, February 12. https://www.politico.com/story/2018/02/12/food -stamps-trump-administration-343245.

Fairclough, Norman. 1989. *Language and Power.* London: Longman.

Fanon, Frantz. 1967. *Black Skin, White Masks.* Translated from the French by Charles Lam Markman. New York: Grove Press.

Farmer, Paul. 2005. *Pathologies of Power: Health, Human Rights, and the New War on the Poor.* Berkeley: University of California Press.

Feagin, Joe. 1975. *Subordinating the Poor: Welfare and American Beliefs.* Englewood Cliffs, NJ: Prentice-Hall.

Feagin, Joe. 2013. *The White Racial Frame: Centuries of Racial Framing and Counter -Framing.* New York: Routledge.

Feagin, Joe, and Zinobia Bennefield. 2014. "Systemic Racism and U.S. Health Care." *Social Science & Medicine* 103:7–14. https://doi.org/10.1016/j.socscimed.2013.09.006.

Feeding America. 2013. "In Short Supply: American Families Struggle to Secure Everyday Essentials." Accessed September 9, 2014. http://www.feedingamerica.org/ hunger-in-america/our-research/in-short-supply/in-short-supply-executive.pdf.

Feeding America. 2014. "Hunger in America 2014: A Report on Charitable Food Distribution in the United States in 2013." Accessed May 22, 2016. http://www .feedingamerica.org/research/hunger-in-america/hia-2014-executive-summary.pdf.

Fisher, Andrew. 2017. *Big Hunger: The Unholy Alliance between Corporate America and Anti-hunger Groups.* Cambridge, MA: MIT Press.

Fiske, John. 1991. "For Cultural Interpretation: A Study of the Culture of Home-lessness." *Critical Studies in Mass Communication* 8 (4): 455–474. https://doi.org/10 .1080/15295039109366809.

FitzGerald, Frances. 2017. *The Evangelicals: The Struggle to Shape America.* New York: Simon and Schuster.

Forbes. 2013. "The Top Skills Every Entrepreneur Needs." https://www.forbes.com/ sites/aileron/2013/11/26/the-top-skills-every-entrepreneur-needs/#1451689576e3.

Fothergill, Alice. 2003. "The Stigma of Charity: Gender, Class, and Disaster Assistance." *The Sociological Quarterly* 44 (4): 659–680. https://doi.org/10.1111/j.1533-8525.2003.tb00530.x.

Foucault, Michel. (1963) 1994. *The Birth of a Clinic: An Archaeology of Medical Perception.* New York: Vintage Books.

Foucault, Michel. 1995. *Discipline and Punish: The Birth of a Prison.* 2nd ed. Translated by Alan Sheridan. New York: Random House.

Frank, Arthur. 1995. *The Wounded Storyteller: Body, Illness and Ethics.* Chicago: University of Chicago Press.

Frankenberg, Ruth. 1993. *White Women, Race Matters: The Social Construction of Whiteness.* Minneapolis: University of Minnesota.

Fraser, Nancy. 1987. "Women, Welfare and the Politics of Need Interpretation." *Hypatia* 2 (1): 103–121.

Fraser, Nancy. 1992. "Rethinking the Public Sphere: A Contribution to the Critique of Actually Existing Democracy." In *Habermas and the Public Sphere*, edited by Craig Calhoun, 109–141. Cambridge, MA: MIT Press.

Fraser, Nancy, and Linda Gordon. 1994. "A Genealogy of Dependency: Tracing a Keyword of the U.S. Welfare State." *Signs* 19 (2): 309–336.

Freire, Paulo. 1970. *Pedagogy of the Oppressed.* New York: Seabury.

Frey, Larry, Pearce, W. Barnett, Pollock, Mark, and Artz, Lee. 1996. "Looking for Justice in All the Wrong Places: On a Communication Approach to Social Justice." *Communication Studies* 47:110–127.

Galeano, Eduardo. 1991. "Celebration of the Human Voice/2." In *Book of Embraces*, translated by Cedric Belfrage. New York: W. W. Norton.

Gandhi, Mohandas Karamchand. 1993. *An Autobiography: The Story of My Experiments with Truth.* Translated by M. Desai. Boston: Beacon Press.

Gandy, Justin. 2016. "Social Entrepreneurship as Spiritual Entrepreneurship." *Journal of Ethics & Entrepreneurship* 6 (1): 149–164.

Garthwaite, Kayleigh. 2016. *Hunger Pains: Life inside Foodbank Britain.* Bristol, UK: Policy Press.

Garthwaite, Kayleigh. 2017. "'I feel I'm Giving Something Back to Society': Constructing the 'Active Citizen' and Responsibilising Foodbank Use." *Social Policy and Society* 16 (2): 283–292.

Ghose, Rina, and Margaret Pettygrove. 2014. "Urban Community Gardens as Spaces of Citizenship." *Antipode* 46 (4): 1092–1112. https://doi.org/10.1111/anti.12077.

Gibson-Graham, J. K. 1996. *The End of Capitalism (As We Knew It): A Feminist Critique of Political Economy*. Oxford: Blackwell.

Giddens, Anthony. 1984. *The Constitution of Society: Outline of the Theory of Structuration*. Cambridge: Polity.

Gilens, Martin. 1999. *Why Americans Hate Welfare: Race, Media, and the Politics of Antipoverty Policy*. Chicago: University of Chicago.

Giroux, Henry A. 2014. "The Militarization of Racism and Neoliberal Violence." Truthout, August 18. http://www.truth-out.org/opinion/item/25660-the-militarization -of-racism-and-neoliberal-violence.

Goffman, Erving. 1963. *Stigma: Notes on the Management of Spoiled Identity*. New York: Simon and Schuster.

Goldberg, David Theo. 2009. *The Threat of Race: Reflections on Racial Neoliberalism*. New York: John Wiley & Sons.

Gordon, Avery. 1997. *Ghostly Matters: Haunting and the Sociological Imagination*. Minneapolis: University of Minnesota.

Gottlieb, Robert, and Anupama Joshi. 2010. *Food Justice*. Cambridge, MA: MIT Press.

Greene, Carlnita, and Janet Cramer. 2011. "Beyond Mere Sustenance: Food as Communication/Communication as Food." In *Food as Communication; Communication as Food*, edited by Janet Cramer, Carlnita Greene, and Lynn Walter, ix–xix. New York: Peter Lang.

Gundersen, Craig, Linda Weinreb, Cheryl Wehler, and David Hosmer. 2003. "Homelessness and Food Insecurity." *Journal of Housing Economics* 12 (3): 250–272. https:// doi.org/10.1016/S1051-1377(03)00032-9.

Guthman, Julie. 2011. "'If Only They Knew': The Unbearable Whiteness of Alternative Foods." In *Cultivating Food Justice: Race, Class, and Sustainability*, edited by Alison Alkon and Julian Agyeman, 263–268. Cambridge, MA: MIT Press.

Hall, Stuart. 1988. "The Toad in the Garden: Thatcherism among the Theorists." In *Marxism and the Interpretation of Culture*, edited by C. Nelson and L. Grossberg, 35–74. Urbana: University of Illinois Press.

Hall, Stuart. 1997. "The Spectacle of the 'Other.'" In *Representations: Cultural Representations and Signifying Practices*, edited by Stuart Hall, 223–279. London: Sage.

Hamm, Michael, and Anne Bellows. 2003. "Community Food Security and Nutrition Educators." *Journal of Nutrition Education and Behavior* 35 (1): 37–43.

Hancock, Ange-Marie. 2004. *The Politics of Disgust: The Public Identity of the Welfare Queen*. New York: NYU Press.

Harding, Sandra. 2004. "Rethinking Standpoint Epistemology: What Is Strong Objectivity?" In *Feminist Standpoint Theory: Intellectual and Political Controversies*, edited by Sandra Harding, 127–140. New York: Routledge.

Harter, Lynn M., Charlene Berquist, B. Scott Titsworth, David Novak, and Tod Brokaw. 2005. "The Structuring of Invisibility among the Hidden Homeless: The Politics of Space, Stigma, and Identity Construction." *Journal of Applied Communication Research* 33 (4): 305–327. https://doi.org/10.1080/00909880500278079.

Harter, Lynn M., Autumn Edwards, Andrea McClanahan, Mark C. Hopson, and Evelyn Carson-Stern. 2004. "Organizing for Survival and Social Change: The Case of Streetwise." *Communication Studies* 55 (2): 407–424. https://doi.org/10.1080/10510970409388627.

Harvey, David. 2005. *A Brief History of Neoliberalism*. London: Oxford University Press.

Hinson, Waymon, and Edward Robinson. 2008. "'We Didn't Get Nothing': The Plight of Black Farmers." *Journal of African American Studies* 12 (3): 283–302.

Holborow, Marnie. 2015. *Language and Neoliberalism*. London: Routledge.

Holt-Giménez, Eric, Raj Patel, and Annie Shattuck. 2009. *Food Rebellions: Crisis and the Hunger for Justice*. New York: Food First Books.

Holton, Avery E., Laura C. Farrell, and Julie L. Fudge. 2014. "A Threatening Space? Stigmatization and the Framing of Autism in the News." *Communication Studies* 65 (2): 189–207. https://doi.org/10.1080/10510974.2013.855642.

hooks, bell. 2004. "Choosing the Margin as a Space of Radical Openness." In *The Feminist Standpoint Theory Reader: Intellectual and Political Controversies*, edited by S. Harding, 153–160. London: Routledge.

Hunger Solutions. 2018. "Food Shelves See Record Number of Visits in 2017." Accessed September 13, 2018. http://www.hungersolutions.org/data-posts/food-shelves see -record-number-of-visits-in-2017/.

Joint Religious Legislative Coalition (JRLC). 2010. "No Poor Among You." https://jrlc.org/wp-content/uploads/2017/09/nopooramongyouc.pdf.

Jones, C. P. 1987. "Stigma: Tattooing and Branding in Graeco-Roman Antiquity." *The Journal of Roman Studies* 77:139–155. https://doi.org/10.2307/300578.

Jones, Trina, and Kimberly Jade Norwood. 2017. "Aggressive Encounters and White Fragility: Deconstructing the Trope of the Angry Black Woman." *Iowa Law Review* 102:2017–2069.

Jost, Timothy Stoltzfus. 2003. *Disentitlement? The Threats Facing Our Public Health-Care Programs and a Rights-Based Response*. New York: Oxford University Press.

King, Martin Luther, Jr. (1955) 2007. "The One-Sided Approach of the Good Samaritan." In *The Papers of Martin Luther King, Jr., Vol. VI: Advocate of the Social Gospel, September 1948–March 1963*, edited by Clayborne Carson, Susan Carson, Susan Englander, Troy Jackson, and Gerald L. Smith, 239–240. Berkeley: University of California Press. https://stanford.app.box.com/s/rxjnkl701cyft7h2ssiodbq3e1jkm7r5.

King, Martin Luther, Jr. 1965. "Sermon at Temple Israel of Hollywood." Accessed September 11, 2018. https://www.americanrhetoric.com/speeches/mlktempleisrael hollywood.htm.

Kirkland, Anna. 2011. "The Environmental Account of Obesity: A Case for Feminist Skepticism." *Signs* 36 (2): 463–485. https://doi.org/10.1086/655916.

Kirkpatrick, Sharon I., and Valerie Tarasuk. 2011. "Housing Circumstances Are Associated with Household Food Access among Low-Income Urban Families." *Journal of Urban Health* 88 (2): 284–296. https://doi.org/10.1007/s11524-010-9535-4.

Kjos, S. A., A. M. Kinney, M. D. Finch, and J. M. Peterson. 2015. "Bridge to Health Survey 2015: Northeastern Minnesota & Northwestern Wisconsin Regional Health Status Survey." Duluth, MN: Generations Health Care Initiatives, Inc. http://www .bridgetohealthsurvey.org/images/pdfs/CountyReports2015/CARLTON_2015%20 BTH%20County%20Report%20Second%20Edition.pdf.

Klein, Naomi. 2007. *The Shock Doctrine: The Rise of Disaster Capitalism*. New York: Metropolitan.

Kluegel, James, and Eliot Smith. 1986. *Beliefs about Inequality: Americans' Views of What Is and What Ought to Be*. New York: Aldine de Gruyter.

Kobayashi, Audrey, and Linda Peake. 2000. "Racism out of Place: Thoughts on Whiteness and an Antiracist Geography in the New Millennium." *Annals of the Association of American Geographers* 90 (2): 392–403. https://doi.org/10.1111/0004-5608.00202.

Kollannoor-Samuel, Grace, Julie Wagner, Grace Damio, Sofia Segura-Pérez, Jyoti Chhabra, Sonia Vega-López, and Rafael Pérez-Escamilla. 2011. "Social Support Modifies the Association between Household Food Insecurity and Depression among Latinos with Uncontrolled Type 2 Diabetes." *Journal of Immigrant & Minority Health* 13 (6): 982–989. https://doi.org/10.1007/s10903-011-9499-9.

Larner, Wendy. 2000. "Neo-Liberalism: Policy, Ideology, Governmentality." *Studies in Political Economy* 63:5–25.

Levkoe, Charles. 2006. "Learning Democracy through Food Justice Movements." *Agriculture and Human Values* 23 (1): 89–98. https://doi.org/10.1007/s10460-005 -5871-5.

Link, Bruce, and Jo Phelan. 2001. "Conceptualizing Stigma." *Annual Review of Sociology* 27 (1): 363–385. https://doi.org/10.1146/annurev.soc.27.1.363.

Link, Bruce, and Jo Phelan. 2014. "Stigma Power." *Social Science & Medicine* 103:24–32. https://doi.org/10.1016/j.socscimed.2013.07.035.

Ludwig, David, Susan Blumenthal, and Walter Willett. 2012. "Opportunities to Reduce Childhood Hunger and Obesity: Restructuring the Supplemental Nutrition Assistance Program (the Food Stamp Program)." *JAMA* 308 (24): 2567–2568. https://doi.org/10.1001/jama.2012.45420.

Lupton, Deborah. 2003. *Medicine as Culture: Illness, Disease and the Body in Western Societies*. 2nd ed. London: Sage.

MacKinnon, Catharine A. 1982. "Feminism, Marxism, Method, and the State: An Agenda for Theory." *Signs* 7 (3): 515–544.

Mansbridge, Jane, and Aldon Morris, eds. 2001. *Oppositional Consciousness: The Subjective Roots of Social Protest*. Chicago: University of Chicago Press.

Massey, Doreen. 2015. "Vocabularies of the Economy." In *After Neoliberalism: The Kilburn Manifesto*, edited by S. Hall, D. Massey, and M. Rustin, 24–36. London: Lawrence & Wishart. Accessed September 11, 2018. https://www.lwbooks.co.uk/sites/default/files/free-book/after_neoliberalism_complete_0.pdf.

Maxwell, Daniel G. 1996. "Measuring Food Insecurity: The Frequency and Severity of 'Coping Strategies.'" *Food Policy* 21 (3): 291–303.

McChesney, Robert. 2003. "Introduction." In *Profit over People: Neoliberalism and Global Order*, edited by N. Chomsky, 7–16. New York: Seven Stories Press.

McCormack, Karen. 2004. "Resisting the Welfare Mother: The Power of Welfare Discourse and Tactics of Resistance." *Critical Sociology* 30 (2): 355–383. https://doi.org/10.1163/156916304323072143.

McKnight, John. 1995. *The Careless Society: Community and Its Counterfeits*. New York: Basic Books.

Meisenbach, Rebecca. 2010. "Stigma Management Communication: A Theory and Agenda for Applied Research on How Individuals Manage Moments of Stigmatized Identity." *Journal of Applied Communication Research* 38:268–292.

Metallinos-Katsaras, Elizabeth, Kathleen S. Gorman, Parke Wilde, and Jan Kallio. 2011. "A Longitudinal Study of WIC Participation on Household Food Insecurity." *Maternal & Child Health Journal* 15 (5): 627–633. https://doi.org/10.1007/s10995-010-0616-5.

Miller, Carol, and Brenda Major. 2000. "Coping with Stigma and Prejudice." In *The Social Psychology of Stigma*, edited by T. F. Heatherton, R. E. Kleck, M. R. Hebl, and J. G. Hull, 243–272. New York: Guilford Press.

Morris, Aldon, and Naomi Braine. 2001. "Social Movements and Oppositional Consciousness." In *Oppositional Consciousness: The Subjective Roots of Social Protest*, edited by Aldon Morris and Jane Mansbridge, 20–37. Chicago: University of Chicago.

Mukerjee, Madhusree. 2010. *Churchill's Secret War: The British Empire and the Ravaging of India during World War II*. New York: Basic Books.

Murray, Charles. 1984. *Losing Ground: American Social Policy 1950–1980*. New York: Basic Books.

Nakayama, Thomas, and Judith Martin, eds. 1999. *Whiteness: The Communication of Social Identity*. London: Sage.

Nestle, Marion. 2002. *Food Politics: How the Food Industry Influences Nutrition and Health*. Berkeley: University of California Press.

NGO/CSO Forum for Food Sovereignty. 2002. "Food Sovereignty: A Right For All A Political Statement by NGO/CSO Forum for Food Sovereignty." Via Campesina. Accessed September 13, 2018. https://nyeleni.org/spip.php?article125 5.

Nord, Mark, Alisha Coleman-Jensen, Margaret Andrews, and Steven Carlson. 2010. "Household Food Security in the United States, 2009." EER-108, US Department of Agriculture, Economic Research Service.

Occhipinti, Laurie. 2005. *Acting on Faith: Religious Development Organizations in Northwestern Argentina*. Lanham, MD: Lexington.

O'Connor, Anahad. 2017. "In the Shopping Cart of a Food Stamp Household: Lots of Soda." *New York Times*, January 13. https://www.nytimes.com/2017/01/13/well/eat/food-stamp-snap-soda.html.

Oliveira, Victor. 2018. "The Food Assistance Landscape: FY 2017 Annual Report." EIB-169, US Department of Agriculture, Economic Research Service.

Parker, Richard. 2012. "Stigma, Prejudice and Discrimination in Global Public Health." *Cadernos de Saúde Pública* 28:164–169.

Parker, Richard, and Peter Aggleton. 2003. "HIV and AIDS-Related Stigma and Discrimination: A Conceptual Framework and Implications for Action." *Social Science & Medicine* 57 (1): 13–24.

Patel, Richard. 2009. "Food Sovereignty." *Journal of Peasant Studies* 36 (3): 663–706.

Petersen, Alan, and Deborah Lupton. 1996. *The New Public Health: Health and Self in the Age of Risk*. Sydney: Allen and Unwin.

Phelan, Jo, Bruce Link, Robert Moore, and Ann Stueve. 1997. "The Stigma of Homelessness: The Impact of the Label 'Homeless' on Attitudes toward Poor Persons." *Social Psychology Quarterly* 60 (4): 323–337.

Pine, Adam. 2016. *Confronting Hunger in the USA: Searching for Community Empowerment and Food Security in Food Access Programs*. Abingdon, UK: Routledge.

Pine, Adam, and John Bennett. 2014. "Food Access and Food Deserts: The Diverse Methods that Residents of a Neighborhood in Duluth, Minnesota Use to Provision Themselves." *Community and Society* 45 (4): 317–336.

Pine, Adam, and Rebecca de Souza. 2013. "Including the Voices of Communities in Food Insecurity Research: An Empowerment-Based Agenda for Food Scholarship." *Journal of Agriculture, Food Systems, and Community Development* 3 (4): 71–79.

Poppendieck, Janet. 1999. *Sweet Charity? Emergency Food and the End of Entitlement*. New York: Penguin Putnam Books.

Pudup, Mary Beth. 2008. "It Takes a Garden: Cultivating Citizen-Subjects in Organized Garden Projects." *Geoforum* 39 (3): 1228–1240. https://doi.org/10.1016/j.geoforum.2007.06.012.

Rastogi, Rahul, and Mohan J. Dutta. 2015. "Neoliberalism, Agriculture and Farmer Stories: Voices of Farmers from the Margins of India." *Journal of Creative Communications* 10 (2): 128–140. https://doi.org/10.1177/0973258615597380.

Religious Action Center of Reform Judaism (RAC). n.d. "Hunger: Introduction & Jewish Values." Accessed January 4, 2018. https://rac.org/hunger-introduction-jewish-values.

Riches, Graham, and Tiina Silvasti. 2014. "Hunger in the Rich World: Food Aid and Right to Food Perspectives." In *First World Hunger Revisited: Food Charity or the Right to Food*, 2nd ed., edited by Graham Riches and Tiina Silvasti, 1–14. New York: Palgrave Macmillan.

Rose, Nikolas. 1989. *Governing the Soul: The Shaping of the Private Self*. London: Routledge.

Rose, Nikolas. 1999. *Powers of Freedom: Reframing Political Thought*. Cambridge: Cambridge University Press.

Rose, Nikolas, and Peter Miller. 1992. "Political Power beyond the State: Problematics of Government." *British Journal of Sociology* 43 (2): 173–205. https://doi.org/10.2307/591464.

Sager, Rebecca, and Laura Susan Stephens. 2005. "Serving Up Sermons: Clients' Reactions to Religious Elements at Congregation-Run Feeding Establishments." *Nonprofit and Voluntary Sector Quarterly* 34 (3): 297–315. https://doi.org/10.1177/0899764005275203.

Saldanha, Arun. 2006. "Reontologising Race: The Machinic Geography of Phenotype." *Environment and Planning D: Society and Space* 24 (1): 9–24.

Sanders, Elizabeth. 1999. *Roots of Reform: Farmers, Workers, and the American State, 1877–1917*. Chicago: University of Chicago Press.

Seccombe, Karen. 2011. *"So You Think I Drive a Cadillac?": Welfare Recipients' Perspectives on the System and Its Reform*. 3rd ed. Boston: Allyn and Bacon.

Sen, Amartya. 1983. *Poverty and Famines: An Essay on Entitlement and Deprivation*. New York: Oxford University Press.

Shiva, Vandana. 2008. *Soil Not Oil*. Boston: South End Press.

Shugart, Helene A. 2014. "Food Fixations: Reconfiguring Class in Contemporary US Food Discourse." *Food, Culture and Society: An International Journal of Multidisciplinary Research* 17 (2): 261–281. https://doi.org/10.2752/175174414X13871910531665.

Silvasti, Tiina, and Jouko Karjalainen. 2014. "Hunger in a Nordic Welfare State: Finland." In *First World Hunger Revisited: Food Charity or the Right to Food*, edited by Graham Riches and Tiina Silvasti, 72–86. New York: Palgrave Macmillan.

Slocum, Rachel. 2006. "Anti-racist Practice and the Work of Community Food Organizations." *Antipode* 38 (2): 327–349. https://doi.org/10.1111/j.1467-8330.2006.00582.x.

Slocum, Rachel. 2007. "Whiteness, Space and Alternative Food Practice." *Geoforum* 38 (3): 520–533. https://doi.org/10.1016/j.geoforum.2006.10.006.

Sniderman, Paul, and Edward Carmines. 1997. *Reaching beyond Race*. Cambridge, MA: Harvard University Press.

Soss, Joe, Richard Fording, and Sanford Schram. 2011. *Disciplining the Poor: Neoliberal Paternalism and the Persistent Power of Race*. Chicago: University of Chicago.

Soss, Joe, Sanford Schram, Thomas Vartanian, and Erin O'Brien. 2004. "Welfare Policy Choices in the States: Does the Hard Line Follow the Color Line?" *Focus* 23:10–15.

Springer, Simon. 2016. *The Discourse of Neoliberalism: An Anatomy of a Powerful Idea*. London: Rowman and Littlefield.

Spurlock, Cindy M. 2009. "Performing and Sustaining (Agri)Culture and Place: The Cultivation of Environmental Subjectivity on the Piedmont Farm Tour." *Text and Performance Quarterly* 29 (1): 5–21. https://doi.org/10.1080/10462930802514305.

St. Louis County Public Health and Human Services. 2013. "Health Is More than Health Care." Accessed August 3, 2015. https://www.stlouiscountymn.gov/Portals/0/Library/Dept/Public%20Health%20and%20Human%20Services/SLC-Health-Status-Report.pdf?ver=2018-04-26-141739-580hx.

Tarasuk, Valerie, and Joan M. Eakin. 2003. "Charitable Food Assistance as Symbolic Gesture: An Ethnographic Study of Food Banks in Ontario." *Social Science & Medicine* 56 (7):1505–1515.https://doi.org/10.1016/S0277-9536(02)00152-1.

Tarasuk, Valerie, and Joan M. Eakin. 2005. "Food Assistance through 'Surplus' Food: Insights from an Ethnographic Study of Food Bank Work." *Agriculture and Human Values* 22 (2): 177–186. https://doi.org/10.1007/s10460-004-8277-x.

Thrush, Glenn. 2018. "Trump's 'Harvest Box' Isn't Viable in SNAP Overhaul, Officials Say." *New York Times*, February 13, 2018. https://www.nytimes.com/2018/02/13/us/harvest-box-snap-food-stamps.html.

Tuck, Eve. 2009. "Suspending Damage: A Letter to Communities." *Harvard Educational Review* 79 (3): 409–427.

Tuck, Eve, and K. Wayne Yang. 2012. "Decolonization Is Not a Metaphor." *Decolonization: Indigeneity, Education & Society* 1 (1): 1–40.

United Nations Human Rights. 2010. "The Right to Adequate Food: Fact Sheet 34." Office of the United Nations High Commissioner for Human Rights. Accessed April 15, 2017. http://www.ohchr.org/Documents/Publications/FactSheet34en.pdf.

United States Department of Agriculture (USDA). 2017a. "Food Security in the United States: Definitions of Hunger and Food Security." USDA, Economic Research Service. Last modified October 4, 2017. http://www.ers.usda.gov/topics/food-nutrition-assistance/food-security-in-the-us/definitions-of-food-security.aspx.

United States Department of Agriculture (USDA). 2017b. "Fraud: How Can I Report SNAP Fraud?" USDA, Food and Nutrition Service. Last modified March 28, 2017. https://www.fns.usda.gov/fraud/how-can-i-report-snap-fraud.

United States Department of Agriculture (USDA). 2017c. "Fraud: What Is SNAP Fraud?" USDA, Food and Nutrition Service. Last modified January 20, 2017. https://www.fns.usda.gov/fraud/what-snap-fraud.

United States Department of Agriculture (USDA). 2018. "Supplemental Nutrition Assistance Program (SNAP): Am I Eligible for SNAP?" USDA, Food and Nutrition Service. Last modified June 27, 2018. https://www.fns.usda.gov/snap/eligibility.

United States Department of Health and Human Services. 2014. "National Healthcare Disparities Report, 2013." Agency for Healthcare Research and Quality. Last modified May 2014. https://archive.ahrq.gov/research/findings/nhqrdr/nhdr13/index.html.

van Dijk, Teun A. 1990. "Social Cognition and Discourse." In *Handbook of Language and Social Psychology,* edited by H. Giles and W. P. Robinson, 163–183. Oxford: John Wiley & Sons.

van Dijk, Teun A. 1993. "Principles of Critical Discourse Analysis." *Discourse & Society* 4 (2): 249–283. https://doi.org/10.1177/0957926593004002006.

van Dijk, Teun A. 1995. "Ideological Discourse Analysis." In "Interdisciplinary Approaches to Discourse Analysis," edited by Eija Ventola and Anna Solin. Special issue, *New Courant* 4: 135–161.

van Dijk, Teun A. 2001. "Discourse, Ideology and Context." *Folia Linguistica* 35 (1–2): 11–40.

Walley-Jean, J. Celeste. 2009. "Debunking the Myth of the 'Angry Black Woman': An Exploration of Anger in Young African American Women." *Black Women, Gender Families* 3 (2): 68–86. http://www.jstor.org/stable/10.5406/blacwomegendfami.3.2.0068.

Washington, Harriet. 2006. *Medical Apartheid: The Dark History of Medical Experimentation on Black Americans from Colonial Times to the Present.* New York: Harlem Moon.

Waxman, Chaim. 1983. *The Stigma of Poverty.* Elmsford, NY: Pergamon Press.

Webber, Caroline B., and Arezoo Rojhani. 2010. "Food or Fuel: Rising Gasoline Prices and Food Access among WIC Families in Non-metropolitan Southwest Michigan." *Journal of Hunger & Environmental Nutrition* 5 (4): 484–497. https://doi.org/10.1080/19320248.2010.527279.

Whitaker, Robert, and Sean Orzol. 2006. "Obesity among US Urban Preschool Children: Relationships to Race, Ethnicity, and Socioeconomic Status." *Archives of Pediatrics and Adolescent Medicine* 160 (6): 578–84. https://doi.org/10.1001/archpedi.160.6.578.

World Health Organization (WHO). 2018. "About Social Determinants of Health." Accessed September 8, 2018. http://www.who.int/social_determinants/sdh_definition/en/.

World Bank. 1986. "Poverty and Hunger: Issues and Options for Food Security in Developing Countries." World Bank/International Bank for Reconstruction and Development. Accessed March 26, 2015. http://www-wds.worldbank.org/external/default/WDSContentServer/WDSP/IB/1999/09/17/000178830_98101901455676/Rendered/PDF/multi_page.pdf.

Yaro, Joseph Awetori. 2004. "Theorizing Food Insecurity: Building a Livelihood Vulnerability Framework for Researching Food Insecurity." *Norwegian Journal of Geography* 58 (1): 23–37.

Zoller, Heather M. 2005. "Health Activism: Communication Theory and Action for Social Change." *Communication Theory* 15 (4): 341–364. https://doi.org/10.1111/j.1468-2885.2005.tb00339.x.

Index

Food, Health, and the Environment

Series Editor: Robert Gottlieb, Henry R. Luce Professor of Urban and Environmental Policy, Occidental College

Keith Douglass Warner, *Agroecology in Action: Extending Alternative Agriculture through Social Networks*

Christopher M. Bacon, V. Ernesto Méndez, Stephen R. Gliessman, David Goodman, and Jonathan A. Fox, eds., *Confronting the Coffee Crisis: Fair Trade, Sustainable Livelihoods and Ecosystems in Mexico and Central America*

Thomas A. Lyson, G. W. Stevenson, and Rick Welsh, eds., *Food and the Mid-Level Farm: Renewing an Agriculture of the Middle*

Jennifer Clapp and Doris Fuchs, eds., *Corporate Power in Global Agrifood Governance*

Robert Gottlieb and Anupama Joshi, *Food Justice*

Jill Lindsey Harrison, *Pesticide Drift and the Pursuit of Environmental Justice*

Alison Alkon and Julian Agyeman, eds., *Cultivating Food Justice: Race, Class, and Sustainability*

Abby Kinchy, *Seeds, Science, and Struggle: The Global Politics of Transgenic Crops*

Vaclav Smil and Kazuhiko Kobayashi, *Japan's Dietary Transition and Its Impacts*

Sally K. Fairfax, Louise Nelson Dyble, Greig Tor Guthey, Lauren Gwin, Monica Moore, and Jennifer Sokolove, *California Cuisine and Just Food*

Brian K. Obach, *Organic Struggle: The Movement for Sustainable Agriculture in the United States*

Andrew Fisher, *Big Hunger: The Unholy Alliance between Corporate America and Anti-Hunger Groups*

Julian Agyeman, Caitlin Matthews, and Hannah Sobel, eds., *Food Trucks, Cultural Identity, and Social Justice: From Loncheras to Lobsta Love*

Sheldon Krimsky, *GMOs Decoded: A Skeptic's View of Genetically Modified Foods*

Rebecca de Souza, *Feeding the Other: Whiteness, Privilege, and Neoliberal Stigma in Food Pantries*

Made in the USA
Columbia, SC
18 November 2023

26704947R00188